M000019926

# CONDUCTING A LIFE

*Reflections on the Theatre
of Maria Irene Fornes*

SMITH AND KRAUS PUBLISHERS
**The Art of Theater Series**


*Accommodating the Lively Arts: An Architect's View*
by Martin Bloom


*Anne Bogart—Viewpoints*
Edited by Michael B. Dixon & Joel A. Smith


*Chekhov: Letters About the Theatre*
Compiled and Translated by Carol Rocamora


*500 Years of Theatre History*
*from The Actors Theatre of Louisville Classics in Context Series*
Edited by Michael Bigelow Dixon


*Women Who Write Plays:*
*Interviews with Contemporary American Dramatists*
Edited by Alexis Greene

If you require pre-publication information about upcoming Smith and Kraus books, you may receive our semi-annual catalogue, free of charge, by sending your name and address to *Smith and Kraus Catalogue, 4 Lower Mill Road, North Stratford, NH 03590. Or call us at (800) 895-4331, fax (603) 922-3348. WWW.SmithKraus.com.*

# CONDUCTING A LIFE

*Reflections on the Theatre*
*of Maria Irene Fornes*

edited by
Maria M. Delgado and Caridad Svich

A SMITH AND KRAUS BOOK

Published by
Smith and Kraus, Inc.
Post Office Box 127, Lyme, NH 03768
www.SmithKraus.com

Copyright © 1999 by Maria M. Delgado and Caridad Svich
Each contributor retains copyright of his or her piece.

All rights reserved. No part of this book may be reproduced or
transmitted in any form or by any means, electronic or mechanical, including pho-
tocopying, recording, or by any information storage and retrieval system, without
permission in writing from the publisher.

First edition: December 1999
10 9 8 7 6 5 4 3 2 1

*Book design by Julia Hill Gignoux, Freedom Hill Design*

Publisher's Cataloguing-in-Publication Data
Delgado, Maria M.
Conducting a life: reflections on the theatre of Maria Irene Fornes /
by Maria M. Delgado and Caridad Svich. —1st ed.
p. cm.
Includes bibliographical references and index.
ISBN 1-57525-204-X
1. Fornes, Maria Irene—Criticism and interpretation. 2. Theater—New York
(State)—New York—Production and direction—History—20th century.
3. Feminism and theater—New York (State)—New York—History—20th century.
4. Women in the theater—New York (State)—New York—History—20th century.
I. Svich, Caridad.  II. Title.

PS3556.O7344 Z64 1999
812'.54—dc21    99-048899

# CONTENTS

# COMMENTARIES

# EXERCISES

# ⊛ LIST OF PHOTOS

# ❀ HOW DOES ONE DRAW
# A PORTRAIT OF AN ARTIST?

MARIA IRENE FORNES' LIFE AND WORK IN
the theatre defies classification. A founder of the Off-Off-Broadway movement, she has built a body of work and created an aesthetic that runs
against the conventions of what an American playwright's (and director's) career "should" be. Thus, we have decided to create a tribute to
Irene Fornes in her own manner. As befitting our subject, throughout
the volume we as editors and the various contributors call her "Maria
Irene" and "Irene." When using the former, we tend to link her formally with her Spanish  heritage, and when using the latter "Irene,"
we are speaking to her and of her in the intimate and familiar American side of her nature — we could even say that the two versions of
her name call attention to the private, and public Irene. The range of
contributors acknowledge the subjectivity of their own positions in this
volume through informed reflections on her expansion of the parameters
of theatrical practice, and open up the discussion of how portraiture
is a many-sided affair depending on who is drawing the portrait.

The "scrapbook" approach in evidence here in this volume speaks
directly to the way in which Fornes formulates her own work as writer,
director, and teacher. Indeed the book is organized to reflect her achievements in these three areas, but all the contributions, in some form, comment on the diverse way these three skills merge and converge. A collagist
by training and by nature, Fornes' is a magpie mind. The diversity of
the contributions in this volume attest to the wide-ranging influence
of Fornes' work and unique artistic sensibility: from scholars like Peggy
Phelan, Jill Dolan, Gayle Austin, Scott T. Cummings, Ruby Cohn, Susan
Letzler Cole, and Stephen Bottoms to actors and playwrights who have
worked or studied with Fornes over the years. Rather than adhere to a
chapter format, this volume posits an alternative means of organizing
and documenting theatrical work that breaks the academic norms toward

a more fragmented, less linear structure, where the varied pieces jut against each other in startling and original ways. The sixty plus contributors all testify to an influence and resonance that transcend admiration and permeate the very structures of how performance is organized, taught, practiced, and performed.

In creating this "portrait" of Irene, we examine her life's work in and out of chronology, and discover how the work she made in the 1960s has affected her ongoing work in the 1990s. Different generations of actors (from John Seitz to Michael Cerveris) testify to her attention to detail, her generosity as a director, the challenges posed by her constant rewriting during rehearsals, her attention to space and place and the intensity of the rehearsal process. A number of her contemporaries (Crystal Field, Lawrence Kornfeld, Caryl Churchill, Terrence McNally, Ellen Stewart, Kate Carney) assess her importance and contribution. For McNally she remains a "classicist" and "modernist" (p. 1) with a unique voice as distinctive as that of her theatrical ancestors. For Stewart she is still the embodiment of the visual site specific, interdisciplinary theatre that the 1960s brought with it. For another generation of scholars and practitioners (Ron Bagden, Oskar Eustis, Lisa Peterson, Gayle Austin) it is *Fefu and Her Friends* that proves a resonant landmark in the dramaturgical landscape and a theatrical model that is now adopted by a range of alternative performance artists.

As we point to the parallels and contradictions that are part of Irene's theatrical vocabulary, certain plays begin to take an overriding significance. Contributors return to *The Summer in Gossensass* (1997 and 1998) and the crop of plays written in the 1980s like *Mud* (1983), *Sarita* (1984), and especially *The Conduct of Life* (1985), which is seen by British dramatist Rod Wooden as putting us "in touch with our secret, unlived life, with the other in ourselves" (p. 75) — a point also made by New York playwright and teacher Martin Epstein about her entire body of work. For Maggie Mackay this play is a powerful Biblical allegory with direct relevance to the social, ethical, and moral decisions that form part of the fabric of our day-to-day lives while Julie Jensen testifies to the change of direction fostered in her own writing by seeing a Chicago production of the play. Fornes' protagonists, as Stephen Bottoms indicates, are often doers, engaged in acts of learning and struggling to find utterance with the few resources available to them. But it is, as Susan Sontag, Peter Lichtenfels, and Jonathan Moscone all note, the compassion, grace and generosity they are often imbued with that sets them apart. Peggy Phelan, Jeffrey Jones, and Crystal Field also indicate Fornes' achievements in placing on the stage the voices of those who are so often erased from its platform.

Oskar Eustis uses "mystery" as a noun to embody her uncanny ability to provide works in which there "never seems a disjunction between the life of the play and how that life expresses itself" (p. 23). Her blurring of the writer/director axis has also probed this very matter. Fornes' exquisite choreography, textured staging, and delicate sense of color and light are testified to by a range of contributors. For Leon Martell, Molly Powell, and Ron Bagden, her astute contemplation of performers, observed as carefully as a painter observes color, identifies her as a director of particular sensitivity and scope. For Heather Dundas it is this astute observation that marks her out; and through the intensity of her gaze we have an indication of the particular vision imparted through Fornes' remarkable work.

Playwright John Steppling posits Irene's "poetics of the almost" (p. 76). And in this, we have to look at the intersecting identities of Irene Fornes as woman, lesbian, Latina, director, writer, and teacher. No one area of her work is separate from the other, and so we find former students like Bernardo Solano and Migdalia Cruz talking about their complicated mentor-protégé relationship with Fornes, as well as director Carey Perloff testifying to Irene's use of domestic space as analogous to Harold Pinter's (p. 125). From stories of thrift-shopping, (which are an indelible part of Irene's social life and impinge directly on her art and sense of design) to the inimitable presence of her mother Carmen, we are able to see the many sides of Irene reflected in differing prisms.

Thus, while we have sought to provide stylistic consistency for the book, we have also attempted to keep the individual contributors' voices and styles veritably intact. Instead of eradicating difference, our goal has been to highlight tensions, frictions, and questions that indicate the variant artistic and critical vocabularies within use among the worlds of academia and of practicing theatre artists. This variance extends to the use of the word *theatre* itself—as how it is differently spelled and understood by practitioners from the United States and the United Kingdom, and how the word is spelled differently to denote inclusiveness and exclusiveness by different authors beyond their ingrained linguistic use of the word. What is revealed in this volume are the open-ended methods of engagement with art and artists' work, not only as it befits Irene Fornes' remarkable trajectory but also as it points to alternative models of examining art.

The book opens with an introduction arguing the influence of Fornes' life and work in the theatre. The first section charts a particular trajectory as observed by those who have worked with her as performers, producers, and designers, as well as more general observations on her influence from a range of critics and contemporaries. The second section records commentaries on her plays and productions from writers, directors, and critics who have chosen to focus on a particular work or group of work(s). The third section serves as way of collecting together some sort of record of the exercises that have shaped a whole generation of dramatists. Workshops and exercises are recalled and revisited by different dramatists and directors whose work in theatre bears the imprint of those encounters. As an epilogue, an extended interview with Irene Fornes records her own views on her career as she prepares for the 1999–2000 Signature Theatre season. Here her own views can be seen to intersect with a range of points, subject areas, arguments, and persons covered in other sections of the book.

We have been assisted in the preparation of this volume by the generosity of all the contributors who have given of their time and scanned their address books to provide us with names and contact details for friends and colleagues whom they felt would wish to be involved in this venture. We would like to extend another debt of gratitude to those who were unable to contribute but voiced their respect and admiration for Irene's work: Anne Bogart, Gabriel Berry, Giles Croft, Nilo Cruz, Ariel Dorfman, Michael Earley, Holly Hughes, Eduardo Machado, Tom McGrath, Pedro Monge-Rafuls, Estelle Parsons, Mark Ravenhill, Marc Robinson, Peter Sellars, Paula Vogel, Lois Weaver, Ella Wildridge and Susan Yankowitz. Olga Celda and David Price-Uden provided an initial transcript of the interview with Maria Irene Fornes; The School of English and Drama at Queen Mary and Westfield College, the University of London, and the Mark Taper Forum offered practical and administrative support; the former institution's Arts Computing Services and the School's Technical Director Gregor Turbyne assisted with the opening of transatlantic e-mails and documents that defied our respective computers; Bruce Whitacre and the staff at Signature Theatre kept us informed on how the season developed; Julia Miles and Lisa McNulty at the Women's Project and Maria Irene Fornes' agent Morgan Jenness graciously answered our queries and questions; Alan McVey and Denise Matthes at the University of Iowa, Len Berkman at Smith College, and Richard Schoch at Queen Mary and Westfield College provided useful information to assist us in compiling the chronology; Henry Little was a careful and attentive proofreader; Anne Militello graciously shared her archival material with us; Maria Irene Fornes' assistant Jocelyn Ruggiero was unfailingly cooperative, supportive, and generous with her time, research, and good will; Marisa Smith, Eric Kraus, Julia Hill Gignoux, and the staff at Smith and Kraus guided the book through its final stages.

Our final thanks go to Maria Irene Fornes, for her friendship, wit, support, and generosity. This book is dedicated to *la maestra* with our love and thanks.

Maria M. Delgado & Caridad Svich
July 1999

# ✿ CARYL CHURCHILL
*playwright*

## A POEM FOR IRENE FORNES

When I feel sick of
plays, writing, theatre,
the whole business, I
sometimes think of yours
and get a flicker
of what it is I
like about it all.


And I liked meeting
you and your mother
in that hotel room.
She was a hundred
asleep on the bed
in her black hat and
woke to say good-bye.


Thank you for both those.

# CONDUCTING A LIFE:
# A TRIBUTE TO
# MARIA IRENE FORNES

FOR OVER THIRTY YEARS, MARIA IRENE Fornes has been carving her own unique place in American theatre with an inventiveness and resilience that has withstood fashion, taste, and the increasing corporatization of the regional theatre movement. An artist who came of age in the early 1960s in the heart of the New York avant-garde, Fornes has been uncompromising in the pursuit of her singular vision, becoming one of the United States' most significant dramatists while at the same time being one of the most underrated among generational peers that include Sam Shepard, Lanford Wilson, and Terrence McNally.

Since her debut in 1963 with the absurdist *Tango Palace*, Fornes' work has been indicative of her time and ahead of her time. Concerned with feminist issues before the word *feminist* entered the national vocabulary, eschewing easy answers in the age of "political correctness," focusing on the human and intimate when theatre was creating commercial behemoths that ignored or devalued the focus on interpersonal relationships—especially if the humans under the lens were poor or disenfranchised, breaking form, when the nineteenth century model of the well-made play resurfaced as the ideal, directing her own work in the age of the director, Fornes has conducted a life in the theatre unlike any other.

While careerism has infected the American theatre with a vengeance, especially in the last twenty years, as fallout from the experiments of the 1960s has given way to the embracing of institutional models, Maria Irene Fornes has refused to deem her work as dramatist, director, and teacher a "career." Hers is a life and the work is part of it, like eating and sleeping. This lack of demarcation between "public" work and "private" life enacts a curious dance in looking at Fornes.

Born in Havana in 1930, she is often labeled a "Hispanic" or "Latina" dramatist, but she rarely uses the term herself, and in fact acknowledges her debt to Chekhov, Ionesco, and Brecht before linking her work to the Iberian or Latin American masters. At the same time, she founded the INTAR Hispanic Playwrights Lab in New York in 1981 with the exclusive purpose of mentoring and training what would become a significant generation of Hispanic dramatists because she felt that emerging Latino writers needed to have a place to develop their unique visions, and because she was "trying to discover a Hispanic sensibility."[1] An acknowledged lesbian, she nevertheless refuses to limit the "reading" of her work to her sexual preference, or to link it exclusively to works by more openly militant artists like Holly Hughes, Lisa Kron, or her protégé Cherríe Moraga. A founder of the Off-Off-Broadway movement, and along with Ellen Stewart of La MaMa, a "mother" of the American avant-garde, she nevertheless enjoys Broadway and its patently glamorous trappings. It is no small secret that one of Fornes' early plays — an absurdist office comedy — was produced on Broadway directed by Jerome Robbins with a cast that included the rueful comedienne Elaine May. A world-class director with a meticulous eye for choreography and the importance of the telling symbolic gesture, she insists that improvisation is one of the most important techniques in her work, and will go thrift-store shopping for fabrics or set pieces that will make their way on stage in her rigorously designed productions.

Maria Irene Fornes is an artist that revels in contradiction. Nothing and no one will pin her down. As Fornes nears her seventieth birthday, and a career-retrospective season is launched in her honor at the Signature Theatre in New York, my co-editor Maria M. Delgado and I have asked writers, actors, designers, critics, and directors to paint a portrait of Irene in her own manner, with the contradictions and multiplicities of experience intact.


## MEETING IRENE

My first encounter with Maria Irene Fornes was on the page. In 1986 PAJ Publications, co-founded by critic Bonnie Marranca, published a collection of Fornes' "mature" works: *Mud, The Danube, The Conduct of Life* and *Sarita* with a revelatory and provocative preface by Susan Sontag (which Ms. Sontag has allowed us to reprint in this volume). I read *Sarita* first and was immediately taken with the dark lyricism, frank humor, and fragmented realism offered by Fornes. It struck me as a remarkable mix of Odon Von Horvath, Wedekind, and García Lorca filtered through the playful mind of a very Cuban artist who was syncretic to the core. Then I read *The Danube* and thought, "This is someone else completely." And so my reaction changed with the reading of each play. But in the end, I kept coming back to *Sarita*, and thought, "This is the same artist. She is simply transforming herself. Changing her guise," for with Fornes, there are recurring concerns, not the least of which is the role women play in our society.

The act of transformation is central to the understanding of Fornes' thirty-plus-year span of work. Each play builds on the other but also strips the former to reveal another side. Under her microscope, the abused girl in *Sarita* can be seen as a reflection of the captive Nena in *The Conduct of Life*, or the "liberated" Marion in *Abingdon Square*. Separated by class, location, and time, each of these characters plays out scenarios that are rooted in the upending of the structures of melodrama, which have defined the "female character" on stage since Ibsen.

It is no accident that Fornes has been driven to *Hedda Gabler* first as director, and later as re-interpreter of the text in her own play *The Summer in Gossensass*. For *Hedda Gabler* was the first play Fornes read, and the imprint of Ibsen's classic and therefore, Hedda's predicament, can be traced in many of her plays and their willful heroines.

In Fornes' work, one is not only watching a character caught in different moments in time, but also watching a very distinct commentary on the theatrical role of such a character through the history of drama. Not consciously meta-theatrical like her peer Richard Foreman, Fornes nevertheless makes clear to her informed audience—and certainly as a director with her use of isolation, stillness, and profound intimacy between characters on stage—that her characters are part of a larger continuum of which they have often no control. The curtains that dwarf Marion in *Abingdon Square*, the high drab walls that contain Lloyd, Mae, and Henry in *Mud* limit the characters' worlds and heighten their thwarted passions. The battles her characters fight for their own spiritual liberation and knowledge are fought in a world that is destined to destroy them, but what counts for Fornes is the fight: the post-existential battle. Sacrifice is part of the bargain.

Sontag wisely notes in her essay on Fornes the Catholic influence in the plays: Fornes' "theater of miracles," Fornes' "catechism" (p. 18). Sacrifice is, of course, central to Western drama. One need only look at the works of Euripides and Aeschylus to note the way the sacrificial act has become a cornerstone of theatre. The fatalistic strain in Fornes' work is also an integral part of the Cuban sensibility, and sense of humor, for if there is bleakness in Fornes' landscape, it is always suffused with an inescapable humor: a compassionate wink from the playwright herself, who understands deeply the vaudeville that is life.

While other American playwrights have become hobbled by the burden of importance that has come to signify "great" theatre in the United States, Fornes has shrugged off the burden, in part, by staying true to her own vision, regardless of trends, and also by staying true to the nature of "play" itself: the exploration of form within the theatrical space. Beginning her life in the theatre on the NYC fringe, she has, except for unfortunately rare instances, continued to work on the margins. While Shepard, Wilson, and McNally and other of her contemporaries from Judson Church and Caffe Cino days have tried to negotiate their visions in larger not-for-profit and for-profit venues, Fornes, by chance and often by design, has remained America's most lauded theatrical "outsider."

After forty hard-won years in the theatre, she retains a youthful experimentation with form, language, and ways of destabilizing preconceived notions of theatre while very much working within a classic American realistic tradition. Fornes, for all her playfulness, rarely loses sight of the human beings at the center of her works. In an age when pornography, nihilism, and disaffected gestures merit much newspaper ink and pundits' praise, Fornes resists the post-MacLuhan "cool" in favor of tenderness, even in the midst of brutality and rage, in favor of the open wound exposed on stage — catharsis of the most basic kind.

# RE-MEETING IRENE

In November of 1988, I caught a glimpse of Irene in a drafty rehearsal room on 53rd Street between 10th and 11th Avenues in New York City. She was dressed casually and was unrolling a straw mat to begin yoga-influenced meditation exercises before the start of another writing workshop at the INTAR Hispanic Playwrights Lab. A handful of "students" had already gathered in one corner of the second-floor room, and as I walked through the door, she turned her mischievous gaze to me. "Are you Caridad?" she said. "Welcome." And she shook my hand.

Just out of the MFA playwriting program at the University of California at San Diego, I was eager to test my writing in a different environment and eager to work under the notorious mentorship of Fornes. The Lab was already legendary, having produced Milcha Sanchez-Scott and her play *Roosters*, Migdalia Cruz's *Miriam's Flowers*, and Eduardo Machado's early burst of plays about Cuba, which were to become his *Floating Islands* trilogy. The impact of *Roosters*, especially, had set a national standard for the emerging next generation of Latino playwrights. This Lab was not only a place to train and develop your writing muscles under a master's guidance and supervision, but also a place where you could upset expectations of what a play could be and be part of a community of writers dedicated, in part, to the forging of an entirely different theatrical language, one that could borrow equally from Iberian and Latin American traditions, and European and American ones. Fornes would often say around the circle of tables where the three-hour writing sessions would be run, "We are writing for the twenty-first century."

Now, of course, the twenty-first century is upon us, and it is ironic indeed that both Fornes and a generation of Latina/o dramatists who were either mentored by her or influenced by her are only now being slowly deemed "ready" for many US stages. But then, US theatre has always been behind the rest of the arts, as Fornes herself has stated, "Theater is one hundred, two hundred years behind the times."[2] While the visual arts, dance, and music have continued evolving, mutating, and reconfiguring essential notions of line, time, space, energy, and presentation/representation — one need only look at the range of work created in the dance world alone from the emergence of Twyla Tharp to the current fascination with British dance-theatre storyteller Matthew Bourne. US theatre, after the experiments of the 1960s and the performance art "crossover" work pioneered by Mabou Mines and The Wooster Group in the 1970s and 80s in New York, has clung quite safely to nineteenth-century models of dramaturgy as a standard to follow. Certainly the mimetic possibilities offered by television and film have encouraged this. But it can also be speculated that the element of risk that is necessary for the creation of art has ever so slowly been eliminated from the "formula" of producing work on US stages, especially as a "for-profit," "corporate," "subscriber-friendly-only" sensibility has infected decision- making, and thus has written one side of US theatre history, while neglecting another.

The other side of the coin, however, is that Fornes is a Latina dramatist, and while she is often dubbed the "American Caryl Churchill," she is certainly not placed at the forefront of theatrical discussion, except in academic or tight theatrical circles. It could be posited that a certain level of discrimination has informed the positioning of Fornes' work in the US canon, especially since Fornes refuses to "fit" into the prescribed dramaturgical boxes set aside for "Latina" dramatists or "lesbian" dramatists. This refusal has to do with a profound mistrust of categorization, which immediately places a limit on the art and defies the nature of the artistic process.

"I feel I've never had any choice. When I'm not doing something that comes deeply from me, I get bored. When I get bored, I get distracted, and when I get distracted, I become depressed. It's a natural resistance and it insures your integrity. You die when are faking it, and you are alive when you are truthful."[3]

Fornes' ruthless commitment to her own voice as an artist upsets the "mainstreaming" notion of art in the United States, and while she is lauded for her integrity, she is also negatively criticized, often within the Latino artistic community, for not being more fiercely "Latina" in her work. The decentralization of her texts angers many, so much so, that she is often dubbed a "Eurocentric" writer rather than a "Latina."

This narrow view of what a writer can or cannot write is particularly aggravated by the tribalism that has dominated the last twenty-odd years of theatrical discourse in the United States. The proliferation of development programs for playwrights of various ethnicities has encouraged many great new voices, but it has also placed an "ethnically specific" limit on the subject matter that these writers could address. Working in such a climate has meant that a writer belonging, by virtue of race, gender, or ancestry, to a specific "non-white" tribe could go so far only if he or she stayed within the prescribed notions set by the dominant culture.

The INTAR Hispanic Playwrights Lab in New York during its long tenure under Fornes' estimable leadership went against these prescribed notions. The six to eight writers from around the United States selected to take part in the Lab every year (with writers often serving consecutive residencies) had to be Hispanic, but the litmus test was always the work itself. Fornes, leading by example, did not require that the playwrights in the Lab address any ethnically specific subject matter or theme. Through daily visualization exercises, the writers were asked to discover the work within them, to create the forms that suited their visions, and under Fornes' rigorous, watchful eye, to speak the truth about their worlds.

A virtual Who's Who of Latino theatre in the United States can be traced back to the Lab. Idiosyncratic, individual voices that range from Eduardo Machado to Lisa Loomer to Migdalia Cruz have paved their own way and sustained Fornes' legacy while at the same time building upon it. The nexus of performers and storytellers that formed part of and were nurtured by the Lab's community included John Leguizamo, WOW Café veteran Carmelita Tropicana, triple-threat (actor-writer-director) maverick Michael John Garces, and designer Riccardo Hernandez.

It is a testament to Fornes herself that the Lab's legacy of playwrights and performers continues to not only produce some of the most distinctive and daring work in American theatre but to incorporate Fornes' teaching methods in their own workshops geared to passing on the tradition to a new generation of theatre artists.

Fornes has also ensured that the work from the Lab find venues in which to be seen by directing it herself: Leo Garcia's *Dogs* at West Coast

Ensemble in Los Angeles in 1990, Ana María Simo's *Going to New England* at INTAR Stage Two in 1990, and my own *Any Place But Here* at Theater for the New City in New York in 1995. Her recognition of the necessary Oedipal impulse in art — as one generation of artists must forcibly step aside to make way for another — is at its most keen in these volatile instances when she directs work from the Lab or ancillary workshops, as the "frisson" of master artist and emerging artist play out their sensibilities on the stage.

In fact, it is "frisson" itself, which seems to be at the center of Fornes as artist and human being. She revels, as most provocateurs and mischief-makers do, in constantly defying expectations. She stages violence with beauty and austerity, moments of Bakhtin-like humor with an odd stillness and gravity (which makes the moments even more hilarious and troubling), and sexual encounters with directness and an almost pre-Freudian sense of innocence. Working over a number of years with a trio of designers who are closely identified with her sensibility — scenic designer Donald Eastman, costume designer Gabriel Berry, and lighting designer Anne Militello — Fornes has developed one of the most unique directorial visions in the United States.

Unfortunately, she is not often thought of as a director in the same breath as a Peter Sellars or Anne Bogart, precisely because she stages, for the most part, her own work as a dramatist, and the "auteur" sensibility is somehow disregarded in US theatrical criticism unless the work is manifestly avant-garde à la Richard Foreman or Elizabeth LeCompte. But Fornes' work as a director must be readdressed and examined. It is a vital part of understanding her writing and her vision.

Much has been made of the fact that Fornes began her artistic career as a painter. Certainly, the painterly eye is always present in her construction of scenes, her delineation of space, and her microscopic attention to gesture and color on stage. But it is how she has transformed the ostensibly static quality of painting to the three-dimensional demands of theatre that are of importance here. Is it any accident that *Fefu and Her Friends* is one of the first site-specific plays in the US theatrical canon?

Fornes is a designer of space on stage. Collaborating intensely with lighting designer virtuoso Anne Militello on plays like *Mud, What of the Night?, Abingdon Square, Sarita*, and her staging of *Hedda Gabler* at Milwaukee Rep throughout the 1980s and early 1990s, Fornes has tested the limits of chiaroscuro lighting on stage — cropping bodies in door-frame windows, or more liminal stage spaces, isolating actors' gestures, exploring the interplay of light and shadow within the staging of a single scene. While her plays are rooted in both the absurdist and realist traditions — and in fact, fuse the two in many instances — her directing of the work places the plays firmly in nonrealistic territory. The disjunction of text and staging is what often gives her work in production a feeling of being constantly on edge. An actor will be discovered in half-light, and play a scene framed in shadow until one forgets they are in half-light at all, then suddenly the actor will step forward and a bank of light will engulf them, and the audience's perspective is changed, or a scene will be cut short by a blackout that will leave the audience "in the dark" for an unconventionally long time, thus testing the notion of "real time" on stage.

Playing with perspective also informs her collaboration with scenic designer Donald Eastman, who with Anne Militello and costume designer Gabriel Berry has contributed to one of the longest-standing collaborations between a playwright-director and a designer in the history of contemporary US theatre. Starting with Fornes' conceptual design imprint on the space — be it a found space or a more conventional one — Eastman has helped define Fornes' worlds architecturally, to once again explore disjunction. Scenes are played out on the edges of the stage or in unlikely contained spaces — a closet, behind or under a piece of furniture, a bathtub — against a large and indifferent visual world. The oversize curtains that dwarf the intimate interactions of the characters in *Abingdon Square*'s first production at the American Place Theatre in New York in 1987 place an even greater obstacle to Marion's liberation. The high, flat walls that frame the trio in *Mud*'s production at Theater for the New City in New York make the characters' increasing isolation even greater and point to the fact that for Mae there will be no way out of this world.

Fornes' preoccupation with obstacles informs her constructions of stage space (with Eastman and other designers). Actors often need to make an entrance through restrictive paths blocked with objects or through perilously narrow doorframes. Angles are slightly skewed in the space and sometimes even a false low ceiling will obstruct passage for a large, tall actor. While it may be said that this preoccupation is playful in the extreme, it also points to Fornes' need to show in actual flesh-and-blood circumstances the difficulty her characters must face to survive their world. Even in the wide, open space offered to Hedda in Fornes' staging of *Hedda Gabler* there is a feeling that the over-abundance of space itself can be a trap. There is a constant awareness of the theatrical event being enacted in Fornes' productions. The audience is not passive but complicit in the knowledge that although an illusory world is being created on stage and very much contained within it, that these are also actors playing a game, and with Fornes' use of light, space, time, and sound, the element of "gamesmanship" remains at the forefront.

One of the seminal reasons for this investigation of space and its uses can be traced directly to Fornes' almost ten-year tenure at the Padua Hills Playwrights Festival in California. Working, for the most part, outdoors (as was an initial mandate of the Festival) Fornes staged early versions of *Mud, The Summer in Gossensass, The Conduct of Life,* and other plays on the expanse of land offered to festival participants, whether it was Padua Hills itself or the grounds of Cal State-Northridge. Founded in 1978 by theatre maverick Murray Mednick, the Festival — which in its early years housed Sam Shepard, John Steppling, John O'Keefe, and Fornes — was one of southern California's most exciting developmental venues. A roving company of actors, some of whom would work with Fornes almost exclusively through the years both in and outside California, performed in evening-long marathons of new plays under the open twilight sky for a devoted, and equally roving audience, which often had to follow scenes from location to location.

Fornes speaks of the importance of Padua in her re-examination of space after working in New York for a number of years as a liberation, as well as attesting to the fact that she used these summer workshops as the place to launch what would become her most important plays. "There's more freedom and initiative to experiment here than anywhere," she remarked when working on her outrageous comedy *Oscar and Bertha*.[4] This sense of freedom allowed Fornes to more fully explore the topography of her work, both as director and writer.

The very fact that Padua was built on the concept of breaking down theatrical barriers, beginning with not staging the work exclusively in a conventionally theatrical setting refocused Fornes to take into full account the geography and climate in her plays. The soft red earth in the promontory described by Fornes in the opening stage directions of *Mud* can be directly linked to the reddish dirt where *Mud* was first performed at Padua in 1983. The ecological use of found text and twilight images in *The Danube* could also be traced to her play's first staging at Padua in 1982.

As a director, the years at Padua also opened Fornes up to the possibilities first hinted at in her site-specific work with *Fefu and Her Friends*. Not only was she able to place scenes in geographical locations but she was able to play with the use of natural light, the randomness of weather, and the vastness of space itself. Distance suddenly became a more overt consideration for Fornes, as actors were placed either huddled together surrounded by empty rolling hills, or standing alone against the wide sky while another actor was speaking a relatively great distance away. The formalized gestures of her early work with Caffe Cino and Judson Church in New York were now giving way to a more fluid, yet still rigorous style. The juxtaposition of the formal and the natural, which had always been an aesthetic concern for Fornes, was now given a perfect forum for expression at Padua and was incorporated into the stagings of her work in the plays' premieres in New York and elsewhere.


## TAKING IRENE'S LEAD

I sit in a room and think of where my writing began, and how it changed from having studied and worked with Irene. As one of the last of the consecutive-year INTAR "Lab-bers" (1988–1992), I was privileged to work with Irene in the 53rd Street rehearsal room where so many wonderful writers had already left their marks. I was privileged also to regretfully witness the end of the INTAR Lab — and how this was to signify a new chapter in Fornes' career — as she was to embark on writing opera librettos like *Balseros* and *Terra Incognita*, complete her epic play *What of the Night?* — which was short-listed for the Pulitzer — and find her way to writing her profoundly witty take on Ibsen and the vicissitudes of the theatrical life in *The Summer in Gossensass*.

As an artist I have always believed in truth telling in the work and finding different forms and voices to enact this truth telling. Working with Irene deepened my sense of truth, enriched my experience of characters as three-dimensional, flesh-and-blood creatures who had wills of their own and would dictate the plays to me rather than the other way around. There was no "central concept" when one would begin a play at the Lab. One wrote and discovered, and tapped the shamed and unspoken parts of the self, or the curious and generous ones, to enable the work to make itself manifest. Once it had done so, the journey of finding the "play" would begin, somewhat akin to finding the rules of a game once the board is placed in front of you. Part of the journey was the daily writing and interaction with a similarly focused group of writers, but the other part was the staging of the work itself.

At the end of a Lab sequence — which could run three months consecutively to nine months — each writer, after an initial cold reading of the text with actors, was handed fifty dollars and free rein of the 53rd Street stage space for a week. In that week, one had to cast the play from the vast NYC acting pool, design the "set and costumes," make decisions with a one-man technical crew about lights and sound, and direct the play. Suddenly, Irene's penchant for thrift-store shopping seemed absolutely essential to the making of art, as my colleagues and I scavenged, scoured, and fought our way for treasures that could be salvaged from a shop's neglect and find their way onto our stage. The responsibility of "designing" and "staging" the work enlivened us in the most practical sense to the importance of spatial and temporal elements in the crafting of a play, to the necessity of thinking of a play as something not only of literature but of performance.

At the end of the week, all the plays from that year's Lab were presented in "book-in-hand" two-day marathon sessions that often went into the wee hours of the morning under Irene's singularly caring gaze. And while there was an inevitable feeling of competition, especially since INTAR's artistic director Max Ferrá was present at these sessions, the mood tended toward the celebratory, and led toward an investigation of what was learned and what now needed to be done.

I half-jokingly would tell my colleagues that the INTAR Lab years were my unofficial "Ph.D." But the joke, more and more, is in earnest, as I write and find myself pulling out of my imaginary toolbox, Lab "tools" for unblocking the writing on a scene, animating a piece of text through the use of an image, or simply focusing the work on the essential that must be communicated between characters in space.

Working with Irene gave me a sense of architecture. Her own preoccupation with the construction of space on stage or outdoors has been one of the most important lessons I could have had as a playwright. In the plays I wrote while in New York at the Lab — *Gleaning/Rebusca, But There Are Fires, Shelter,* and *Any Place But Here* (which Irene was later to direct at Theater for the New City in 1995) — stage time is cut into discrete pieces, and space, both physical and spiritual, serves as the locus where the tension between and among the characters resides. To this day, these plays have the splendid habit of waking me up, of making me pay attention to what's important on stage and to my own vision — all by reminding me of where the plays came from, and how Irene would smile as I sat next to her in the circle of creaky wooden tables at the Lab as I wrote and read my raw work out loud. That smile in my memory reminds me of mischief and delight, two qualities that are the very essence of Irene, and her theatre.

A testament to Fornes' influence is the wide range of artists that openly acknowledge her impact on their work or sensibility. From directors seeing her work for the first time to critics who have been forced by the delicate, subversive nature of the work itself to reposition themselves in regard to conservative views of what playwriting can or should be in the American theatre. However, nowhere is the influence more apparent than in the flourishing generation of playwrights and storytellers that have emerged from the INTAR Lab or other venues in which she has taught.

While Fornes' own legacy of work is estimable indeed, her force as teacher and mentor has often been the only way her vision has had an opportunity to be visibly expressed in a country where her work as a playwright has been pushed to the very fringe of theatrical experience. The articulation of her aesthetic has been made manifest in her hands-on work as a teacher, and therefore is an essential, inextricable part of her work as playwright and director.

Working from a private, intuitive place of visualization where the ego must be bypassed to give way to the imagination, Fornes' writing exercises focus on impulse, knowledge, and the openness to surprise or discovery, all of which are elements of her own creative process. From intensive sessions five days a week at the INTAR Lab, for example, Fornes was able to test and retest over a number of years not only how a specific writing exercise was perceived, but how it could evolve over time as different writers took the same exercise and formed their own unique response to it. These exercises are what Irene has called the "anatomy of inspiration,"[5] and if one were to look at the array of artists who have studied that anatomy, one would be looking at some of the most dynamic, daring, and unique writers in the American theatre.

From the INTAR Lab years alone, one can look at Fornes' legacy through the works of Cherríe Moraga, Nilo Cruz, Ana María Simo, Migdalia Cruz, Eduardo Machado, and Bernardo Solano, and see how each playwright has taken a bit of Fornes into their own work and transformed her influence into something wholly their own — whether it be the elliptical, short-scene structure of her plays, the concern with formal experimentation, or the use of language as provocation.

From her teaching years at Padua and other venues, the legacy can be traced to a possibly even more diverse group of playwrights like Luis Alfaro, Elizabeth Wong, Jennifer Maisel, and Paula Cizmar who have taken Fornes' example as a working artist in an increasingly "corporatized," "Disney-fied" theatre "market" as proof that one can find one's own path, and remain true to it, despite often crippling pressures to succumb and subsume one's vision to a larger, treadmill-paced entertainment structure.

In the visible and not-so-visible trenches of American theatre, these playwrights are paving the way for the next and next generation. The post-Fornes upstarts, who perhaps tired of the self-rationalizing, madly trendy, pop fizzy plays of the near future, will go back to Fornes' stark, achingly human, defiant texts and those of her acknowledged or more veiled protégés, and refind the heart of US theatre for another century.

Caridad Svich

1. Maria Irene Fornes, in Kathleen Betsko and Rachel Koenig, *Interviews with Contemporary Women Playwrights* (New York: Beech Tree Books/Quill Edition, 1987), p. 157.

2. Maria Irene Fornes, in a private conversation with Caridad Svich in New York at INTAR, 1988.

3. Maria Irene Fornes, in Kathleen Betsko and Rachel Koenig, *Interviews with Contemporary Women Playwrights* (New York: Beech Tree Books/Quill Edition, 1987), p. 167.

4. Maria Irene Fornes, quoted in Maryl Jo Fox, "Stage Hand," *LA Weekly*, July 21–27, 1989, p. 33.

5. Maria Irene Fornes, in a private conversation with Caridad Svich in New York at INTAR, 1991.

# ✹ MAKE YOUR OWN FORNES
## H.M. Koutoukas
### dramatist, director, performer

ON VARIOUS COLORED BITS OF PAPER, write the following phrases, each on a separate bit of paper. Then visit your most beautiful museum or cultural venue. Place the bits of paper in the most priceless vase or amphora, preferably Hellenic. Shake bits of bits of paper — draw. You will then create your own portrait of Maria Irene Fornes.

A daughter of De Beauvoir.

A life experiment in haute humanism.

Her eyes alert like a young girl who has been made aware of life's cruelty and instability too early.

Bathed in the kind of muted light that seems to hover within Judson Church at teatime.

Brave as only an only sister can be.

Her direction is as the Muses' harpoon.

Indefatigable is her war against writing by number.

The girl is into physics, but she has not yet written the axioms.

Earnest and appreciative of each new brick wall she encounters, and happy to toil at what she loves.

Often escorted by her mother, who had a sweet smile and a prayer for everyone.

Aristocratic, Castillian, and en peinetada*.

Life is veiled, she needs no veil.

She knew the joy of comforting a parrot.

Not the sort of person to hold resentments.

Instead she turns her grievances into fuel for her work.

Deadly work.

Plays lurk everywhere before they take a vocation and mindsurf in theatre writers' brains.

With a light green butterfly net, she catches stars and a planet or two, releases fireflies, from glass canning jars.

Her work carries its own light.

The old, the Every Day, become new and electric.

She glows in the dark.

There are many Fornes parables. Each has his own personal one.

There will be many more.

*from peineta: an Andalucian tortoiseshell comb.

Enough for each of the few who worship the original story, life, or person.

Each line an experience.

She is a humanist indeed.

And the kind of girl one would like to give one's grandmother's cameo to.

She stands securely in her own space, brave enough to create her own time and make a fool of history.

She is our little sister of the arts.

She is a joy.

She has given us enough rope to hang ourselves.

# ✵ TONY KUSHNER
*playwright*

## ONE OF THE GREATS

AMERICA HAS PRODUCED NO DRAMATIST
of greater importance than Maria Irene Fornes, a statement with which
no serious person familiar with our literature and stage practice could
disagree. She's one of the greats: Her accomplishment is unimpeach-
able, enduring, protean. She ranks with Albee, Guare, and Mamet; with
Caryl Churchill in England and the late Heiner Müller in Berlin. I have
loved her work since I first started studying and thinking about playwriting. Her plays and productions profoundly altered my understanding
of what theater is; what it aims at accomplishing; what it may demand
of its audience; how it speaks to the political through the personal and
vice versa; and the role that beauty plays in the political, redemptive,
transformational power of art. Fornes is a creator of worlds of tough,
exigent, overwhelming beauty.

## ❀ MIGDALIA CRUZ
*playwright*


A DOUBLE HAIKU FOR IRENE
BECAUSE SHE DETESTS THE ORDINARY...
FROM HER ETERNAL FAN, MIGDALIA

In six lines or less —
I must honor the teacher
who gave me the moon.
It was an honest,
clear, yet savage light, poured from
desire's heart-fire.

# CONDUCTING A LIFE:
## *Reflections on the Theatre*
## *of Maria Irene Fornes*

# OBSERVATIONS

# ✸ TERRENCE McNALLY
*Playwright*

MARIE IRENE (THAT'S WHAT I CALL HER; don't know why; it just comes trippingly off my tongue) has been a friend and colleague since the Good Old Days when we all worked (or wanted to work) at places like Caffe Cino, Judson Poets Theatre and La MaMa. She was always a star in that particular firmament. She still is. She had her own very specific voice before a lot of us had even learned to speak and when we did it was often in the rhythms of our immediate ancestors: Beckett, Ionesco, Genet, Albee, Pinter. Not Marie Irene. From the first she sounded like Marie Irene. She was a grown-up early on. I have always admired the sheer joy and self-confidence she brings to the theater. Those two aspects of her craft have never dimmed. If anything, they burn brighter than ever. She manages to make playwriting seem the most personal form of expression while reveling in its most public, ritualistic aspects. She is a classicist and and a modernist at the same time. I have always admired her work. I am sometimes baffled by it but I have never for an instant doubted its integrity, intelligence, or power. Of course, I usually enjoy her work tremendously too, and she can be one hell of a funny girl, this Marie Irene, but since this is a scholarly tribute we don't want to go into that. I have been proud to be her colleague for forty years. I know for certain that her best is yet to come.

# ✹ ELLEN STEWART
*Founder/Director, La MaMa*
*Experimental Theater Club, New York*

IRENE FORNES, HER MOTHER, AND I MET IN 1961 when we were part of the group that sailed to Tangiers on a Yugoslavian freighter. The voyage was nine days and I spent eight of those in the bottom of the ship — seasick out of my mind. Irene's mother was so very kind to me.

In Morocco I had a very strange experience that made me decide to return to the United States to do something with my life. On my return on the Holland/America, Irene's mother was on the same boat and I talked with her, told her my plans. She was very loving and encouraging. My plan was to start a project that somehow would help "would-be" theater artists. I called my plan my pushcart. She told me she would pray for me and on each occasion that I saw her after, until almost the day that she died (and she was over 100 years old) she would pray for me. She is very dear to La MaMa.

I feel more comfortable saying Maria Irene Fornes because I have always called her Maria Irene. She is equally dear to La MaMa. She returned from her trip and became one of the lead artists at Judson Memorial Church. The program was directed by Al Carmines. The Judson works were certainly considered much more professional in the early years than ours and Maria Irene and her multi-talents certainly helped to strengthen this conviction. In the 1960s she already thought of visual theater. She loved working with text, music, and dance. The Judson had a big performance area, lights, sound, and Al Carmines was a very talented composer and director. The work that came from their productions is the reason why we have the term Off-Off-Broadway. Jerry Talmer, who was a critic, coined that term for their theater and later it was subsequently used as a label for all of us who were down here below 14th Street attempting to do theater.

Maria Irene Fornes did a beautiful piece, *Red Burning Light,* at La MaMa in 1969 and it was a gorgeous production. Richard Peaslee and John Bauman composed the music; Remy Charlip was the show doctor and Ralph Lee was Private Macoo.

In these years, the 1960s, she and Tom O'Horgan were doing site-specific work that by now has become very much a part of today's theater. *Fefu and Her Friends* was a brilliant example. Maria Irene's works, for the most part, were music-theater, highly political and very successful. Her success in theater has never stopped. She is very prolific. Most of her plays have been published and she is one of the best teachers in drama that exists.

Maria Irene's play *St. Joan* (1986) was a prophetic insight into the political exploration of the creative and revolutionary influence of women.

*Sarita* was a portrayal of a Hispanic family of single women, endeavoring to break the social boundaries that imprisoned them. The love/hate relationship that developed between Sarita and her lovers was a creative parallel, which depicts the emotional conflicts that exist in the young and the demands that traditions make upon them. At the time this play was written single mothers and their problems had not as yet taken their place in the public domain as we know it.

To Irene, Bravo.

The Judges, actors George Bartenief (kneeling) and Benis Masdem (standing)

*A MATTER OF FAITH*
Theater for the New City, New York City, 1986

Photo by Anne Militello

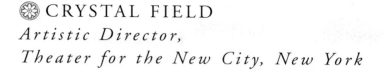

# CRYSTAL FIELD
*Artistic Director,*
*Theater for the New City, New York*

THE FIRST TIME I WORKED WITH IRENE
Fornes was at Judson Church. I had just started at Lincoln Center and
at the same time, discovered the Judson Dance Group, a troupe of radical dancers and choreographers whose staunch opposition to the rigid
Martha Graham techniques in which I had been schooled, produced
thrilling and wild dances and poetry in the very sanctuary of Judson
Church.

It was here I first met Al Carmines who wrote music to every sort
of play's dialogue and finally a fabulous score for a new musical called
*Promenade,* written by Irene Fornes.

I had sung in a Mass that Al had written for one Sunday at a Judson Service, and I was enthralled. I had suffered such hardships through
college and in the commercial theater because of my unorthodox views
relative to the aesthetics of both dance and theater, and lo and behold,
I had found a group of artists espousing a cause I had fought for, alone
and without a true philosophy to back me up, but only an instinct that
told me "something's up" in this world, and it's too strong a pull for
me to accept the status quo as it was handed out to me on every side.

Holy Moly! Sex without guilt — Joy without guilt, Food without
guilt — Break the fourth wall — Poetry without guilt — Politics! Friendship! All new and, of course, when we began rehearsals for *Promenade,*
a rehearsal process I had never known before.

I remember when Irene and Al came in with the "Ha! Ha!" Song.
It was a song whose chorus was laughter set to music. And the joy of
singing that song put me on a pink cloud of total ecstasy.

Then, one day, Irene came to me and said, "I am going to write a
song for you, but not just for you, but also about you, and it will be
the real you. This song will be you — so tell me all about yourself."

And I told her my life story. All my trials and tribulations. All my longings and desires. All my philosophical struggles since my professional career at the age of three as a modern dancer with Klarina Pinska. What was my surprise when, a week later the "Cigarette Song" appeared on my rehearsal chair:

> To walk down the street
> With a mean look in my face,
> A cigarette in my right hand
> A toothpick in my left;
> To alternate between the cigarette
> And the toothpick,
> Ah! That's life.
>
> Yes, I have learned from Life.
> Every day I've learned some more.
> Every blow has been of use.
> Every joy has been a lesson
> Yes, I have learned from life.
> What surprises me
> Is that life
> Has not learned from me.[1]

---

1. Maria Irene Fornes, *Promenade* in *Promenade and Other Plays* (New York: Performing Arts Journal Publications, 1987), p. 22.

# ❀ RUBY COHN
*Critic*

## A FORNES CALENDAR

> Critics need to feel more love for the theater and writers. When they *harshly* criticize writers I get upset. If critics loved the theater then they and writers would write to each other the way we write to friends.
>
> 

Fornes quoted in *Theater Week*
Oct. 26–Nov 1, 1987, p. 20

BASED AS I AM IN SAN FRANCISCO AND London, I have loved Irene Fornes mainly through her work, so I thought that her admirers might value a few notes and dates on her impact, mainly far from New York.

1963 — For no reason I can recall, I hosted a party to which my friend Herb Blau brought a playwright whose work was in rehearsal at the San Francisco Actor's Workshop. Over thirty-five years later my only recollection of that party is Irene Fornes. Shy, slim, and looking eighteen years old (at thirty-three!), she failed to nibble at the small talk or to drain the large drinks of party fare at that time. In an awkward attempt to befriend Irene, I asked about her background, and we discovered that we had overlapped in Paris in 1954. And that we had both been dazzled by the complex simplicities of Roger Blin's production of *En attendant Godot.* So I was predisposed to love her play *There! You Died* (later revised to *Tango Palace,* but I cherish the original title).

And love it I did. Today I marvel that logocentric Blau virtually choreographed the play. Although I had to refresh my memory on the actors' names — Robert Benson and Dan Sullivan as Isidore and Leopold — I can still see aspects of their duel, with a towering Benson intimidating a lithe Sullivan, as ingenious cards slowly littered the stage floor. Instead of yielding to Fornes' inventive imagery, I compared her pair to Beckett's Vladimir and Estragon. Like Richard Gilman and Toby Zinman after me, I too easily pigeonholed her as an Absurdist (replete with a metaphysical context that I manufactured).

1965 — For all the absurdities (small a) of *The Successful Life of 3*, the label was clearly wrong for the zany intricacies of Fornes' triangle play, which was not as innocent of psychology as she later claimed. (There was a lot of print about regional theater in the 1960s, but if you loved the theater in the USA, you still had to manage a trip to New York, and it was there I saw Fornes' winsome threesome.) In the "Introduction" to Fornes' first collection of plays, Richard Gilman has described the playfulness of his production, but I saw Joe Chaikin's original Open Theatre version; it was the first time I was aware of him as a director of a play, as well as of a company. Chaikin's production sparkled with Transformation Technique as an actor's tool toward quick shifts of mood, filmic parodies, and musical mockeries. The lovable characters (yes, characters!) radiated a compendium of erotic triangles from the Trojan War to B-movies. Although Fornes was to be claimed by feminists, her "She" consistently "thinks with a stupid expression,"[1] and She triumphs in the final "Song To Ignorance" (pp. 64–5). Deliciously light, *The Successful Life of 3* punned theatrically on a "three," whose theatrical life was "successful." Although Fornes' *Promenade* of the same year has received more acclaim — perhaps because of Al Carmines' music — the witty economies of the triangle should appeal to today's budgets. How I'd love to see it again.

1967 — Irene could be grave as well as funny. I saw her at close quarters in the Angry Arts production of *A Vietnamese Wedding*, which lists no director. Irene cites the 1968 production of *Molly's Dream* as her first directorial credit, but in her version of *A Vietnamese Wedding* she enacted a director who actually functioned as a director. It is the only time I saw Fornes direct. She doesn't seem aware of how much she offers to other directors.

Western United States was more prescient than the East about the cruel idiocy of the Vietnam War, and I was a veteran of protests by the time I absorbed Irene's simple, formal initiation into the wedding — her gentle way of protesting. I think that 1967 predated the phrase — "The personal is political," but I know of no performance that embodies it more fully than *A Vietnamese Wedding*.

1975? — During Irene's fallow years, when she headed Theatre Strategy, a New York actress performed a "Sixties Medley" in San Francisco, enacting Dr. Kheal in frayed tuxedo and wire-rimmed glasses. Perhaps that feminine touch softened my view of the beleaguered professor whose name contains the contradictory elements of "heal" and "kill." I no longer possess the program of a therefore anonymous medley, but its performance causes me to reject the usual unloving reduction of Dr. Kheal to his last line: "Man is the rational animal."[2] Although Dr. Kheal is always arrogant and often ridiculous, she begins to falter when examining the human will. She grows abusive to her invisible audience, urinating like a dog, but some of her declarations make sense, or perhaps have a significance beyond sense: "A thing not named and the same thing named are two different things" (p. 132) "That is truth…elusive" (p. 132). For Dr. Kheal love emerges from mathematics, and hope from a drawing of a sunny swim. Dr. Kheal's truths may be elusive, but they are truths for all that.

*Dr. Kheal* was brought briefly to the Bay Area by a visiting New Yorker, but in the 1980s Fornes was produced indigenously — by small, struggling theaters. In the meantime I met Irene at TNT (The New Theater) in Baltimore, Maryland.

1977 or 1978 — My memory is hazy for the context of two dominant impressions of Irene at TNT, but the impressions are vivid. Janitorial help was scarce on the campus where TNT took place, and early one morning I walked into a refuse-strewn room to find Irene busy with a broom. A little later she might have wished for a metaphoric broom to sweep away the antagonisms between those who advocated "pure" theater and those who insisted on a social purpose for theater. As tempers flared, I can see Irene's pained face: "This is a *terribly* unfortunate thing to happen." I wish I could report a happy ending, but TNT died soon afterward.

1981 — Fornes usually dates her more serious plays from *Fefu and Her Friends* in 1977, but it took four years for that groundbreaker to reach the Bay Area. Credit should be given to the director Alma Becker, who was not intimidated by an eight-strong cast in five different settings. Designed by Patrick Monk in the church that was then the home of the Eureka Theater, *Fefu* was a risky and expensive undertaking for a ninety-nine-seater, whose ninety-nine seats were not always full. By and large, Fornes stages the surfaces of her characters in the auditorium-living-room, and their more intimate revelations in kitchen, study, bedroom, and lawn. In these inner scenes at Trinity Methodist Church, we were so close to the actors that it seemed like eavesdropping on privacy. Yet Fornes returns us to the auditorium for the shocking climax, where Fefu's offstage shot kills Julia onstage, and the play ends on a horrified tableau.

Looking back on that play set in 1935, which quotes from a book written in 1917, I feel a slight nostalgia for an age that could swallow a sentence like: "A sense of life universal surges through our life individual." And I realize once again that theater is the most ephemeral of goods. I dropped two names that are unfamiliar to you — the director Alma Becker and the designer Patrick Monk, both of whom disappeared from the Bay Area theater scene, perhaps from theater itself. Of the eight sterling actors of *Fefu and Her Friends*, Linda Hoy-Fefu and Lorri Holt-Christina have had long, active careers in the Bay Area, but are unknown outside it. The Trinity Methodist Church, so hospitable to the Eureka Theater, burned down four months after *Fefu* closed. The play itself, so brightly analyzed by Scott T. Cummings, Deborah Geis, William Gruber, Beverly Pevitts, Marc Robinson, Ross Wetzsteon, William Worthen, is rarely revived. I wonder how many of these critics have actually *seen* the play.

1985 — Sometimes one can love a play in spite of a production. Three years after Fornes directed *The Danube* in Padua Hills, California (where she has worked intermittently), it arrived in San Francisco. The Eureka Theater had just opened its new home in a converted garage, and it turned valiantly to Fornes to fill 200 seats. However, lacking the exterior-interior contrasts of *Fefu*, and not knowing what to make of the language-tapes, the director conducted a reading rather than a performance. An unanimated reading at that. Dry ice smoking through the floorboards was the signal for a change of scene, but dialogue continued in the same flat tone. Only Larry Pisoni (of the Pickle Family Circus) gave physical vigor to a waiter, a doctor, a barber, and Mr. Kovacs.

Although I sensed a dark undercurrent in *The Danube*, only in reading it afterwards was I aware that Fornes had dramatized the death of Europe during World War II. The physical disintegration of the principals precedes their relegation to puppet status. For Eve's father: "There's no place to go."[3] Even if Eve and Paul escape to America, the life of the Danube dies beyond resurrection.

1989 — Sometimes a little theater can achieve an impeccable production. Although the London-based Shared Experience's *Abingdon Square* (directed by Nancy Meckler) later transferred to the Royal National Theatre, I saw it at the small Soho Poly, where the designer Lucy Weller miraculously produced an all-white set bounded by right-angled flowerbeds. Looking nothing like a room in an actual Abingdon Square mansion, the space was a frame for Fornes' formal and understated words. Meckler, an American with decades of British stage experience, adapts her directing style to the particular playwright, and for *Abingdon Square* she found a naturalistic kernel within each controlled action. Or rather, she guided the actors to do so, individually and severally. Fornes' scenes are so short that the actors resort to a modified transformation technique to negotiate the emotional rapids. The word "stylized" seems to me a cop-out term for non-naturalistic acting that resists description; yet I don't know what other adjective to use. Rarely have I seen a more coherent production. When Philip Voss as Juster dies at the end of this cruelly tender play, his unfaithful wife cries out: "He mustn't die!"[4] For me at least he will never die. *Abingdon Square* is my pinnacle of Fornes productions.

1990 — But *Mud* follows hard behind. Fornes wrote the play in Padua Hills in 1983 although the verb *wrote* fails to convey how objects triggered her scenes, which went into workshop while she was still composing. Daytime performance originated the eight-second freezes that end each of her seventeen scenes, and she liked the effect enough to retain it. When *Mud* migrated to Northern California, it was to the non-Equity Magic Theatre, where the casting was a triumph of transplantation. Local director Mary Forcade imported Gregory Pace, the original Lloyd of Padua Hills. Bay Area–veteran John Robb played Henry. And from New York came Wendy vanden Heuvel, graceful in her ungainly movements, resonant in her effortful speech. Ironing mechanically, reading painfully, she was at once naturalistically credible and radiantly ambitious.

*Mud* causes most critics to invoke Beckett, and like that master Fornes "vaguens" the setting of her elemental characters. Although the quasibiblical mud was offstage, its traces were evident on Mae's feet and Lloyd's clothes. Mae wishes not upon a star, but upon the description of a starfish in a book. Her rival lovers, sick Lloyd and insecure Henry, grow increasingly dependent on her. Barely articulate, muddy and muddled, they may read like our inferiors, but Forcade's direction imbued them with a hard tenderness that was more eloquent than their language. Perhaps the whiteouts contributed to this hermetic world that reflected our own in its brutal hunger for love. Nearly two decades after her Open Theatre play, Fornes dramatized the unsuccessful life of three.

1996 — My last Fornes date links up with the Open Theatre. For the 25th anniversary performance of *Terminal,* directed by Joe Chaikin, Open Theatre members traveled to San Diego from the far corners of the country. The radically revised *Terminal* belied its title, with young actors newly initiated into a theater that they found experimental. However, they were confronted with exclusionary reminiscence when aging panelists underlined their own uniqueness. But not Irene Fornes, who spoke briefly of the freedoms implicit in Chaikin's sometimes dictatorial Open Theatre exercises. She was no longer shy or slim, but her large dark eyes carried the fervor of youth. "How do you manage to look so young?" I teased her, but Irene is impervious to flattery. Looking me square in the eye, she responded sternly: "I'm sixty-five." A good age to write a play, and with a little luck I'll see it and love it.

1. Maria Irene Fornes, *The Successful Life of 3* in *Promenade and Other Plays* (New York: Performing Arts Journal Publications, 1987), p. 48. Subsequent references are parenthesized.

2. Maria Irene Fornes, *Dr. Kheal* in *Promenade and Other Plays,* p. 135. Subsequent references are parenthesized.

3. Maria Irene Fornes, *The Danube* in *Plays* (New York: Performing Arts Journal Publications, 1986), p. 64.

4. Maria Irene Fornes, *Abingdon Square* in *Womens Work: Five New Plays from the Women's Project,* ed. Julia Miles (New York and Tonbridge: Applause, 1989), p. 42.

# ❀ KATE CARNEY
*Actor*

## IRENE FORNES:
## PATIENT, CATALYTIC GENIUS

IRENE FORNES' ORIGINAL AND BRILLIANT mind has challenged and changed me more than once. We worked together in the Open Theatre in the 1960s and enjoyed talking when we met at Greenwich Village copy shops and bookstores.

When I was looking for a piece of hers to perform in a one-person show about New York experimental theater, she suggested *Dr. Kheal*. It became part of *Off-Off-Broadway!* several times, in Europe and then New York.

In the winter of 1973, Irene had to find a quick replacement for her half of a Sam Shepard/Irene Fornes double bill at Theatre Genesis. She called on a Tuesday, "Could you perform *Dr. Kheal* by Friday?"

"Yes," I said, "if Michael [Smith], my director has time." Irene said she'd be happy to direct too. I was thrilled, but outnumbered by directors, I felt swamped. It was too much attention for both were exacting. If Irene would say, "That's ha, ha, ha, ha, not ha, ha, ha," Michael would affirm the value of the fourth "ha" and find other omissions.

A year or so later, at a rehearsal at her studio apartment, I asked her how *Dr. Kheal* came to be.

In an apothecary's cabinet of drawers, which filled a whole wall of her studio apartment, she stored ideas and images, different drawers for different plays. One drawer was overflowing with snippets that had not fit into any other play. This drawer had gotten so full that it could barely be closed, but she could not bear to throw any of the insights away. A friend had suggested she put the bits together as a teacher's lecture. *Dr. Kheal* was born.

Rehearsal space at Irene's was a problem. There were tables piled with thick file folders, full of plays in progress, the apothecary's cabinet, a settee, some chairs, and myriad costumes for shows she was working on.

One gray, wintry, Saturday afternoon, the space seemed more impassable than ever. It was hard to make a properly assertive entrance as Dr. Kheal must. Irene suggested I enter from the kitchen, a space so densely packed with a tiny stove, refrigerator, and sink that it must have once been a closet.

I inserted myself into the space between the stove where a stew — Cuban menudo? — bubbled and a windowed wall with narrow shelves full of crockery. There was barely room in which to turn around before I was to sweep in through the louvered swinging doors.

Rehearsal began. Irene stopped me before I got through the first sentence, time after time. I was sure I was doing everything as she'd directed me. It had worked well for audiences.

With each retreat to the tiny kitchen, I saw more breakables that might topple if I moved an inch in the wrong direction. With each failed attempt I grew more and more inhibited. The gray afternoon light was begining to fade and I saw us grinding away at this entrance deep into the night. We'd never get to the rest of the play. I dreaded the thought of inching through the thirty-five minute piece. I was sure the frustration was mutual. I despaired of ever getting off the treadmill of shuttling between that claustrophobic kitchen and the cluttered living room. If she would just let me get past the beginning, I'd get into it, I'd be fine. But she was not going to let me until I got the entrance right.

Back in the kitchen for the fifteenth time, I turned, ducking the hanging vegetable basket, the simmering menudo pot at my right, and the trembling crockery on my left.

Then it hit me: "This woman has the most interesting mind I know. I will enter into it. I will let go of what I think works. I will go into Irene Fornes' brain." Why hadn't I thought of it before?

Suddenly everything seemed easy — but risky. My body charged through the swinging doors and I played the opening just as I'd been doing all afternoon — except that my mind was different. She did not stop me.

After I'd finished, she said, "That was fine, right from the entrance.

The spirit was right. My notes are little things, nothing worth stopping for."

Now, when I rehearse *Dr. Kheal*, I let go. It's out of my hands. I move into Irene's eccentric, argumentative, and paradoxical mind — and trust in her challenge — that she and Dr. Kheal are almost always right.

# ❀ SUSAN SONTAG
*Critic, Writer*


## ON MARIA IRENE FORNES


FOR MANY YEARS MARIA IRENE FORNES HAS been conducting with exemplary tenacity and scrupulousness a unique career in the American theater.

Born in Havana, Fornes arrived in this country with her family when she was fifteen; in her twenties she spent several years in France (she was painting then), and began writing plays after she returned to New York, when she was around thirty. Although the language in which she became a writer was English, not Spanish — and Fornes' early work is inconceivable without the reinforcement of the lively local New York milieu (particularly the Judson Poets Theatre) in which she surfaced in the early 1960s — she is unmistakably a writer of bicultural inspiration: one very American way of being a writer. Her imagination seems to me to have, among other sources, a profoundly Cuban one. I am reminded of the witty, sensual phantasmagorias of Cuban writers such as Lydia Cabrera, Calvert Casey, Virgilio Piñera.

Of course, writers, these or any other, were not the conscious influences on Fornes or any of the best "downtown" theater of the 1960s. Art Nouveau and Hollywood Deco had more to do with, say, The Theater of the Ridiculous, than any plausible literary antecedents (Tzara, Firbank, etc.). This is also true of Fornes, an autodidact whose principal influences were neither theater nor literature but certain styles of painting and the movies. But unlike similarly influenced New York dramatists, her work did not eventually become parasitic on literature (or opera, or movies). It was never a revolt against theater, or a theater recycling fantasies encoded in other genres.

Her two earliest plays prefigure the dual register, one volkisch, the other placeless-international, of all the subsequent work. *The Widow,* a poignant chronicle of a simple life, is set in Cuba, while *Tango Palace,* with its volleys of sophisticated exchanges, takes place in a purely theatrical space: a cave, an altar. Fornes has a complex relation to the strategy of naivete. She is chary of the folkloristic, rightly so. But she is strongly drawn to the preliterary: to the authority of documents, of found materials such as letters of her great-grandfather's cousin that inspired *The Widow,* the diary of a domestic servant in turn-of-the-century New Hampshire that was transformed into *Evelyn Brown,* Emma's lecture in *Fefu and Her Friends.*

For a while she favored the musical play — in a style reminiscent of the populist parables in *musical-commedia* form preserved in films from the 1930s like Rene Clair's *À Nous la Liberté.* It was a genre that proclaimed its innocence, and specialized in rueful gaiety. Sharing with the main tradition of modernist drama an aversion to the reductively psychological and to sociological explanations, Fornes chose a theater of types (such personages as the defective sage and the woman enslaved by sexual dependence reappear in a number of plays) and a theater of miracles: the talking mirror in *The Office,* the fatal gun wound at the end of *Fefu and Her Friends.* Lately, Fornes seems to be eschewing this effect: the quotidian as something to be violated — by lyricism, by disaster. Characters can still break into song, as they did in the dazzling bittersweet plays of the mid-1960s, like *Promenade* and *Molly's Dream* and *The Successful Life of 3.* But the plays are less insistently charming. Reality is less capricious. More genuinely lethal — as in *Eyes on the Harem, Sarita.*

Character is revealed through catechism. People requiring or giving instruction is a standard situation in Fornes' plays. The desire to be initiated, to be taught, is depicted as an essential, and essentially pathetic, longing. (Fornes' elaborate sympathy for the labor of thought is the endearing observation of someone who is almost entirely self-taught.) And there are many dispensers of wisdom in Fornes' plays, apart from those — *Tango Palace, Dr. Kheal* — specifically devoted to the comedy and the pathos of instruction. But Fornes is neither literary nor antiliterary. These are not cerebral exercises or puzzles but the real questions, about… the conduct of life. There is much wit but no nonsense. No banalities. And no non sequiturs.

While some plays are set in never-never land, some have local flavors — like the American 1930s of *Fefu and Her Friends*. Evoking a specific setting, especially when it is Hispanic (this being understood as an under-privileged reality), or depicting the lives of the oppressed and humiliated, especially when the subject is that emblem of oppression, the woman servant, such plays as *Evelyn Brown* and *The Conduct of Life* may seem more "realistic" — given the condescending assumptions of the ideology of realism. (Oppressed women, particularly domestic servants and prostitutes, have long been the signature subject of what is sometimes called realism, sometimes naturalism.) But I am not convinced that Fornes' recent work is any less a theater of fantasy than it was, or more now a species of dramatic realism. Her work is both a theater about utterance (i.e., a meta-theater) and a theater about the disfavored — both Handke *and* Kroetz, as it were.

It was always a theater of heartbreak. But at the beginning the mood was often throwaway, playful. Now it's darker, more passionate: consider the twenty-year trajectory that goes from *The Successful Life of 3* to *Mud,* about the unsuccessful life of three. She writes increasingly from a woman's point of view. Women are doing women's things — performing unrewarded labor (in *Evelyn Brown),* getting raped (in *The Conduct of Life)* — and also, as in *Fefu and Her Friends,* incarnating the human condition as such. Fornes has a near faultless ear for the ruses of egotism and cruelty. Unlike most contemporary dramatists, for whom psychological brutality is the principal, inexhaustible subject, Fornes is never in complicity with the brutality she depicts. She has an increasingly expressive relation to dread, to grief, and to passion — in *Sarita,* for example, which is about sexual passion and the incompatibilities of desire. Dread is not just a subjective state but is attached to history: the psychology of torturers *(The Conduct of Life),* nuclear war *(The Danube).*

Fornes' work has always been intelligent, often funny, never vulgar or cynical; both delicate and visceral. Now it is something more. (The turning point, I think, was the splendid *Fefu and Her Friends* — with its much larger palette of sympathies, for both Julia's incurable despair and Emma's irrepressible jubilation.) The plays have always been about wisdom: what it means to be wise. They are getting wiser.

It is perhaps not appropriate here to do more than allude to her great distinction and subtlety as a director of her own plays, and as an inspiring and original teacher (working mainly with young Hispanic-American playwrights). But it seems impossible not to connect the truthfulness in Fornes' plays, their alertness of depicting, their unfacile compassionateness, with a certain character, a certain virtue. In the words of a Northern Sung landscape painter, Kuo Hsi, if the artist "can develop a natural, sincere, gentle and honest heart, then he will immediately be able to comprehend the aspect of tears and smiles and of objects, pointed or oblique, bent or inclined, and they will be so clear in his mind that he will be able to put them down spontaneously with his paint brush." Hers seems to be an admirable temperament, unaffectedly independent, high-minded, ardent. And one of the few agreeable spectacles that our culture affords is to watch the steady ripening of this beautiful talent.

First published as the preface to Maria Irene Fornes, *Plays* (New York: Performing Arts Journal Publications, 1986).

# ✺ JULIA MILES
*Artistic Director, The Women's Project,*
*New York*


## AN INVESTIGATION
## OF MARIA IRENE FORNES


IN NOVEMBER 1997, THE WOMEN'S PROJECT
held a conference entitled "Women in Theatre: Mapping the Sources
of Power." Maria Irene Fornes was on the Playwrights Panel and spoke
of the process of writing a play. For her, "it is somewhat like an investigation — find out why this thing interests me, and ultimately, an audience." I'm "investigating" my great admiration, respect, and love for
Irene's plays and for this truly remarkable and exhilarating playwright.

Irene's plays are unique in form. Images are as important as
text, perhaps more so. Character is supreme, and the language is poetic
and often irreverent. I saw Irene's *Promenade* (with Al Carmines' music)
at the Judson Church in the mid-1960s but missed her one and early
Broadway production *The Office*, so Irene and Broadway are not part
of my "investigation." Just as well! She is an Off-Broadway star with
many, many, many Obies to prove it.

In 1974, I got to know this lady when we produced *Dr. Kheal*
at the American Place Theatre when I was the Associate Director. A
few years later costume designer Willa Kim and I went to see a play of
Irene's in an apartment. I could not articulate my reasons — I didn't
know what it meant really — but I knew that I had to produce this
play *Fefu and Her Friends* with its women and their contradictions,
and we did the play at the American Place Theatre in 1978, the year
that I founded the Women's Project. Of course, Irene directed, and I
remember the Stage Manager taking Polaroids of the positions of the

actors, so the director could be certain they would take the exact same positions every time!

The American Place Theatre produced *The Danube* in 1984, a powerful and scary play, and the Women's Project produced *Abingdon Square* in 1987. This was the year we became independent from APT and rented the theater from them to do the play, because, well, it was the right stage for it.

Irene always directs the original productions of her work, and she should. Of course, when other playwrights ask if they can direct the work, I reply: "No, you're not Irene Fornes." And it's true. It's also true, as my investigation proved, what interests Irene, interests me — always.

# OSKAR EUSTIS
*Artistic Director, Trinity Rep*
*Providence, Rhode Island*

## MYSTERY

IN THE LATE 1970S, MY FRIEND JIM LEVERETT, now a Professor at Yale and Columbia, asked me to come see a production of a new play by Maria Irene Fornes, *Fefu and Her Friends*. He told me that he wasn't certain that I would like it, but that if I didn't, we would no longer be friends.

He didn't need to worry. That production, the original incarnation of what is perhaps Irene's most widely known work, was an absolutely seminal theater experience for me. I had never seen intelligence and intuition, history and character, environmental and realistic theater, narrative and experimental techniques combined in such an extraordinary way. What was clear to me that night has remained clear ever since: Irene Fornes is a dazzling, unique artist, both of her time and completely individual.

Tony Kushner once remarked to me that Irene's unconscious must have a structural density that most of us lack, and I know what he means: Her plays create a language of their own, are each experiments in which the form seems reinvented to carry the specific content and characters of that particular piece. From *Promenade*, to *Fefu*, from *Mud* to *Sarita*, from *The Danube* to *The Conduct of Life*, each of Irene's plays seem as organic and inevitable as classic art works, seamlessly constructed so there never seems a disjunction between the life of the play and how that life expresses itself. And yet each play is also wholly itself: Rarely have we had such a self-consciously inventive and experimental writer. She is a mystery in many ways.

As such, she has also been a writer's writer. She has always been more appreciated within the profession than outside it: Sometimes I think no one who has not wrestled with problems of narrative and representation in our post-modern world can completely appreciate the magnitude of her achievement. But she has also been enormously influential within the profession: No teacher of her last generation has had a more profound impact on young writers than Irene. The purity of her example, the generosity of her teaching, the radicality of her methods are all things that have made her workshops legendary.

Irene's magnificent body of work and her sometimes lonely, always principled career, stand as a constant reminder to us of what the theater is capable of, even in this diminished era. She is the model of an artist who can follow her own vision and still have a powerful impact on those around her. We are lucky to have her among us.

# ❀ MARTHA BOESING
*Playwright, Actor, director, Founder
and Artistic Director of At the Foot of
the Mountain, the longest running
professional women's company in the USA*

I FIRST HEARD OF AND BRIEFLY MET IRENE
in the sixties when she came to the Firehouse Theater in Minneapolis,
for a production of *Tango Palace*. Later Paul Boesing, who performed
in her first (I believe) Off-Broadway production, *The Successful Life of
3,* and I were to become core members of the Firehouse Theater Company. In 1970, when the Firehouse Theater left for San Francisco and
Paul and I stayed in Minneapolis to pursue a musical theater career,
he directed and I performed in *Promenade* for the Cricket Theater. Our
paths crossed over the years, but it wasn't until 1985, when I played Fefu
in Irene's production of *Fefu and Her Friends* for At the Foot of the
Mountain — Minneapolis' professional women's theater where I had
recently reigned as playwright and Artistic Director — that I really got
to know her.

Irene arrived with her mother, many suitcases, and a head full of
very clear ideas about how this production should look. She chose the
venue (another old firehouse, where the Mixed Blood Theater had set-
tled); she designed the set and carefully watched over its construction;
she went shopping in all the secondhand rag shops the city has to offer
for the costumes; she meticulously hunted down the props; and she
directed the play with attention to every gesture, every nuance of voice.
If this sounds dictatorial, it was. Many of us had been dallying At the
Foot of the Mountain's more collaborative playing field and I in particular would jump in with ideas and images every time Irene asked a
question (which she did, out loud, with great frequency, talking — it
turned out — to herself) only to be told that she was the director, not
I, and that she would make all the decisions, thank you very much.

But she was the warmest, the funniest, the most kind-hearted dictator any of us had every met, and we all fell in love with her. *Fefu* was a huge success and Irene was the toast of the town. She took it all in stride and, generously sharing the accolades, hosted us all at a banquet at a gourmet restaurant down the river a-ways, after the last show — an event none of us will ever forget.

The day she won my heart was the day we had a fiercely screaming fight in the parking lot behind our theater. It went on for what seemed like hours to me. It was about whether any "true" theater art can be created by collaborating on the ideas or the script or the directing, which Irene, upholding the stance of the true individualist, was convinced it could not. All art, she maintained, needed the singular mind of one artist behind it to achieve anything worth calling art, whereas I, coming from a history of collaboration from both the Firehouse and At the Foot of the Mountain theaters thought this was so much capitalist bunk. It was a glorious argument — free from personal garbage, passionate and impetuous. We never came to an agreement. But I thought she was magnificent to take me on and stick to her case, refusing to be intimidated by me. So I bought her a bouquet of flowers immediately afterwards, by no means as an apology for fighting but just to celebrate who she was.

Irene is an amazing woman — ardent, intelligent, witty, opinionated, and generous — a rarity.

# ✸ JOSEPH CHAIKIN
*Actor, Director, Founder of*
*The Open Theatre*

IRENE FORNES IS REMARKABLE. SHE IS ONE of my two favorite playwrights. Working on her plays in the days of the Open Theatre was special. Now I look forward to working with her again, at the Signature.

# ✾ ALICE TUAN
*Playwright*

TO BE AROUND IRENE FORNES IS TO LEARN how to write from the marrow.

# ❂ MAC WELLMAN
*Playwright*

SIMPLY PUT, AMERICAN PLAYWRITING WOULD be unimaginable without Irene Fornes. In her best plays (my favorites are *Fefu* and *Abingdon Square* and *The Danube*) she manages a crystallization of behavior, emotion, and idea that is rare in any art, but almost unknown in the theater. Her writing is wry, comic, complex, and scary. Her writing is also never hectoring, knee-jerk, or merely of the moment; hence the gravity of the plays, their refusal to be anything other than what they are.

Irene Fornes may be our only truly indispensable playwright. Certainly no one I know of has brought more dignity to the craft, in our time, than she.

Madeleine Potter (Marion) and John Seitz (Juster)

*ABINGDON SQUARE*
The Women's Project and Productions, at the American Place Theatre,
New York City, 1987

Photo by Anne Militello

# ✹ DAVID HARROWER
*Playwright*


"You have to know how to enter another person's life."[1]


THIS LINE, SPOKEN BY MARION IN FORNES'
*Abingdon Square* has stayed with me since I read it and in the strange alchemical process by which poetry works has come to affect my approach to writing drama.

"You have to know how to enter another person's life."

The attitude that Fornes' characters strike in relation to the play; how they seem to step aside from dramatic dialogue and so beautifully suggest ideas to each other. How Fornes has for so long subverted the traditional motivations and easily readable psychologies — what a character "wants" that so often seems to limit them to drives and dullness, robbing them of potential and possibility. Fornes has done so much to subvert this — her characters find so much else to dwell on — they positively seem to study the world around them. But above all, it is the presence of the other characters around them, and how these people must be taken into consideration that finally determines how any of Fornes' characters are "like" themselves. This is what is truly important, they seem to say — how I am touched upon by others. The presence of other characters around them continually occupies them and how only the briefest meeting with another person can change the direction of anyone.

"You have to know how to enter another person's life."

In my own writing this line has taught me the importance of "entry points." Where exactly to start each character's life, when to enter and present the world — exactly how much needs to be revealed to an audience to move them, to involve them absolutely. How characters are "reached"; how they contradict themselves, continually evolving and growing within the journey of the play. Where the play is begun and where it is ended.

1. Maria Irene Fornes, *Abingdon Square* in *Womens Work: Five New Plays from the Women's Project*, ed. Julia Miles (New York and Tonbridge: Applause, 1989), p. 17.

# ✺ MURRAY MEDNICK
*Director, Producer, Los Angeles*


## ON MARIA IRENE FORNES


I AM FORTUNATE IN BEING ABLE TO CLAIM a long asssociation with Irene Fornes, dating back to the sixties, but the impression regarding her that seems to come most readily to mind occurred in 1994 at the penultimate Padua Hills Playwrights Workshop/Festival. We were at a place called Woodbury University in Burbank, thirty miles from downtown Los Angeles, and were rehearsing plays outside all over the campus. I was working at a switchback walkway that connected the soccer field with the building facilities. Behind me was a swimming pool. Just down the way, Irene was transforming the side of an embankment to the soccer field. Students streamed through by the hundreds in every direction, planes flew overhead, and a steady hum from the nearby freeway caused us to sometimes shout lines and direction. We often rehearsed at the same time. Our actors could hear each other, as could Irene and I, and I could not help frequently glancing in her direction to see what she was doing, partly out of interest, but mainly for the relief and support of seeing her there with that characteristic valor and determination of hers, that call to intelligence and taste that she seemed to make with every directorial gesture. She appeared to thrive amidst the chaos and adversity, her voice ringing out with authority and the joy of working. Of course, these qualities of Irene's had given us all strength for years, and even now, remembering that scene in Burbank, I feel encouraged by her example — as did Padua's many audiences and students — and privileged to be her colleague.

# ✹ MARTIN EPSTEIN
*Playwright, Teacher of playwriting and dramatic literature, Tisch School of the Arts, New York University*

SUMMER, 1984. IRENE WAS DOING HER first (outdoor) production of *The Conduct of Life* for the Padua Hills Playwrights Festival at Cal Arts. The school, in Valencia, is situated on a rising promontory of rock and dirt, surrounded by insulated clusters of beige ranch-style housing developments with brownish lawns, dark picture windows and never a soul in sight. Irene was still searching for a performing space, and I called her attention to a large grassy field that extended back to a two-lane highway. The terrace we were standing on was where Irene eventually chose to put the audience, as well as stage the indoor family scenes, while members of a death squad seized and carried people off in the field below. The final scene, played around sunset, had Nena (Sheila Dabney), running up the empty highway, right to left, while the death squad, driving slowly in a large car, bumped her to her knees several times before throwing her inside and driving off. It was a devastating ending, made more so for one particular performance when a local jogger in red shorts suddenly appeared and continued his slow inclining trot in the wake of the car. So the audience thought they were watching Irene's final providential touch. And who's to say they weren't.

# ✸ LEON MARTELL
*Actor, Playwright*

## WORKING WITH MARIA IRENE FORNES

I FEEL SO LUCKY TO HAVE WORKED AS closely and for as many times as I have with Maria Irene Fornes. Though most consider me a writer, to Irene, I am an actor. Our relationship started in 1982, when I was invited to do one of my plays, *Hoss Drawin'* at the Padua Hills Playwrights Festival. In those years, Padua was a fearless endeavor, people wrote and directed a play while acting in another and teaching classes. There was nothing else to do out in Claremont, but make theater and engage in drunken art fights. It was a glorious time. I was the junior writer, Murray Mednick and Irene were the spiritual Mom and Dad of the place, and the rest of us found our place in the dramatic spectrum. The students at the time included Jon Robin Baitz and Kelly Stuart among others.

Since it was already written and my wife, Beth Ruscio, and I had performed it before, there was not the usual festival hysteria involved in mounting the piece. The festival was a "creative community" that put on the plays…everyone wore many hats, and accordingly, it wasn't surprising that I would be auditioning for one of the other playwright's plays. I can't remember the audition, but the play was *The Danube*. I think at that time it was called "You Can Swim in the Danube, But the Water Is Too Cold." The entire play is made up of dialogue originally gleaned from "Learn to Speak Hungarian" records, which Irene found at a garage sale.

'Garage saling' was one of the biggest pursuits in Claremont. Looking for inspiration, and cheap props, at garage sales. Irene never failed to be inspired. Irene said that when she listened to the recording, she saw a strange world. The man spoke in a monotone, and said things like "The weather is bad." What is "bad" weather? Inclement? Evil?…

She recorded the record onto tape and then edited the tape, sometimes in the middle of the night in her room, using ordinary scissors and scotch tape, until it finally told the story of Mr. Alexander, his daughter Eve, and Paul, the visitor from America. I think I got the role because I was a farm boy from Vermont, and in some ways it still showed. Irene wanted guilelessness and simplicity. "When these people ask, 'How are you?' they are really inquiring about your health." Every line in the play was said on tape, in English, and Hungarian, before the live actors said it. It was a very tenuous spell to maintain. The audience knew our lives, before we did. The surprises came in who would be speaking. The same man, in slightly cheerful monotone gave each line on the tape, but any one of us on stage could deliver it. Innocence, simplicity, and love. Paul fell in chaste, simple, love with Eve in this world, which slowly began to fill with smoke from pots below the outdoor stage. By the end of the play, the characters are all wearing gas masks, still trying to connect. In the hands of anyone else, it could have been a disaster, but, this was Irene. From the beginning, she knew this world, these people, and as an actor I quickly learned, that *nothing* we did was taken for granted or overlooked. Irene had been a painter, and she watches her actors as carefully as a painter observes color.

I don't mean this to sound manipulative. She has very deep intuitions about the characters, she knows what's right when she sees it, but we bring ourselves to the roles. She expects such deep commitment to each gesture, that the actor needs to fill in a complete internal life to achieve the correct externals, to stay with the music of the piece. Irene didn't seem concerned about how we got our performance. She treats actors like professionals and assumes that's your job, to find a way to give a desired performance for the piece. I was simply pleased to have a director who paid such strict attention *and* who knew what this play was, beyond a literal understanding. A writer/director who had such a deep sense of style.

I told one interviewer years ago that I felt like Irene's pit bull. By that I meant that I was free to let myself go, to give over to the process and trust completely, because I knew that there was a strong and confident hand on my leash. I wouldn't go over the top, I wouldn't fall outside what was needed in the play. I could try anything, knowing that

Irene would not allow anything that wasn't right for the play, and that absolutely everything I did as an actor would be noticed, considered and directed, by a master. What a gift.

After *The Danube* I worked on several Padua projects with Irene, but the quintessential experience came in 1992 at the Festival Dionysia in Siena, Italy. Irene had been invited to represent the United States, and I was lucky enough to be invited by her to be one of her actors. There were five of us, Leo Garcia, Shauna Casey, Kimberly Flynn, Steve Hofvendahl, and myself. Irene had written an opera for a project for 1992, which was the five-hundredth anniversary of Christopher Columbus' voyage to the New World. As she often does, she was reworking that project, this time stripping away the music and working with the text as a play. The opera was in its very early stage and everything was to be rearranged, rewritten, rethought. Knowing that it had been an opera text, one could feel the arrangement of arias, duets, trios...but I doubt that an audience would ever have noticed. There were elements of the play that Irene manipulated and repositioned as she had the tape in *The Danube*.

The play *Terra Incognita* was set in a street cafe in Europe. Three friends — a brother and sister, and her best friend, traveling together — have stopped for tea. They talk about their trip, shopping, postcards, journal entries, the mundanities of tourism...and the brother reads newspaper articles aloud, concerning the Iraqi soldiers who were killed during the Gulf War, thousands of conscripts, buried alive in trenches by bulldozer tanks. They are interrupted by a rancid-smelling street person, (my part), who badgers them with his opinions on sailing and geography. He can't imagine that anyone wouldn't share his enthusiasm for his ideas. At a nearby table sits a man alone. On occasions, he quotes from the letters of Bartolomeo de las Casas, a monk who documented the slaughter of the Caribbean Indians as a protest to the King of Spain. De las Casas was the first to sound the alarm, that the Spanish in the New World had lost all regard for life, that what they were doing was, without a doubt, evil, and if the Indians were not treated with at least simple compassion, the Spanish Empire would, without a doubt, incur the wrath of God, collapse, and the Spanish nation burn in hell for all eternity. De las Casas' letters brought about a change in official policy but only after thousands of innocents had been butchered. He was later canonized and is the patron saint of the Indians. Now, how do these elements come together? To explain the play, even if I could, is not the play, and all this set up is only to bring you to share a moment of creation with Maria Irene Fornes.

We rehearsed the play, as it existed, in pieces, for a week in New York, then flew to Italy. We touched down in Rome and went right from customs to a bus that whisked us across the countryside and past Siena to the little farming community of Castelnuovo Berardenga. We were to live and rehearse here for the next three weeks until we performed in Siena. As we piled off the bus, I remember one of the Nigerian actors exclaiming, "As far as we have seen, Italy is an entirely agricultural country!" He was right, we had gone from the airport, through farm country, to farm country and now we were put up at a *fattoria,* a farming community, some of the stone buildings dating back to the fifteenth century. The American men and the Poles stayed in a modern version of the stone bunk houses, with stove, showers and all the modern conveniences, the American women stayed in the ancient manor house (or whatever ones calls that in Italy, the main house) that had been outfitted with the same. The buildings were often rented out to vacationers who came to enjoy the countryside, rolling hills covered with grape arbors and wheat fields.

We began rehearsing as soon as we got off the bus. Irene's energy is boundless. We had flown all night, taken the bus from Rome, and Irene had the energy to conduct a rehearsal *and* make edits, rewrites, and changes on the script as we rehearsed. I have to admit, for the first and only time in my career, I feel asleep during a rehearsal, while on stage. I was wasted. We survived the first rehearsal and caught up with Irene's energy, refining older scenes, adding new lines, re-ordering, and refining. While Irene did rewrites in the mornings, we would first do yoga for an hour, led by Kimberly, who taught yoga in New York, then I would walk on the country roads, going over my lines and preparing for rehearsal.

It was actor heaven, aside from the fact of having to "represent the United States" at the end of this process. Here were superb actors from all over the world, whom we were getting to know at our communal dinners every evening, so there was definite pressure to have this play, which we were still fashioning, be great. Each evening, the entire festival, all actors and playwrights, were loaded onto a bus and shuttled to a big cafeteria in Castelnuovo Berardenga where we all ate together. Many days, I sat with Irene, for the forty-five minute ride along the mountain road into town, and as she talked about what we had done that day, where the play was going, what was missing… I learned more about writing than at any other time and place in my life.

A few days into rehearsal Irene's mother, Carmen, flew in to be with us. Carmen was, I believe, one hundred and one at the time. I'd known her since she was a girl in her early nineties. Despite the fact that she had trouble hearing and seeing and spoke limited English, she was very funny, a shameless flirt, and commanded deep respect from everyone. At an age when most people have been, yes, dead for twenty years, she was flying around the world to see what Irene was doing. When she arrived, it was the usual pattern. On the first day, she reclined on a row of chairs while watching rehearsal. On the second day, she sat up. On the third day, she was arguing with Irene about directing choices. It was apparent where Irene had gotten her fire.

The play was taking shape nicely, but as anyone who works in a nontraditional way can attest, the hardest part is, the ending. How does it come together? What does it add up to? We all trusted Irene to know, inside, what would bring the vectors together in an organic way. A few days before the performance, various endings had been tried and rejected. Irene had a look on her face that I had seen before, the look that generals probably have before battles. It shows they have the situation under control, but they also acknowledge that they have to pull a miracle out to make this work. I had seen Irene produce miracles on a regular basis, but knowing that it would have to eventually come through us actors, we were all sweating.

As I remember it, it was the final day before tech. We were to do our play on a stage that had been erected in a fourteenth-century courtyard of the Public Palace in Siena. It's off the Plaza Del Campo where the Palio, Siena's famous horse race, has been run since the Middle Ages. Theater artists from all over the world were coming to an ancient and historic place to see our play, and it didn't have a satisfactory ending.

We were rehearsing in the "American men's" kitchen. That's when the storm hit. It was midday, but the sky turned black, completely blotting out the sun. The rain and wind came up, horizontal weather, wind blowing the rain so hard that it pounded straight against doors and windows. Lightning flashed all around followed by immediate thunder. The storm was all over us. Irene was trying to reshape the end of the play. Of course, the power went out and it was midnight-on-a-country-road dark. Luckily, the house had candles, so we continued by candlelight.

The ending was really on Leo and Steve, the brother character and the reincarnation of de las Casas. The brother had been cynical throughout the play and fixated on death statistics in the Gulf War. The sister and friend leave for a moment, and the brother confided to the man, that he has AIDS. Everything made sense, both intellectually and emotionally. Now what? The rain started to come in under the door. I put a couple of our towels down to block the flood. Irene had Steve do one of de las Casas' speeches depicting the slaughter of the innocents. There was still something missing. The flame on the candles was blown horizontal by the wind tearing through cracks in the wall. The water overwhelmed the towel dam in minutes. During any pauses I used our remaining towels to bail water that was flooding the room into the kitchen sink. We were all huddled within a few feet of each other, in candlelight, in a tempest.

Irene had Steve do the speech again, and this time, she told Leo, your clothes begin to burn your skin, you have to get free of them. The brother wore an impeccable summer suit. Steve did the speech again, telling of the gentle, naked people of the Caribbean, hacked to pieces by the merciless Spanish soldiers and Leo tore at his clothes until he was huddled, and helpless, squatting on the floor. Everyone was weeping. Everything came together, and the lightning flashed all around.

We went on to do the play a few days later, with much success, but nothing will compare with experiencing Irene birth the end of the play in the lightning storm. The next year, Irene worked on *Terra Incognita* as an opera again and in 1994, at the Padua Festival, I got to work with her on it, again, as a play. There are few enough people who are even "very good" in the theater, and a only handful who are truly "great." I feel so lucky to have sustained a relationship with someone for whom

I can have unquestioned respect. Her strength makes me feel strong. I look forward to another chance to work for her, but I doubt the circumstance can ever be as inherently dramatic as rehearsing in the lightning in Italy.

# ✸ BETH RUSCIO
*Actor*

## A HUMBLE HAIKU FOR IRENE

At Padua
We dine on yard sales
and Irene's magic
hat
hat
hat!

# ✸ OLIVER MAYER
*Playwright*

I remember Carmen.
The sexiest 102-year-old I ever met.
An on-the-lips kisser. A fancy dancer. A Spanish speaker.
So light she might fly away on the Santa Ana wind.
So strong she wouldn't let go of this life.
Why should she? It was far too much fun.
I remember how she slept, and how she woke in a roomful of
    writers. How our scribbling neither kept her up nor helped
    her sleep, but how she was always there.
How Irene almost seemed to be her mother.
And Carmen seemed the youngest person in the room.
She gave birth to Irene, who gave birth to so many of us.
Which makes Carmen our grandma.

When I think of Cuba, I think of her.
The female Cuba. The muse Cuba. The immortal Cuba.

Carmen Fornes and Maria Irene Fornes
New York City, 1988

Photo by Jim Kent

# ⚘ LEO GARCIA
*Playwright, Actor*

I'VE BEEN BLESSED, AND I DON'T USE THE word "blessed" often, but it is the word when it comes to having worked with Irene as a student, as a playwright, and as an actor over the last fifteen years. I was a member of INTAR's Hispanic Playwrights-in-Residence Laboratory under Irene's direction for four sessions. I acted in her adaptation of Virgilio Piñera's *Cold Air* at INTAR Hispanic American Arts Center, was directed by her in her play *Terra Incognita* at the Dionysia World Festival in Siena, Italy, and again at the Padua Playwrights Festival in Los Angeles, and have had the distinct honor of having my play, *Dogs* directed by her at the West Coast Ensemble Theatre in Los Angeles. Beyond our work together, I've come to respect and to love my friend Irene.

I'd like to share a thought about Irene's mother, Doña Carmen Fornes.

The first time I saw Carmen was in 1983 at INTAR's art gallery at the opening night reception of Irene's adaptation of Virgilio Piñera's *Cold Air*. She wore a black floor-length skirt, a black jeweled blouse, a black leather skull cap, and was attended to by an entourage of admirers.

I thought, "Who is that Warholian woman with Irene?"

"Who," I asked, "Who is that woman?"

"Carmen," someone said.

"Who's Carmen?" I had to know.

"Irene's mother," someone else said. "She's ninety."

"Oh," I said and pieced it together and said, "Oh," again, then took another look and said, "Oh," one more time.

I thought, "Hmmm. Carmen. Three times my age and infinitely more alive."

I had to meet her.

Irene said, "Mama. This is Leo. The poet." She told her that because I played one in her play *Cold Air*.

Carmen remembered. Everything. In that moment I saw the entire play flash through her eyes. She smiled and put her hands on my face and spoke to me in Spanish. I didn't understand her words completely, but I understood her hands on my face. It was a royal touch.

Years later, I sat with her in Siena, Italy, at a round table in a Tuscan country hotel as we waited for guests to arrive and take their seats. The dinner was to honor the playwrights who had been invited to the first Dionysian World Festival. The guests included Nigeria's Nobel Prize–winner Wole Soyinka, England's Howard Barker, Poland's Slawomir Mrozek, and Irene, who had been invited to direct her play, *Terra Incognita*.

Carmen wore a navy blue dress with light blue flower print and hand-sewn black buttons and a belt, a beige jacket, a beret that matched the jacket, and a gold chain with a medallion that wrapped around her neck at least twice. (I remember what she wore because when I'd visit Irene, I had on more than one occasion caught a glimpse of Carmen constructing her outfits. In those moments I'd recognize the activity of simply doing and better understood the simple process of creating.)

At the dinner, the tables were set, the glasses were filled with water, and the bread was on the bread plates. Carmen and I talked a bit about the pretty men and women. She seemed to particularly love pretty Italian men that evening. Then, I picked up the butter knife, dipped it into the butter, and spread the butter on the bread. Suddenly, Carmen slapped my hand. Hard.

All at once the bread fell onto the table, the knife fell against the butter dish, I was startled, and Irene protested, "Mama!"

Carmen said to me, with her hands, "What are you doing?"

Then to Irene, still with her hands, "What is he doing?"

Her little hands were talking out loud.

It seemed, I wasn't supposed to eat the bread until everyone had been seated. So, I placed the butter knife and the bread back on the plate.

Irene said, "Mama. He's a grown man. He can eat the bread if he wants to."

But, I immediately conceded: No eating before everyone is seated. When a woman into her second century slaps your hand, it's best to pay attention. There's something to it if she says so.

I look back and am awed by her, by those hands — those tiny, gossamer-like, vein-draped, velvet-soft hands that held firmly and solidly to my arm as we'd walk to dinner or to a rehearsal or to wherever I might have had the honor of escorting her and holding onto her as she told me a joke — either clean or naughty. I recognized our strength together in the balance-off balance of our walk. I treasure my memories of Carmen and cherish her steady, solid, playful assurance that "it" — whatever "it" was — is, was, and will be all right. Don't worry.

So, I remember and miss my time with Doña Carmen Fornes and I am grateful and thank her for having a beautiful daughter in my *maestra* Maria Irene Fornes.

With respect and love.

Always.

# ❋ JULIE HÉBERT
*Playwright, Director*


## SATURDAY WITH THE PROS


I WAS RUNNING LATE AS USUAL AND ALEXIS, sullen from being awakened too early on a Saturday morning, gave me one of those mothers-are-not-supposed-to-do-this looks as I insisted she finish her breakfast in the car so we could hurtle up the freeway for a rendezvous with one of the living legends of the American theater. It seemed critical to arrive within an acceptable window of lateness. When I had suggested I come by at nine o'clock, Irene had been adamant, "No, no, no. It opens at nine. We have to leave here at least ten minutes before that."

At 8:53 I pulled onto the private college campus that was hosting Padua that year and seriously considered resetting the car clock to read 8:49. Shaken out of her glum silence, my daughter actually turned hostile, yelling "Mo-om!" when I drove a little too quickly over the so-called speed bumps. There is no way I could explain to her the moment we were in. She and I were good, we were canny, we were sharp, with discriminating eyes and silly songs we had shopped thrift stores across the country, but we were about to pick up a couple of total pros and we mustn't show our lack of seriousness by arriving like the ten o'clock scholar.

As I rounded the bend I saw Irene and her mother, Carmen, waiting anxiously at the curb. I pulled up in front of the dorms, trying to be nonchalant as I opened the door, helped Carmen in and joked that I was only three minutes late, pointing to the clock, which thank God still read 8:53. Irene was not impressed.

Driving down the tree-lined back streets of Burbank, with Irene staring straight ahead in deep and forbidding concentration and sweet 100-year-old Carmen, speaking English with a heavy Cuban accent, attempting to engage my recalcitrant twelve-year-old in pleasantries, I tried to recall what had possessed me to suggest this four-generational outing. I turned on the radio to ease our nerves.

Suddenly, monumentlike, there it was...The American Way Thrift Store on Magnolia near Hollywood Way. Enormous orange letters in the window screamed "Saturday – Seniors 50% OFF!!!" This is what had brought us here, Carmen was a senior. Our strategy was to make our selections and then have Carmen buy it all for us at half off. I'm certain we were the only ones with this plan. I parked. Alexis and I lagged behind as the Living Legend of the American Theatre and Her Spry Mother hurried in.

By the time we were in the front door, tiny Carmen, with her own big cart, was rapidly disappearing into an overstuffed aisle of dresses. Always in need of a plan, I nabbed Irene and asked her how much time she wanted. With a wild look in her eye as if I was insane to ask the question and even crazier to detain her at this critical juncture, she mumbled, "An hour, maybe two. I don't know." And with her own empty red plastic supermarket-sized rolling basket she was off in a different direction than Carmen. It hit me like a bolt, this was a competition.

Two hours later I nervously located Irene and we quickly agreed we needed another hour. Carmen flew by, in her own world, until Irene called to her. We had a show-and-tell meeting in the middle of the store, commenting freely on the booty and mostly convincing each other to buy more. While we were far from finished, the profound calming effect of successful treasure hunting washed over all of us and there was a new camaraderie and mischievousness as we suggested outfits for each other. Carmen had picked out several dresses for Irene, a blouse for me and a coat for Alexis. Her eye for size was dead-on; her sense of style on the other hand was uniquely her own. She reminded me of my grandmother who many years before had admonished me that as long as my clothes fit and were clean and pressed I shouldn't be ashamed if they were patched. Irene and Alexis rejected Carmen's offerings outright. Outspoken and laughing, they said "No way." I, naturally, with cowardice and good manners, put the blouse in my basket and said I'd think about it.

Around noon, exhilarated and starting to get hungry, we reconvened. Now came the critical decision making and possible bartering.

Irene had scored a pair of king-sized feather pillows that were to die for. Really. Thrift stores never have such things, in perfect shape, practically brand new. I tried to quell my envy.

Each of us examined our goods, eliminated borderline cases, analyzed price-tag colors, calculated the discount, and came up with our must-haves and our discussables. The pillows were in Irene's must-have pile. I asked her how she was going to get them back to New York. She scoffed at my feeble attempt. "Carry-on. And if that doesn't work, I'll buy a suitcase for them!" No hope there.

Carmen waited in line with two baskets overflowing. Irene stood with her as Alexis and I returned the unwanted items to the racks. When I took the blouse Carmen had suggested for me and started to hang it up, she asked if I was sure about that. I hesitated. "She's good color for you and silk." She was absolutely right. I neatly laid it atop my must-haves.

Before we could eat we had to make two quick stops at smaller thrift stores in the neighborhood, a kind of dénouement after the climactic American Way. When we were done, finally, we drove around until we found a suitable restaurant to reward ourselves for hard work and determination, a nice-looking Indian place with pink table cloths and fresh flowers. I parked the car a block away, we walked over, and to our dismay discovered it was closed between two and five in the afternoon. By this time we were starving. I immediately began looking around for an alternative, but I had underestimated my compadres. Irene banged loudly on the locked glass door and gave me a daring look that said "Watch this." As the perturbed proprietor pulled back the curtain, Carmen transformed in front of my eyes into the frailest, tiniest most desperate little woman I had ever seen. She began pleading with him in Spanish, which of course he did not understand. Irene translated. "Please, sir, we want to come in and have lunch. My mother is very hungry and as you can see, she's 100 years old." He shook his head, no. I suddenly realized what it meant to be 100. This babbling crone in no way resembled the aisle-darting energized Carmen of an hour before; now she seemed truly ancient and ready to faint. Irene begged, "Please, then, only a glass of water. She needs a glass of water. It's very hot out here. Please." How could he say no. He opened the door.

Later as we finished our fine Indian meal, Carmen and Irene regaled us with their story of Mario Cuomo. Irene was to accept an award from the New York State Council for the Arts and was looking forward to meeting the charismatic Governor. When the moment came, she shook his hand and introduced him to her mother, who began flirting furiously with the tall, dark Italian. She told him her amazing age, which he announced to the audience who then gave Carmen a standing ovation. "Hey, wait a minute!" Irene protested, pretending to be upset, using a fake tough-guy accent, "This is my award!" Carmen lowered her gaze coyly, what could she say, her power over men was legendary. Alexis giggled. The eavesdropping restaurant staff smiled shyly on these unabashed, joyous women. Irene and Carmen parried and sparred, enjoying each other completely, a team, a couple of must-haves.

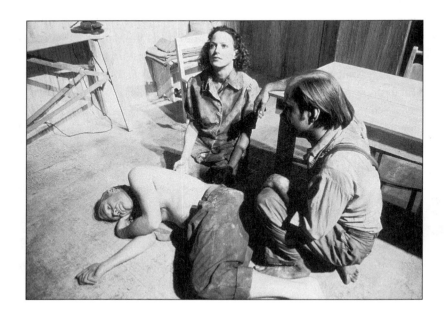

Alan Nebelthau (Henry), Patricia Mattick (Mae),
and Michael Sollenberger (Lloyd)

*MUD*
Theater for the New City, New York City, 1983

Photo by Anne Militello

# COMMENTARIES

## STEPHEN J. BOTTOMS
*Department of Theatre, Film, and Television Studies, University of Glasgow*

## HOW TO DO MORE WITH LESS

MARIA IRENE FORNES LOVES WORDS. THE first time I met her, in the summer of 1994, in the fabled Tiffany's restaurant in Greenwich Village, I was startled by just how much she likes to talk. Her taut, verbally precise plays had led me to expect someone who speaks as she writes: using a few words to maximum effect. However, after an interview lasting five-and-a-half hours, in which I myself said very little, I was both exhausted and exhilarated by the seemingly limitless stream of insights, observations, witticisms, and playful gossip that I had prompted. I left making a mental note that the distinctive economy of her language on the page was clearly a very deliberate creative choice rather than simply a reflection and extension of her everyday personality. Later that same day I was forcibly reminded of the impact a few carefully chosen words can have when I was mugged on the New York subway. "Give us your money," I was told quietly by the guy with the razor blade: "Give us your money." That was it: four words. What more would you need to say?

The fact that language, given the right conditions in which to operate (a subway, a knife), can perform a direct action with consequences, in addition to (or instead of) simply communicating information, has been a key issue on the critical-theoretical agenda since J. L. Austin's lecture series *How to Do Things with Words* was published in 1962. Over roughly the same period, the American theater has seen the emergence of a number of significant playwrights whose work can often be seen to demonstrate much the same point. Edward Albee's *Who's Afraid of Virginia Woolf?*, for example, bewildered its first audiences (also in 1962) by offering them not a quantifiable dramatic statement or message (a

"constative," as Austin might put it) but three-and-a-half hours of ver-
tiginously "performative" language games, whose alternately mesmeric
and bludgeoning impact on listeners was in many ways the play's rai-
son d'etre. Similar observations could be made about the work of subsequent great white hopes like Sam Shepard and David Mamet, whose
uses of spiralling, rhythmic versions of American vernacular often create the impression that their characters are making themselves up through
language as they go — performing themselves into existence. Irene Fornes
shares a similar sense of the "doing" potential of language, but what
she *does* is very different from the work of her male counterparts. Rather
than assaulting audiences with violently insistent and prolific verbal pat-
terns, she offers something far more minimal and controlled: Worlds
in which the impact of language in performatively shaping reality is
felt most acutely by the speakers themselves. Shepard or Mamet characters may create themselves through language but rarely seem to have
trouble in *finding* the words to do so. Fornes' protagonists, conversely,
tend to be only too aware that their own limitations in vocabulary and
expression are the very factors that effectively restrict their ability to
comprehend and transform their worlds. In seeking to acquire more
language and more control over their language, they also seek to empower
themselves. Fornes' work, as Susan Sontag once put it, "is both a theater about utterance and a theater about the disfavored."[1]

This sense that characters are held back by linguistic limitations
has been a part of Fornes' writing from the very outset: In *Tango Palace*
(1963), for example, Leopold can only ever speak words that, it emerges,
are already scripted for him on cards held by Isidore. Yet Fornes never
subscribed to the attitude — common among many of her contemporaries in the 1960s — that language was to be distrusted as a trap, a
mechanism by which the powerful control and contain the majority.
"There was an ambivalence about words because we had been lied to,"
notes fellow playwright Jean Claude van Itallie: "Yet the very words that
we were being lied to with were the words that we had to use to speak."[2]
Fornes, however, took a somewhat different attitude: As a Cuban immigrant who had had to teach herself to speak English, who had actively
fought through the process of *finding* the words she needed for any given
circumstance, she saw the idea of bemoaning the limits of language as

an indulgence of the privileged. "You *are* trapped by language," she explained to me in our 1994 interview, "but in the way that in a city you're trapped by streets. You cannot walk across a building. But you wouldn't say, 'Oh, that's not fair, I wanted to walk *this* way but there's a building in the way.' You'd just walk around the building."[3]

But how, in terms of language, does one "walk around the building"? The desire to find the words by which one can adequately express oneself and one's view of the world, both to others and to oneself, is one of the most persistent tropes in Fornes' writing. In an early work like *Promenade* (1965) this is seen in a primarily playful form, as the escaped prisoners 105 and 106 — really more the archetypal innocents abroad than experienced criminals — watch and listen to the people and events around them in order to learn how to speak and behave: "I have just discovered what life is all about ..."[4] However, it is in Fornes' later, more overtly serious work in which the liberation that comes with being able to do things with words becomes more apparent. Her 1983 play, *Mud*, for example, can be read as dealing almost paradigmatically with this question, as Mae gropes toward the articulacy through which she might be able to see herself more clearly.

Mae, Lloyd, and Henry live in poverty, in mud (on that brilliantly surreal promontory of moist red earth), deprived of enlightenment or a decent education, operating with the sparest of vocabularies. The men understand on a basic level that the control of language can be a source of performative empowerment, but seek simply to control or impress others with their words rather than developing themselves. Lloyd, for example, senses that reality is a malleable concept, that saying something is true can *make* it so, but he lacks the wit to carry this off for himself: "Didn't I say I got it up yesterday!" he demands of Mae in Scene 1: "OK! So I did!"[5] As with J.L. Austin's account of the "unhappy performative," the conditions do not exist here for the verbal action to have actual effect: Mae is unimpressed by Lloyd's vehemence, and he thus remains impotent, in both senses of the word. Henry's arrival on the scene *does* impress Mae: His superior vocabulary enables him, initially, to assume a position of superiority over her, and she willingly accedes to his advances, both sexual and territorial. It quickly becomes clear, however, that Henry does not fully understand many of the words he utters and thus lacks the power properly to control their use: His attempts at looking wise come to appear doubly foolish.

Mae, by contrast, is interested not so much in using words to control or dominate others (the near-obsessive concern of so many protagonists in Albee, Shepard, Mamet), but in educating herself — reaching toward real understanding. On one level, it is clear that this concern opens her up to abuse, as in her acceptance of Henry, from whom she initially thinks she can learn. In seeking education, she makes herself vulnerable to the verbal actions of those she accepts as superiors: "The teacher says I have no memory. And it's true I don't" (p. 26). The power of suggestion here contributes to holding her back, keeping her in her place, and yet it is also Mae's acute awareness of her own intellectual limitations that gives her such a heightened sense of the potential for expression latent in the simplest of words. She seizes on whatever verbal images and concepts she stumbles over — however banal or clichéd they might seem to a more jaded ear — as tools to aid her in her quest no longer to be "hollow and offensive" (p. 24).

Treating these found phrases much as collage artists (Fornes herself included) use found objects, Mae patches them together to build up a picture of her situation. In Scene 5, for example, she is reduced to tears by contemplation of the beauty of Henry's words when he says grace before a meal: "Oh give thanks unto the Lord, for he is good: his mercy endures forever. For he satisfies the longing soul, and fills the hungry soul with goodness" (p. 26). These are rote words that Henry has memorized but seemingly never thought about; audience members too would not give them a second thought if not for Mae's request that they be repeated. In that context, they suddenly acquire real performative power, the potential to speak for her inchoate spiritual hunger. Likewise, Mae's reading aloud of a standard biology textbook is, Fornes informs us in the stage directions to Scene 6, "inspired" (p. 27). The inspiration she draws from it finally becomes apparent to the audience when it is these words that she adopts for her own self-describing epitaph at the end of the play: "Like the starfish, I live in the dark and my eyes see only a faint light. It is faint and yet it consumes me" (p. 40).

What is perhaps most fascinating about these final lines, however, is that she seems, performatively, to be taking responsibility for, and thus ownership of, even her own death. She makes no mention of the fact that Lloyd has just shot her, only that her desire for more light has "consumed" her. In one sense, moreover, this is completely true. Mae has by this point learnt for herself how to effect real change with the words available to her. In Scene 15, she watches the now wheelchair-bound Henry struggle to possess her verbally and sexually, before announcing simply "You can walk, Henry. You took my money" (p. 37). She has no concrete evidence as to the constative "truth" of either statement, any more than Lloyd had proof that he had "got it up." In this case, however, Mae has acquired sufficient control over herself and the situation that the words become a "happy" performative; in the self-empowering act of speaking them, she is able to free herself from her sense of obligation toward Henry. These few words become the vehicle by which she can leave these clinging, helpless men. Tragically, ironically, the only response remaining to them is to shoot her. Mae's death is thus a strange liberation, but a liberation nonetheless, because she is, finally, able to name it as such: "I long for [the light]. I thirst for it. I would die for it" (p. 40).

It might, perhaps, be seen as condescending on the part of an alert, articulate author like Fornes to write so directly about the poor and undereducated who have to struggle to acquire the linguistic tools by which to comprehend or realize themselves. Yet *Mud* is only one play, and in others, Fornes explores how similar situations apply, in different ways, in other social strata. In *The Conduct of Life* (1985), for example, Leticia too seeks to educate herself, although this time the goal is university-level learning. The mistress of an apparently well-to-do household, she is nonetheless dissatisfied with herself, with being unable to articulate her sense of the injustices at large in the dictatorship that is her homeland. Yet if Leticia, like Mae, hopes to acquire new tools, Fornes does not pull punches in demonstrating that, however well-intentioned, she is also unthinkingly implicated in the abuses of the social structure she abhors. Her language, and thus her mindset, is too individually oriented, too bourgeois, to enable her to see far past her own immediate (dis)comforts. It never occurs to her, for example, to question the dismissively presumptuous way in which she takes the servility of her house-keeper, Olimpia, for granted. (Olimpia's long, repetitive monologue in

Scene 4 is a wonderfully extended example of an "unhappy performative," as she insistently attempts to attract Leticia's attention while apparently knowing all along that she is simply not listening.) Later, in describing the horror of seeing mangled, tortured bodies lying in city streets, Leticia seems more concerned with the idea that her husband, Orlando, is implicated, than with the fact of the brutality itself: "How awful, Mona. He mustn't do it. I don't care if I don't have anything. What's money! I don't need a house as big as this! He's doing it for money!" (p. 85).

Picking up on this darkly ironic undertow to the play, David Savran suggested in a 1986 interview with Fornes that Leticia is shown to be helping maintain the existence of an oppressive regime. Fornes, however, pointed out unequivocally that this spin on the situation was judgemental and condescending; are we not *all* restrained by the concepts, words, and mindsets that condition us? "Are you supporting Reagan because you don't go out and shoot him?" she demanded of Savran,

> Do you know how many people in other countries think that you are? Because you are going around with your little tape recorder and doing your little interviews instead of fighting.... Leticia is just an ordinary woman who doesn't know anything.... Do you expect her to be political?... I expect you to be political. I expect me to be. We're supposed to be.[6]

From those who have much, much shall be expected. One of the underlying challenges of Irene Fornes' work lies in her insistence on pointing out to her "enlightened," "educated" theater audiences that the "disfavored," those who have to struggle to find utterance, frequently *do* far more with the few words available to them than the supposedly articulate and literate do with their many. As I discovered for myself one night on the subway.

1. Susan Sontag, Preface to Maria Irene Fornes, *Plays* (New York: Performing Arts Journal Publications, 1986), p. 9.

2. Jean Claude van Itallie, interviewed by Stephen J. Bottoms, New York City, 14 September 1995.

3. Maria Irene Fornes, interviewed by Stephen J. Bottoms, New York City, 17 August 1994.

4. Maria Irene Fornes, *Promenade and Other Plays* (New York: Performing Arts Journal Publications, 1987), p. 22.

5. *Mud* in Maria Irene Fornes, *Plays*, p. 19. Subsequent references are parenthesized.

6. Maria Irene Fornes interviewed by David Savran in his *In Their Own Words: Contemporary American Playwrights* (New York: Theatre Communications Group, 1988), pp. 68–9.

# ✸ JULIE JENSEN
*Playwright*

IS THERE ANY WOMAN IN THEATER THAT
has not been profoundly influenced by Irene? I swear not a one.

✸

I had my first commission to write a play and had worked hard all summer. But the thing was going nowhere. Inert is a word that comes to mind.

The deadline was approaching, school was starting, and I was frankly embarrassed to show my play to anyone. Panic was setting in.

That's when I saw a production in Chicago of Fornes' play, *The Conduct of Life* (1988). And it made all the difference.

I never looked back.

I started all over and wrote a new play. That play was *White Money*, which won the Award for New American Plays and had a dozen productions throughout the country. *Snake Eyes* is part of that longer piece.

But the important thing to acknowledge is that *The Conduct of Life* was swimming around in my head the whole time.

I remember the production to this day. I remember the props, the colors, the way the actors moved. It was an old story — the struggle between a man and a woman. But it was also completely original. Its intensity, its rhythms, its precision. I'd never seen anything like it. It affected not only the play I was writing, but everything I would ever write.

## SNAKE EYES

ELLA: The second guy I married, he was a grim bugger. He was forty-five and I was nineteen. He drove PIEs for a living Pacific Intermountain Express. Trucks. He never laughed. He put me up in this trailer park outside of Wendover, Nevada, because he had this other girl-friend that was ready to kill him. And so he was hiding out. Bet you was never in Wendover, Nevada. All's I can say about Wendover, Nevada, is if you was hiding out, Wendover, Nevada, would be the place to do it. The flies don't even want to fly in Wendover, Nevada. Now this guy I married. I called him Snakes. Drove trucks. Used to be gone five days, home two.

*(Enter SNAKES.)*

He'd come home, dump his stuff on the floor, take off his hat, take off his shirt, put on his hat, get a beer, open it, take a slug, burp, turn on the television set.

*(And he does.)*

That television only get one channel?

SNAKES: Only need one channel.

ELLA: Professional wrestling?

SNAKES: Killer Bovine and his wife Seattle. The next tag-team champions of the WWWW.

ELLA: Killer Bovine and his wife Seattle are parading through the people. They got tiger clothes on with their names wrote across the front. Killer Bovine is the strongest man on earth, he says.

SNAKES: Killer Bovine is the strongest man on earth.

ELLA: He ain't the strongest man.

SNAKES: He's the strongest man on earth.

ELLA: You sit there long enough in front of a television set and something happens to your blood. Them little lights or something turn your blood.

SNAKES: Blood is blood.

ELLA: What's that mean?

SNAKES: It means I don't want the third degree.

ELLA: Killer Bovine and his wife Seattle are parading through the people. The crowd is going wild. Making signs with their hands. You're near having a heart attack with how you smoke all the time. And drink beer and never do nothing with your body.

SNAKES: I do all I need to with my body.

ELLA: The A-number-one type for getting a heart attack.

SNAKES: I'll outlive you twice over.

ELLA: I'll outlive you twice over, he says. You already have, I said. That's how he talked all the time. Nothing ever happened.

*(SNAKES exits. Sound of peeing.)*

After I cleaned the damn trailer and swept the damn lawn, there wasn't nothing to do. Nothing grew out there. You just kinda spit in your front yard and hoped it would quit blowing in your front door.

*(SNAKES enters.)*

Everytime he would come home, dump his stuff on the floor, take off his hat, take off his shirt, put on his hat, get a beer, open it, take a slug, burp, turn on the television set.

*(And he does.)*

Just then Killer Bovine took out BoBo the Beast with a chain. So I says to him, why don't you tell me something about what happens to you on the road?

SNAKES: Nothing happens on the road.

ELLA: Denver, Colorado, and Cheyenne, Wyoming? Reno, Fresno, Barstow? And nothing happens?

SNAKES: The trees on the side of the road change. Nothing happens.

ELLA: What kind of trees they got in Barstow?

SNAKES: None.

ELLA: What kind of trees they got in Cheyenne?

SNAKES: Green ones. I don't know nothing about trees.

ELLA: What about them truck stops? Eat. Diesel.

SNAKES: No one eats diesel.

ELLA: Television does something to your mind.

SNAKES: It does not.

ELLA: It does.

SNAKES: Doesn't.

ELLA: Does.

SNAKES: Television don't do nothing to your mind.

ELLA: Makes you pissed off all the time.

SNAKES: Do I look pisssed off?

ELLA: Either pissed off or bored.

SNAKES: I ain't either pissed off or bored. I'm tired.

ELLA: Television makes you tired.

SNAKES: No it don't.

ELLA: It does.

SNAKES: TELEVISION IS RELAXING!

ELLA: Television makes you pissed off, bored, boring, and tired.

SNAKES: You make me pissed off, bored, boring, and tired.

ELLA: That's always how he made jokes. Change one word in a sentence and repeat it. Why don't you get yourself another job, I says to him.

SNAKES: All jobs the same. Set behind a desk. Set behind a wheel.

ELLA: Set behind a television set.

SNAKES: Set behind your rear end.

*(SNAKES exits to bathroom. Sound of peeing.)*

ELLA: See, that's how it would go. That's how he would talk. Nothing ever happened. That summer was the year they invented Fresca. So I mixed it with vodka, set my Shay's Lounge out in the sun, and baked myself into a Mexican tar-tilla. You don't hear much about Fresca anymore. It was a Coca-Cola product.

*(SNAKES enters.)*

Then he'd come home, dump his stuff on the floor, take off his hat, take off his shirt, put on his hat, get a beer, open it take a slug, burp, turn on the television set.

*(He does.)*

Television does something to your o-zones.

SNAKES: Sun done something to your o-zones.

ELLA: It takes seventeen minutes.

SNAKES: I know what takes seventeen minutes.

ELLA: After seventeen minutes, you don't have a memory of what happened.

SNAKES: I just spent a hundred and twenty-three hours in a truck. I don't mind not having a memory of it.

ELLA: That's how they get you to do them kinda jobs. They give you television sets so's you don't remember them.

SNAKES: I remember plenty.

ELLA: If you don't do something else sides watch TV and drive that truck, you'll probably die doing one of them two.

SNAKES: I'll die doing one of you two.

ELLA: That's how it went on. That's how he talked. Nothing ever happened. Then one day when he was gone, this woman comes up on my porch. I'm laying there on my Shay's Lounge. She says she's got something in the back of her truck she wants me to see. *(NERVENE enters.)*

NERVENE: You live here?

ELLA: Yeah, I do.

NERVENE: Well, I got something in the back of my truck I want you to see.

ELLA: What is it?

NERVENE: Guts or something.

ELLA: Why you want me to look a some guts?

NERVENE: Because they could easy belong to that some-bitch you live with.

ELLA: Right then, I think, oh hell, this is the crazy bitch he's been hiding from. Nervene. I called her Nervene because I blamed her for everything that had gone wrong in my life. If she wouldn't of left him, I wouldn't of found him, then I wouldn't of got married to him, and I wouldn't be setting here in Wendover, Nevada, looking at her because of him.

# ✺ ROD WOODEN
*Playwright*


## THE CONDUCT OF YOUR LIFE


MARIA IRENE FORNES' SET FOR *THE CONDUCT of Life* is of a wholly interior world: living room, dining room, hall-way, cellar, warehouse. Doors lead to the exterior, in one room there is a telephone. Apart from this, Fornes allows us no contact with the outside — but then she does not need to, because the outside world is brought to us on the lips of her characters. It is a world of terror, of nightmare, of which the world of the play is a microcosm. But in a sense this microcosm of the play is even more terrible than the world outside, because one cannot escape it. In *The Conduct of Life* there is no sky for the characters to turn their eyes toward, there is no God to pray to, there is no distracting clamour in the streets. The sun does not shine here. There is only artificial light, or darkness. And so in this com-pressed space the terror that exists outside on the streets becomes mag-nified, as if under a microscope. The world of the play not only reflects the terror outside, it *is* that terror, it is more than that terror even. What is within is always darker than what is without, and more frightening. Oneself is the only thing one cannot escape from. And in *The Con-duct of Life* there is no escape: neither for ourselves as we read or watch it, nor for the characters. There is no escape because Fornes does not provide one.

It is an upper-middle-class family, with a servant. Orlando, the hus-band, is an army officer; he is sensual, ambitious for promotion, cal-culating. His wife Leticia is also ambitious — not for a career, but for knowledge:

> I want to study. I want to study so I am not an ignorant per-son... I want to be knowledgeable. I'm tired of being ignored.[1]

The person who is ignoring her is Orlando. He is ten years younger than Leticia and has no sexual interest in her; he does not love her, she says, he merely wants her to run the household. A smoothly run household gives the appearance of normality. But Orlando is frustrated, sexually. And Leticia is frustrated, because she loves him but he does not love her. She wants to escape this domestic claustrophobia. She is a sensitive, caring person, someone who feels the pain of other human beings, of animals:

> What! Me go hunting! Do you think I'm going to shoot a deer, the most beautiful animal in the world?... I'd run in front of the bullets and let the mad hunters kill me — stand in the way of the bullets — stop the bullets with my body. I don't see how anyone can shoot a deer. (pp. 68–9)

Her friend Alejo tells her not to worry about any of this, about getting an education, anything:

> Why do you want to worry about any of that? What's the use? Do you think you can change anything? Do you think anyone can change anything? (p. 70)

But Leticia does worry. We know that she worries because she tells us that she does. Like all the characters in the play, she often tells us what she feels, what she is thinking. What she says seems to come directly from the unconscious, or: from the part of the unconscious that she is conscious of. Sometimes these statements are made to another character, but they are not part of a dialogue. Rather, they are an expression of something, an expression of the innermost heart. This expression may be directed toward another character, but it seldom amounts to dialogue because the other character usually does nothing with it. What is being said often appears to be spoken for the speaker's ears only, and for the audience. Characters listen to each other, they may even comment from time to time on what is being said to them, but they do not *hear*. They do not hear because what is being said to them is often too painful, which is why there is nothing they can do with it. The unconscious is exposed briefly, and then life goes on as normal. (But not normal). If the characters really heard what each other were saying, they would run screaming into the street. But no one does, either hear or run screaming. My own pain is enough, I cannot cope with anyone else's. And so the pain goes on, the pain of the world goes on.

There is something else that is unusual about Fornes' use of dialogue. Or: not dialogue. Just as there is often no naturalistic exchange between the characters, so there is no subtext under the text. Instead, the subtext *is* the text. Which means: no safety net. Under the text there is only the real thing: darkness. Listen, this is the darkness of my life. And then you realize: the subtext does not exist line by line, throughout the play, but rather under the whole play itself. Under the expressed darkness, the unexpressed: that all this horror is being allowed to continue. I speak to you out of my heart, but you do not hear me. You speak to me: the same. So all this will continue, there will be no end to it, not within the four walls of the play, nor in the streets outside, nor in the world beyond those streets, *our* world. Because we also listen; whether we listen in the theater or whilst we are reading the text, we listen. Oh, how hard we listen. But we do not hear. If we could hear, just once, then these horrors could surely not continue. But they do continue.

> We're blind. We can't see beyond an arm's reach. We don't believe our life will last beyond the day. We only know what we have in our hand to put in our mouth, to put in our stomach, and to put in our pocket. We take care of our pocket, but not of our country... We don't think we have a country. Ask anybody, "Do you have a country?" They'll say, "Yes." Ask them, "What is your country?" They'll say, "My bed, my dinner plate." (p. 75)

This is Leticia speaking. And then, talking to Alejo, she goes on to say:

> But, things can change. They can. I have changed. You have changed. He has changed. (p. 75)

What does she mean by this? It sounds optimistic. It seems to mean: In spite of all the evil that is happening around us, things can change for the better — just as I have, you have, just as Orlando has. And yet things have not changed for the better, they have got worse. Orlando has just been transferred to a new department within the army, a department that carries out torture. We know this because we have just heard him describing something he has witnessed, a scene of pain and sexual humiliation:

He was pouring liquid from everywhere, his mouth, his nose, his eyes. He was not a horse but a sexual organ. — Helpless. A viscera. — Screaming. Making strange sounds. He collapsed on top of her. She wanted him off but he collapsed on top of her and stayed there on top of her... She was indifferent. He stayed there for a while and then lifted himself off her and to the ground. (p. 74)

Leticia has heard this. So why does she imply that things can change *for the better?* Because: She wants to believe that they can. Just as she wants to believe that she would have run in front of the hunters, to stop them killing the deer. She wants to believe that she is fundamentally a good person. And Orlando wants to believe this of *him*self, also. Even though he has taken Nena, a twelve-year-old girl from the streets, and imprisoned her in the warehouse so that he can force himself upon her sexually, he still wants to believe this. Like Leticia, he desperately wants to believe that he is a good person, someone with ideals. Fornes makes us watch what he does with Nena, in all its depravity: We watch as he pushes his pelvis against her; he reaches orgasm, and we are still watching. And the astonishing thing is: Fornes does not judge him, she does not condemn. She merely: presents. And in spite of the horror of the act, we, the watchers, do not judge or condemn either. The act, yes; the one who commits it, no. Because to judge or condemn someone, one has to feel morally superior to that person. And Fornes does not want us to feel morally superior, she does not allow us that escape route. Rather, by presenting Orlando to us so nakedly — in all his need, all his vulnerability — she makes us think the unthinkable: that a torturer can be a human being. Here is Orlando speaking to Nena in the basement:

> What I do to you is out of love. Out of want. It's not what you think. I wish you didn't have to be hurt. I don't do it out of hatred. It is not out of rage. It is love. It is a quiet feeling. It's a pleasure. It is quiet and it pierces my insides in the most internal way. It is my most private self. And this I give to you. — Don't be afraid. — It is a desire to destroy and to see things destroyed and to see the inside of them. — It's my nature... I was born this way and I must have this. — I need love. I wish you did not feel hurt and recoil from me. (p. 82)

It is terrifying, what Orlando is saying. Terrifying because it has — and Fornes, mercilessly, makes us see this — a terrible logic to it. It is the logic of fascism, the logic of the good husband who is also a torturer. When Leticia mentions the bodies that are now being left in the streets, we know that this is the thinking that has put them there. But now the terror is no longer just in the streets, it is spreading; like blood seeping under a door, it is now in the house also. It is there in the person of Nena, in what is being done to her; firstly in the warehouse, then in the cellar under the house, and now, creeping ever nearer, in the house itself. It is even going to be given a coating of respectability, because, as Orlando tells Leticia:

> She's going to stay here for a while. She's going to work for us. She'll be a servant here. (p. 82)

And Leticia allows it to happen. This woman who said that she would stop the hunters shooting the deer is allowing her husband to sexually abuse a twelve-year-old child in her own house. And she continues to make excuses for him, to claim that it is "they" who are changing him, that he is "too trusting," that she has to look after him. It is like a mother making excuses for a wayward son, a son who has gone off the rails temporarily. She sees the bodies in the streets, she sees the abused child in her own dining room, and yet she still cannot *see* them.

She talks about nothing else, and yet she is still on the outside of the experience, wanting to normalize it, wanting to resist its true horror.

But the true horror cannot be avoided. It is brought to us by Nena, whilst she is sitting at the dining room table with the servant, Olimpia. They are separating stones from dry beans. After telling Olimpia of her life on the streets, of how she used to look after her elderly grandfather, Nena speaks of Orlando:

> …he beats me. The dirt won't go away from inside me. — He comes downstairs when I'm sleeping and I hear him coming and it frightens me. And he takes the covers off me and I don't move because I'm frightened and because I feel cold and I think I'm going to die. And he puts his hand on me and he recites poetry… He puts his fingers in my parts and he keeps reciting. Then he turns me on my stomach and puts himself inside me. And he says I belong to him. (p. 84)

It is terrible, because we know it is the truth. Not a sentimental truth, a truth that has been exaggerated to evoke our sympathy, but simply — and the more terrible for it — the truth. And immediately after it comes the most heartbreaking speech in the play (heartbreaking *because* it comes after it), again from Nena:

> I want to conduct each day of my life in the best possible way. I should value the things I have. And I should value all those who are near me. And I should value the kindness that others bestow upon me. And if someone should treat me unkindly, I should not blind myself with rage, but I should see them and receive them, since maybe they are in worse pain than me. (pp. 84–5)

Again it is the truth, but a different kind of truth. Not a factual truth but her own truth, Nena's truth, something she longs to live by. But heartbreaking. Heartbreaking because we, the listeners, know that she will never be able to put it into practice; because she will never, not be, abused. And yet Fornes gives her the opportunity to voice it, this truth of hers, just as she gave Leticia and Orlando the chance to voice theirs. As if to say: Look, the most beautiful things can exist in the darkest places. All they need is to be allowed to grow. Attention must be paid to this child. Because she is what is most precious in this world: the other. Because she is, in the words of Sylvia Plath, the baby in the barn:

> …Let the mercuric
> Atoms that cripple drip
> Into the terrible well,
>
> — You are the one
> Solid the spaces lean on, envious.
> You are the baby in the barn.[2]

But no one in the play does pay attention. In the final scene the nightmare comes into the heart of the house — into that room of death, the living room. Orlando accuses Leticia of having a lover. (Why? Fornes does not tell us. Why? Because we do not need to know. Not everything is explained, as in life. And just as in life, Fornes knows that our imaginations will go to work on the mystery.) He begins to interrogate her. He is expert, professional. Leticia begins to confess. Her confession could be the truth, or, more likely, it isn't — there is no lover. Again, it doesn't matter. The streets have invaded the living room, the torture chamber has invaded the living room. The truth does not matter, only the confession matters. So, Leticia makes the confession. And then Orlando has one terrible, final question:

Was he tender? Was he tender to you? (p. 88)

But tenderness cannot be admitted here, either as a lie *or* as the truth. Leticia cannot answer. And Orlando cannot ask another question, because without an answer to this one, there *is* no other question. So in lieu of the question, he puts his hand inside her blouse. He has done this before, in other rooms, to other victims. Leticia knows this; suddenly she *knows* it, the thing she has so often spoken about. Suddenly she knows Orlando, what he is, and she also knows herself, what she is. She is a victim, just another victim. In the words of Fornes' stage direction, "She lets out an excruciating scream" (p. 88). Orlando turns away, Leticia takes a gun from a drawer and shoots him dead. The torturer has been killed by his victim. It is the end, we want it to be the end, but it is not the end. The nightmare has entered the house and must have its fill of blood; Orlando may be dead, but there is no killing the nightmare. The game has to be played out according to the rule of the nightmare, which is: Everything must be blamed on the powerless. So Leticia hands the gun to Nena, saying just one word: "Please…" Whether she means Nena to take the blame for killing Orlando, or whether she wants Nena to kill her, Leticia, as well — none of this is clear. But then it does not have to be. In fact, it has to be not clear, because that way the dilemma that Nena — and the audience — is left with is even more terrible. And either way, Nena is doomed: She will either take the blame for killing one person, or for killing two.

The nightmare, the weather in the streets,[3] has invaded the house, and Leticia — the one person who could have stopped it — has allowed it to happen. But what is this nightmare, exactly? Killing and torturing people, yes, but at the heart of it is: denial of the other. Fornes is resolutely on the side of the other in life, and her plays — particularly *Mud* and *The Conduct of Life* — read like reports from the front line of a battlefield where the other is under constant threat. She speaks for the powerless, for sensitivity, for the feminine. And she is against everything that would seek to deny these things their otherness: power, particularly the masculine abuse of it, and also the law — the law that power hides behind. But although she is on the other side, the seldom-voiced side, rather than *this* side, the always-voiced side, she does not weight the argument. She does not present things as she would like them to be; she merely: presents. She sees and sees and hears and hears; then she presents. She presents the evidence. It is the audience who must decide. Which is why her texts have so much power, so much power on the side of the powerless.

I said at the beginning of this essay that Leticia is a sensitive person, someone who feels the pain of other human beings, of animals.

She appears to be, certainly. But the pain she feels most of all is her own. She is trapped within the walls of her own pain, unable to move outside it, unable to act. Like Nena, Leticia wanted to conduct her life in the best possible way, but the prison of her own pain has stopped her doing so. All through the play she has reached out toward the other, toward the possibility of a life other than this one; but between her and Nena — that other life's living embodiment — there has been no contact. A single gesture toward Nena, a word to her even, could have done it: not only change life for Nena, but for Leticia as well. It hasn't happened. She has heard Nena's screams, and she has done nothing — apart from saying to Orlando, "Don't make her scream," "Don't make her cry." But at the very end of the play she does notice her; she reaches out to Nena, and she does make contact: She gives her the gun. She does not give the gun to Olimpia, the belligerent, outspoken servant; she gives it to Nena, the one who is the least powerful, the most sensitive, the most hurt. And addressing Nena for the first time in the play — *seeing* her for the first time in the play — she says, "Please…" Please release me from this. Please take this most potent symbol of masculine power and use it, to release me from this. It is not a gesture of empowerment; by handing the gun to Nena, Leticia is looking for a way out of her own pain. She is using Nena, in the same way that Orlando did. Leticia still cannot see the other, even when it is standing frightened and trembling in front of her. Or rather, she cannot see it for what it is in itself, but only for how she can use it. The other has no use for guns. As a result of Leticia's action, the other is doomed — just as Nena is doomed.

It is in this way, through these acts, that the weather in the streets is created. By action, or by lack of action. Perhaps mostly by lack of action, by ignoring, by denial; by allowing a moral vacuum, which is then filled by something else. It is an easy thing to ignore, the weather, until it comes into your living room, and up to that point Leticia has ignored it very well. She has heard it howling, she has complained about it, but she has ignored it. Her own pain, the frustration she feels at being rejected by her husband, has predominated; her own hurt has prevented her from seeing the hurt of other people. And so she has ignored the suffering child, the baby in the barn. And that is why the weather in the streets persists, because we ignore it. According to how we conduct our lives, the weather in the streets either persists or it doesn't. It is hard to believe this, just as the truth of Fornes' reports from the battlefield is hard to believe; because, if we do believe it, we have to — in the phrase of Clarice Lispector — "believe and weep."4 It is always easier to ignore something, to deny something. What happens in *The Conduct of Life* is happening now, all around us; the thinking, rational part of ourselves will deny this, but there is one part of us, the most secret, hidden part — the other in ourselves — that will say, "Yes, this is the truth," and this is the part that Fornes touches. Which is why she is such a great playwright: because she puts us in touch with our secret, unlived life, with the other in ourselves. In *The Conduct of Life*, Fornes renews our contact with the most powerful part of ourselves — the part that is the most vulnerable, the least concerned with power. The part of us from which, if we choose not to ignore it, we can conduct our life.

1. Maria Irene Fornes, *The Conduct of Life* in *Plays* (New York: Performing Arts Journal Publications, 1986), p. 70. Subsequent references are parenthesized.

2. Sylvia Plath, "Nick and the Candlestick" in *Collected Poems* (London: Faber and Faber, 1981), p. 242.

3. A phrase taken from the title of Rosamond Lehmann's 1936 novel, *The Weather in the Streets* (London: Collins, 1936).

4. "One cannot prove the existence of what is most real but the essential thing is to believe. To believe and weep. This story unfolds in a state of emergency and public calamity. It is an unfinished book because it offers no answer. An answer I hope someone somewhere in the world may be able to provide." From the Author's Dedication, Clarice Lispector, *The Hour of the Star (A Hora da Estrela),* trans. Giovanni Pontiero (Manchester: Carcanet Press, 1986), p. 8.

# ⊛ JOHN STEPPLING
*Playwright*

IRENE IS DELIVERING MESSAGES FROM THOSE outposts where the buses do not run. She hand-delivers them while astride thrift-store chairs carried on the backs on phantom sherpas, and she is insisting that everyone hold their hand just so. It is important, the way a finger is held, sometimes it is the most important thing in the universe. Sometimes the destiny of whole societies hang in the balance, and sometimes nothing hangs in the balance. On stage there should not be any behavior, that would be to suggest that popular delusions are real, and Irene knows even the real isn't real. There is no behavior in Fornes' theater, there is only the meaning of a language that can't be spoken. It is a poetics of the almost, and it hangs precariously somewhere, just about ready to crash…but…but…but…

# ✸ RON BAGDEN
*Actor*

SINCE COMING TO NEW YORK IN 1977 TO
pursue a career in acting I've followed Irene Fornes' work beginning
with the marvelous *Fefu and Her Friends*. That production started in
someone's home, a loft space in downtown Manhattan. (It eventually
played The American Place Theatre, where I also saw it.) After watching the first act, which included all the characters and took place in
Fefu's living room, the audience was divided into four groups and rotated
to four other rooms (one was actually the garden) in Fefu's house. Each
of the four short scenes in this second act was therefore played four
times simultaneously by the actors to accomodate each group. For the
last act the audience reassembled in the makeshift proscenium theater
that had been constructed in the loft with Fefu's living room as the set.
I remember being thrilled by the whole experience. Being in those rooms
with the characters was more intimate than anything I had experienced
in the theater. I instantly became a fan of Irene's work.

A while ago I had the opportunity to work with Irene at The
Women's Project in New York in a workshop production of a play of
hers in development, *The Summer in Gossensass*. It takes place in London in 1891 and I played David, a fictional actor supremely dedicated
to the theater and the art of acting, who's enraptured by the real life
American actress, Elizabeth Robins after seeing her perform. Upon meeting her at her home he's given to extremely theatrical displays of grand
gesture and emotion and literally lies at her feet and kisses her shoes
in adoration of her talent.

Irene was meticulous in her staging of these scenes and with the
movement of each actor individually and in relation to the others. Her
goal was to get the overall "painting" of the character's sincerity and
ridiculousness in the scenes perfect. She gave us images over and over

to help us capture the feeling of what she was after. In trying to stay true to her vision, I gave myself fully to her way of working as she molded and shaped my performance. I also gave myself permission to fly away with new ideas that set off in Irene new inspiration and direction for the scenes, as if a painter had discovered a whole other set of colors to paint with. She kept rewriting and tinkering with words and small gestures until the time came to present our work to an audience. It was a process that led to a production rich in detail, style, and theatrical rewards. The audience found those particular scenes hysterically funny and the characters very human. Irene had a blast working with us and infected me with her childlike joy and sense of play. Irene was very supportive and nurturing to the actors throughout this process.

# ❀ SUSAN LETZLER COLE
*Professor of English and
Director of the Drama Concentration,
Albertus Magnus College*

## MARIA IRENE FORNES: SIGHTINGS

MARIA IRENE FORNES HAS SAID, "THE QUESTION
of theater — the question of art in general — is a question of honesty.
I don't see how a dishonest person could possibly write."[1] It sounds like
a remark made by a character in one of her plays, or the playful, faux-
naïf comment of a coy playwright. But it is neither fiction nor posing.
It is, somehow, I don't know how, the quintessence of Irene Fornes as
I have observed her work in rehearsal for over a decade.

When I first called Irene Fornes in the summer of 1987 to inquire
if I might observe her rehearsals of Chekhov's *Uncle Vanya* and her own
play, *Abingdon Square*, that autumn in New York,[2] she immediately
agreed, but then asked if I could type. Not well, I replied nervously.
Typing would be a useful contribution, she pointed out: Did I not know
that it was a gift to observe rehearsal work? Years later, when I reminded
Irene of this conversation (I never did any typing), she was marginally
embarrassed, adding that she hadn't really known who I was. But she
was right. The gift she offered me, seen more clearly now than was possible then, seems even more of a miracle after having observed her recent
work in rehearsal.

Maria Irene Fornes' new play, *The Summer in Gossensass*, is about
two actresses, Elizabeth Robins and Marion Lea, and their small circle
of interested eccentrics — Elizabeth's brother Vernon, Lady Bell, and
David — who are involved in arranging for the triumphant London
production of Ibsen's *Hedda Gabler*. (Gossensass was the Austrian summer

resort where Ibsen met Emilie Bardach, a young woman who inspired his creation of Hedda Gabler.)

*The Summer in Gossensass* enfolds and unfolds Henrik Ibsen's *Hedda Gabler*. It is a play in which the love object is a play. And it is a play of vampires, demon lovers: The actress Elizabeth Robins is possessed by Ibsen; an eccentric character named David is possessed by Hedda Gabler. Fictional characters in Fornes' play are vampirized by other fictional characters in Ibsen's play; actors are possessed by playwrights. As Irene says to the cast in rehearsal on March 14, 1998: "There are many Draculas in this play." I too have been possessed. In scene 5 of the April 25, 1998, rehearsal script of *The Summer in Gossensass*, David says:

> What an opportunity! Because how often does one have the chance to be possessed by someone else?…or destroyed… That is how you are reborn. You die and then you are reborn… As yourself…reborn…wiser…with ten hearts! (pp. 19–20)

The astonishing last four words illuminate what has attracted me to Maria Irene Fornes and her work in and for theater.

In the winter of 1997 and in the winter and spring of 1998, I observed rehearsals of *The Summer in Gossensass*, presented as a workshop production at the Harold Clurman Theatre in New York on February 1, 1997, and, over a year later, with a largely new cast, given its world premiere at the Judith Anderson Theatre, also in New York, March 31–April 26, 1998. What follows are selected "sightings" of Maria Irene Fornes working as playwright-director in these rehearsals.[3]

During a break in rehearsal on January 31, 1997, Irene says to me: "If you write the mystery of a character under whose spell you are, you can actually get in touch with the essence of a person by a detailed attention to voice, pace of speech, face…" This way of "[getting] in touch," as a writer, with what is essential also characterizes Irene's work as a director.

During rehearsal on March 14, 1998, I hear Irene give notes on voice and pace of speech. She tells actor Joseph Goodrich, playing David: "Think of it anew. You have to break the rhythm of your present phrasing." To Molly Powell, playing Elizabeth Robins, she says: "Lower pitch."

"Lower pitch." "Hands go up higher and voice goes lower. So you become like Dracula, not Ibsen." "Maybe just inhale and exhale." She gives this note to Clea Rivera, playing Marion Lea: "Say the name, 'Thea Elvsted,' like a melody."

Detailed attention to "voice," to "pace of speech," and to "face" keep company in this striking exchange between the director and actress Molly Powell in rehearsal on March 22, 1998:

> Irene: When you speak of a young Viennese girl, let us see her in your eyes.
> Molly: But very slow?
> Irene: Yes. It is only if it is slow that we can see a person in a person's eyes... It's almost as if it's a vision you see but a voice that comes through you.

During a break in rehearsal on January 31, 1997, Irene says to me: "A line might work if the actor is standing up, not sitting down. Sometimes it's a matter of inches. I don't know how that works, but a line can work if a person is a few inches further away from the table." This is dramatically, and meticulously, illustrated over a year later in Irene's directing of two actresses on the first night of rehearsal in the Judith Anderson Theatre on March 26, 1998: "Take a half step more toward center stage, Marion... A little less... And, Elizabeth, don't come toward this table *because you might be blocking her [Marion's] fantasy world... Even a quarter of a step further upstage* [emphasis added]." Then Irene addresses the entire cast: "The space makes demands. You probably feel different demands from the demands I feel down here [speaking from the auditorium to the actors on stage]. I feel currents from the door [on the set]...[To one of the actors during a break in rehearsal] I really don't know the currents until I see people on the set."

To actor Ron Bagden, playing Judge Brac in the workshop production, Irene says in rehearsal in the performance space on January 31, 1997: "From your stomach the venom comes up to your shoulder. Then your head moves... Even slower." To another actor, she says: "You feel your own vitality up from your groin to your chest to your ear." During a break in this rehearsal, she says to me: "It's like a photographer who takes thirty shots and then later chooses the perfect shot. He didn't know in advance or he would have taken one photo. But in directing you have to construct it yourself. The camera just clicks."

Actress Irma St. Paul, playing Lady Bell in the workshop production, describes Irene after rehearsal on January 31, 1997: "Her sense of timing, gesture, speech, and body is to the microsecond and to the micrometer. She has a perfect sense of what's going to work, e.g., 'Tilt your chin; move your feet two inches to the right.' She reminds me of Meyerhold."

On March 6, 1998, the first day of putting the play on its feet in rehearsal for the world premiere production, stage manager Bryan Scott Clark asks Irene: "How do you want to proceed? Shall the actors move at will?" Irene, in a tone of mock-horror: "At *will?*" There is loud laughter from the cast.

During a break in rehearsal on March 22, 1998, actor Joseph Goodrich tells me: "…with Irene…movement is character. That's where character is found… It's all about alternating from being hunched or low to arms up [stretched] or in motion."

I ask Irene to talk about the difference between writing and directing on January 31, 1997:

> For the director it's seeing the character in the person of the actor… As a writer you have to be inside your character and observe from the outside. That's a trick! You have to write from a character's mind and from a character's heart. You think in the third person yet you feel it in your heartbeat but you're watching it from outside. It's like watching someone step on a nail and your foot goes like that [gestures]… The difference is a matter of degree. The observation is more important for the director. For a writer the identification with one character and then another is more important, but then one character is observing another character. It's very difficult. The more I talk about it, the more I think there is something demented about the whole experience.[4]

Over a year later, I ask Irene: "What do you hear in your mind when you write words a character says? When you write, do you hear your words in your own head with your accent?"[5] Irene responds, "What accent?" and then she says:

> I hear the state of mind. It produces a mood, a tone, a particular reading with stresses in my mind when I write. It's not my accent. It's not anybody else's voice. I don't hear a voice.[6]

Remarkable examples of Irene's directing a "state of mind" occur in rehearsal. On March 14, 1998, the director says to Joseph Goodrich, playing David to Clea Rivera's Marion: "Everything she says is angels talking to you." On March 13, 1998, the director interrupts actress Molly Powell: "A little too hot. It's really peaceful. Almost religious. *Every word is a different landscape* [emphasis added]."

Two hours later an extraordinary directorial note is given to the same actress. Irene dictates a new stage direction during rehearsal: "Pause. Dark thoughts." The authorial stage direction is conventionally explicit. Then Irene gives actress Molly Powell a directorial note on her new stage direction: "A cloud passes through you." Later, when I check this quote with Molly, she says: "I wrote it down, too! It's wonderful!"

Another illustration of the director's providing a suggestive supplement to her own text occurs unexpectedly during rehearsal on March 12, 1998. Irene, sitting at the director's table, suddenly interrupts the actors as they begin playing Scene 7: "Take a little moment. Because the sentence doesn't lead you to what I'm asking you to do. [The lines are: "Well this is it. This is the night."] So you create it when you say, 'This is the night.' Think of a magician who brings forth a tiger and the woman disappears because the tiger has eaten the woman." The actress reads the next speech: "That's what we call opening night. We say *the night*."[7] The scene and lines have nothing to do, literally, with magicians and tigers. Irene continues: "Don't lose your magician. You're still there waiting for the next miracle."

Even more unexpected and unprecedented is Irene's announcement in rehearsal on March 20, 1998, that Elizabeth's lines (including the lines quoted above) in Scene 7 are reassigned to her brother, Vernon, and

Vernon's lines in this scene are reassigned to David.[8] In response to the actors' initial dismay, Irene says: "Anybody can play these lines," and, later, "Let's talk about the lines, not about the character who says them."

This switch in speech tags elicits clearly distinct responses in the two actors most affected by it. Daniel Blinkoff, playing Vernon, tells Irene in rehearsal on March 20, 1998: "I feel as if I'm on unstable ground because you've given me lines that another character was speaking." Joseph Goodrich, playing David, tells me during the lunch break on March 21, 1998: "That kind of switch embodies the idea that character is mutable... [It] breaks the back of expected behavior. So characters cannot merely contradict themselves but assume a different character which to a realistic actor or dramaturg would appear to be bad or faulty playwriting. 'He or she just wouldn't *do* that,' is a typical response... This [Irene's] kind of approach to acting and to the liquidity of the script is second nature to me. It's certainly my preference as a way of writing and a means of acting. It's certainly more interesting." The next day he brings me a copy of Roger Shattuck's *The Banquet Years* with a quote from Max Jacob's *Art poétique:* "Personality is only a persistent error."[9]

During lunch break on March 5, 1998, Irene tells me why she makes changes in the script during rehearsal:

> I make changes in rehearsal because it's coming at me. If I see the actor misinterpret the mood, I would see if by revising it I could make it clearer what mood it is, because when I'm not directing it, the director may not see the mood I intended. I want to make things clear to the actor, not the director. Sometimes when I add or take out a word, I'm doing that rather than saying, 'Change the mood or tone.' I don't tell them why I make a change mostly because I think it's obvious. I want to make it clear for other productions.

On March 7, 1998, I watch Irene make a series of changes in the dialogue in scene 1, p. 9, of the current rehearsal script. Her primary assistant, Dawn Williams, writes down the revisions as Irene speaks. These changes, composed in her mind, first take the form of dictation written down not only by her assistant but also by the stage manager, the assistant stage manager, and the actors. Then it "[comes] at [her]" in the voices of the actors reading the words aloud in rehearsal for the first time. The playwright-director hears the changes in the script in the context of what she has already seen and heard in rehearsal, and makes further revisions as she listens and watches. The "final" version, whatever and whenever that will be,[10] is shaped by repeated voicings and repeated listenings in which the director-playwright and the actors continually exchange roles, each at some point listening and voicing and writing. Irene listens to the actors and writes; the actors listen to her voice and rewrite the script; Irene listens to new voicings of what has been newly written, rewrites, redirects. This is a very complicated process, of course, and at one point in rehearsal on March 20, 1998, an actor, taking down dictation of that day's changes, asks: "Which revised script are we revising?" On the first night of rehearsal in the theater, an actor misses his cue in Scene 1. From backstage he calls out: "What happened to 'wild in the parlor'?" An actress on stage replies, laughing: "That's been gone for days."

I ask Clea Rivera during a break in rehearsal on March 13, 1998, if she thinks of Irene as a director when she gives blocking and as a playwright when she gives textual revision. The actress replies:

> She is a director who might also change lines and she's a playwright who likes to get involved with the way these lines are spoken and with the way the actors move. And she's just a full entity unto herself.

During lunch break on March 12, 1998, actress Molly Powell says:

> No one that I've worked with works like Irene... I feel that she works very viscerally, like a little animal that is entirely alert. All of her senses are working. There's a kind of animal focus: She's very, very, very focused on what's right in front of her. Everything that we do in rehearsal — every tone of voice or tilt of the head or angle of the body — somehow lands on her, is perceptible to her. So she starts sorting and pulling and sifting and extending what we do... When we do work on longer

stretches, her attention expands to look at the whole arc. *But right now each little second is passionately looked at* [emphasis added]. That's how I experience it. I don't know what it looks like.

I reply that this is *exactly* what it looks like to me, as we are called back into the rehearsal room.

Here are only a few of the occasions when each second is passionately looked at in the March 7, 1998, afternoon rehearsal. Directing "to the micrometer," Irene tells Clea Rivera: "Go... go...go...go...turn your head... Take one step less, Marion... Turn the body...just a little less. The head is fine." Directing Joseph Goodrich, Irene gives these notes as he performs the role of David: "There are energies that make you move... It's not just from you... A little more like frogs falling. They go up and then they move... It's the elbow. Let the forearm just follow. [She demonstrates at her seat behind the director's table. The actor tries it.] No. The hands were leading." A little earlier in this rehearsal, Irene enters the playing area, stands next to the actress playing Marion, to whom David is bowing in obeisance, and directs the placement of her left elbow, wrist, and hand; the tilt of her shoulders and head; the position of her right foot. Irene demonstrates the placement of the feet and left arm. She watches the actress assume an approximately equivalent position, then removes the script the actress is holding in her left hand, adjusts the left arm, seems to approve, then says, "There is something wrong with the left arm," and readjusts it. The actress moves her left arm slightly and Irene and Molly Powell, who is watching offstage next to me, say simultaneously, "Oh yes." The script is then handed back to the actress in the playing area who as she takes it with her left hand slightly alters the position so painstakingly found. But this is live theater, not film, and the actress will have to find that position over and over again, with and then without her script. In rehearsal on March 12, 1998, Irene moves into the playing area and directs minutely a silent scene: "Eyes open wider... Mouth open more, very slowly... No, no, the eyes open."

Joseph Goodrich, who is a playwright as well as an actor, tells me after rehearsal on March 6, 1998: "With other playwrights they bring in a block of ice and chip a little away. For practical reasons, an actor can't say a line a certain way, or the theatre couldn't afford a door. But Irene is willing to melt the block office and it's not a question of hesitation or indecision or lack of concern for what she's written, for the vision that she brought into the theater. What it is is a willingness to surrender to the moment." This willingness to surrender to what's "coming at me" characterizes Irene as playwright-director throughout rehearsal. On March 6, 1998, she interrupts the playing of scene 3: "That's bad playwriting. Take out 'In Norway?'" On March 13, 1998, rehearsing scene 1, Irene changes Lady Bell's line, "Yes Marion, I'm listening," to "What Marion?"[11] She then adds Marion's line, "Elizabeth says that Ibsen was observant like an ape," and Elizabeth's response, "I didn't say he was observant like an ape. I said he was [changed in rehearsal to "is"] observant. Like an ape." These new lines and surrounding dialogue undergo many revisions. Finally, Irene says, "This joke is not working. Drop the lines about the ape." The actors respond in spontaneous chorus: "No." Irene agrees to "keep trying." After a while she says, "I'm sorry. I think the ape is not such a great idea. Let's take out all the ape references." She changes the line from "Observant. Like an ape." to "Observant.—Like a wild animal."[12] The actors say they like this revision. Rehearsal continues. At one point Irene cuts most of what she has newly added along with certain lines in the last revised draft. One page of dialogue greatly expands and greatly contracts within half an hour, its numerous transformations all now erased by the actors and assistant to the director. There is no copy of the sequence of textual transformations that I witness, except my own transcript, and I have inadvertently erased a few of the intervening revisions as the dialogue changed from 61 to 99 to 36 words.

I believe that for Irene Fornes rehearsal is a means of completing the writing of her own plays: Her directing is writing in another mode. Irene has said in public that she is "usually very unhappy" when she sees productions of her plays by someone else.[13] She is also becoming more upset, she tells me earlier, when critics, however intelligent, "write about my works in ways that misinterpret them…ignoring things that are in the play because it destroys their theory, their agenda." She explains that in writing *The Summer in Gossensass*, she "wanted to clarify the question of what comes out of the words of the text." What she wishes from readers, critics, and interpreters is that they "do an honest reading of and an honest listening to the play.[14] It is this kind of "honest reading" that she herself demonstrates in her responses to Ibsen's Hedda Gabler.

Irene reads Hedda as agoraphobic, suicidal, not pregnant, and "a little kinky for her time period." Irene asks me pointedly if I remember the scene in which Hedda asks Lovborg to tell her about his experience with prostitutes. (I don't.) "People don't remember it because they don't want it to be there."[15] On March 5, 1998, the third day of rehearsal at table, Irene says to the actors: "My interest in writing the play has to do with interpretation and misinterpretation of *Hedda Gabler*... There are things in that territory [Ibsen's play] which are mysterious and odd rather than good or bad."

*The Summer in Gossensass* presents acts of reading and rereading as discovery. In scene 4 of the April 25, 1998, script, Vernon, studying a few pages of an English translation of *Hedda Gabler* that Marion has stolen, says: "You can tell when a person doesn't like another just from the lines. Isn't that amazing. You can tell when a person doesn't like another just from reading the lines. Isn't that amazing?" (p. 8). Like the stolen pages from which two actresses, Elizabeth Robins and Marion Lea, are trying to reconstruct Ibsen's play, the continually revised pages of the rehearsal script of *The Summer in Gossensass* must be studied and restudied, figured and reconfigured, read and reread in every rehearsal.

When I enter the rehearsal room, before the actors arrive, on Saturday morning, March 14, 1998, Irene is talking to her assistant, Dawn Williams, about gambling. She says that Hedda is a gambler and that for a gambler the thrill is the moment of greatest risk, where you either live or die, win or lose. The thrill is not the winning itself. I ask if she herself has ever gambled. No, she says, except for a lottery ticket. But her mother at the age of ninety-nine asked Irene to drive her to Los Vegas to gamble at 2:00 A.M. and they did.

On the following Saturday, March 21, 1998, a revised script appears with a new speech by David:

Now, I understand in this play there's also a character of a woman who is a gambler… I believe Ibsen has written about gambling as a natural although unusual instinct in mankind. More common among men, but women have a more intense, although secret, yet untapped gambling instinct. In a sense, something like a religious drive — an urge to stand on a line so fine, a tightrope that lifts upwards and upwards even further, higher and higher. In a state of balance so perilous, and yet so consuming that rather than wish for safety, one is greedy for more height, more distance from the land. More at risk of death and yet attracted to the ascension while fearing the fall. Being pulled to more height and yet in horror attracted to the fall. That vertigo is what a gambler feels at that moment when he has put all his chips on one number, the roulette is turning the click click click click click sound speeds up, then it starts to approach the end. Omnipotence. The moment of bliss. — A deal.[16]

In the late afternoon, I am asked to sit in the playing area and read the part of Lady Bell during rehearsal of the new speech on gambling. My lines are: "Yes!" "Yes!" "As someone else," "You have an interesting mind, David," and "Yes!"[17] For twenty minutes I am directed by Irene Fornes standing a few feet away from me. It is uncanny. I feel the currents of energy I have only guessed at from my usual seat outside the playing area to the right of the director's table. As Joe Goodrich performs David's new lines over and over, and Clea Rivera lies curled and motionless on the floor, I am caught as if in a kind of wind tunnel. I sit unmoving in a chair. Being still in performance is difficult work. Finally, I come to know how much one feels simply sitting quietly in a Fornes play.

Being directed by Irene Fornes in a play by Irene Fornes is a gift no amount of typing can repay.

1. Maria Irene Fornes, "Creative Danger." Originally published in *American Theatre*, vol. 2, no. 5 (September 1985). Reprinted in *The Theatre of Maria Irene Fornes*, ed. Marc Robinson (Baltimore and London: Johns Hopkins University Press, 1999).

2. For accounts of Maria Irene Fornes' rehearsals of *Uncle Vanya* and *Abingdon Square*, see Susan Letzler Cole, *Directors in Rehearsal: A Hidden World* (New York and London: Routledge, 1992), pp. 35–54.

3. For a fuller, more detailed account of Maria Irene Fornes as playwright-director in rehearsal of *The Summer in Gossensass*, see Susan Letzler Cole, *Playwrights in Rehearsal* (New York and London: Routledge, forthcoming).

4. Irene Fornes, interview after rehearsal, January 31, 1997. Irene's statement that as a playwright "you feel it in your heartbeat but you're watching it from outside," recalls Diderot's characterization of the actor who "must be two people at once, the one immersed in his role and the other coolly observant and critical outside it." (Diderot, *Paradoxe sur le comedien*) translated by David Cole and quoted in David Cole, *Acting as Reading: The Place of the Reading Process in the Actor's Work* (Ann Arbor: University of Michigan Press, 1992), p. 73.

5. Irene was born in Havana and emigrated to New York when she was fifteen. She speaks slightly Cuban-accented English.

6. Interview during lunch break between morning and afternoon rehearsals, March 5, 1998.

7. March 12, 1998 rehearsal script: scene 7, p.1.

8. In the February 27, 1998 script, Elizabeth, Marion, and John — now called Vernon — were in scene 7. On March 20, 1998, the lines in the scene remain the same but Vernon takes over Elizabeth's lines and David, who was not in scene 7, now takes over Vernon's lines. Marion is removed from the scene, her one speech reassigned to David.

9. Roger Shattuck, *The Banquet Years* (New York: Vintage, 1955), p. 39. On March 26, 1998, during a break on the first night of rehearsal in the theater, Irene says to me and her assistant, Dawn Williams: "In my other plays the characters serve the play... In this play they're eccentric for their own purposes. They don't care about the play."

10. In answer to a question from a member of the audience at a colloquium entitled "Focus on Fornes: A Colloquium on the Obie Award-Winning Playwright and Director," Lang Recital Hall, Hunter College, New York City, April 8, 1998, on the afternoon after the opening night performance of *The Summer In Gossensass*, Irene says: "I

do rewrites during rehearsal and during subsequent productions and even after the plays have been published. The perspective you have when you've just completed something is different from your perspective later on.... Twenty years after *Fefu* I was finally able to revise it the way I had always intended." She adds, characteristically, that she thinks the revisions she makes are right. And, indeed, when just before the Colloquium begins, I protest the cutting of a certain line from scene 6 in *Gossensass*, Irene defends the cut. I continue to protest and she says, "I am certain I am right."

11. March 10, 1998 rehearsal script: scene 1, p.4.

12. These lines appear in scene 1, p. 4, of the March 13, 1998 rehearsal script and remain, unchanged, in the April 25, 1998 script. It is interesting that actress Molly Powell experiences Irene's gaze ("she works very viscerally, like a little animal that is entirely alert") in the same way that her character, Elizabeth Robins, describes Ibsen's gaze.

13. Irene Fornes, in response to a question from a member of the audience at the colloquium, "Focus on Fornes..." Hunter College, April 8, 1998.

14. Interview, January 31, 1997.

15. *Ibid.*

16. Scene 5, p. 21. These lines appear verbatim in the April 25, 1998, script.

17. April 25, 1998, script: scene 5, p. 20.

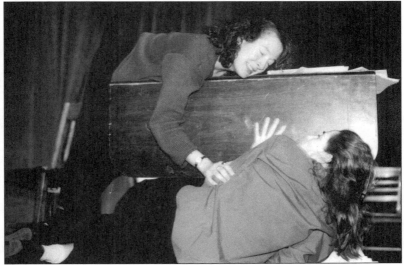

Rehearsal photos of Molly Powell as Elizabeth Robins playing Hedda Gabler leaning over Aime Quigley as Marion Lea interpreting Thea Elvsted

*THE SUMMER IN GOSSENSASS*
The Women's Project and Productions, The Harold Clurman Theatre, New York City, 1997

Photo by Maria M. Delgado

# ⊛ JOE GOODRICH
*Actor, Playwright*

IT'S VERY EASY TO SAY A LOT ABOUT IRENE —
and hard to say just a little. Her generosity of spirit, the plenitude and
fecundity of her talent, her charming and singular personality are easily written or spoken of at length, but defeat any kind of thumbnail
description or easy summation.

But I'll try.

I've had the pleasure of working with Irene on several occasions,
the most recent being her production of *The Summer in Gossensass*, which
was presented by the Women's Project at the Judith Anderson Theatre
in NYC in March and April of 1998.

She delights in language, in the innocence and danger and weight
of speech.

Language inhabits two worlds (as does Irene, born in Cuba and a
resident of New York City for the last fifty-four years): that of the flesh,
and that of the mind. Our words are carried on the breath of our lungs;
through a vast, tiny, complicated system of physical reactions called hearing, we are able to comprehend — sometimes — the thoughts of others. It is the very physicality of speech, which is the stage's greatest asset,
that makes the theater Irene's natural and undisputed home.

Her concern for and attention to the permutations of thought and
action that make up character means that she is always looking for just
the right words, the right actions, and the right combination of the two.

I'd like to describe briefly one of those quests to find the right words.
(Though I've focused on language, Irene is just as meticulous with physical movement — with the way the fingers of a hand are spread on a
collar, say, or the swish and twirl of a skirt in motion... Even with the
quality of the fabric of the skirt itself. Everything that goes into a piece
of theater comes under Irene's gaze.)

On the day of the first preview of *Gossensass*, Irene wasn't yet satisfied with certain parts of the text. One of them was a speech of mine, and she asked if it'd be all right to keep working on it even though we'd be opening the door to the public for the first time in just a couple of hours.

"Sure, Irene."

"You won't have to say it tonight," she said. "Tomorrow night will be fine."

She then proceeded to write each of the lines of the speech in question on a separate strip of paper, and to arrange the strips in different combinations, looking for the right order, waiting for the right order to emerge.

I went to the dressing room downstairs to do whatever it is that actors do before a show. A half-hour or so later I passed through the lobby of the Judith Anderson again — and Irene was still standing there, dressed to the nines for the evening's performance, arranging and re-arranging the lines of the speech while the box office staff swept the floor, put flowers in vases, folded programs.

Later that evening, after the show, I was given a sheet of paper with a new version of my speech on it.

Irene had found just the right words in just the right order.

Her unceasing efforts to "Get It Right," the level of questioning and experimentation she's willing to embrace in the writing and production of her work, the sheer joy she continues to find in the whole process of making theater can serve as an example to us all.

She is a beautiful woman, a beautiful writer, a canny and intuitive director. Working with her is delightfully easy — and there's a very simple explanation for that.

We love Irene, and want to please her.

## ❀ MOLLY POWELL
*Actor*




What makes the Ireneness of Irene? Those of us who have been lucky enough to work with her seem to have a shared shorthand: Irene is Queen, Irene is Irene, La Grande Irene, the inimitable Irene — our monikers affectionate and probably a little proprietary. Not that we are acolytes. Irene eschews guruism. She is too mercurial to lead any school or cult. But we do revel in our shared experience working with her. We trade stories, fall into bad approximations of her accent, retell punch lines from her stories, never quite doing them justice. We pronounce her name with added emphasis, "Ireeene," as though it is a title. All ways of saying, "Wowee! What a force!" She is deeply herself — brilliance, eccentricities, and all. We understand that it is rare, in or out of the theater, to encounter someone whose complicated humanity is so on the surface of their everyday personality.

Two images spring to mind when I think of Irene in the rehearsal room. The first is from a rehearsal for *Springtime*, her short play about an ill-fated love relationship. At the end of the play Greta opens a book and finds a letter from Rainbow, who has left her. Greta, alone and bereft, reads the letter then looks out the window past which Rainbow walked when she left the house for the last time. At the end of a stumble-through, I go toward Irene and see that she is crying. She sighs and says, "Ah! Why must love be so painful?" This is not a proud or showy moment. It's not that she's pleased her play has moved her. Nor is she embarrassed by her tears. It's a very simple, deeply felt and open-hearted sadness that she doesn't think to cover up in front of us. There's something a little witty in her tone, and she seems to be laughing gently at her own absurdity, the absurdity of it all. The moment passes quickly and we're on to notes.

The second image is from a rehearsal for *The Summer in Gossensass*, her new play about the premiere of *Hedda Gabler* in London. Joe Goodrich is playing David, a man who adores actors and the theater and is extremely eager to be somehow involved in this premiere production. David has hunted up whatever second- and third-hand scraps of information he can find about Ibsen, who is still relatively unknown in the London theater world. He is bursting to share his precious portfolio of research with everyone in the room. In an excess of zeal Joe/David leaps downstage to the table, where he is poised to open his precious package of papers. The movement is very gangly and odd and somehow froglike. Irene is electrified. She shrieks with laughter, leaps onto the stage and starts a little amphibious movement improvisation with Joe. Now both are laughing. They spend a good deal of time cavorting goofily and bouncing about, refining this bodily gesture of self-abandon. Irene is having a ball.

Many directors are reluctant to get too closely involved in the mess of an actor creating a role. Irene loves involvement. Minute details others would never spend time on she will labor over for hours: whether to turn your head a half degree to the light on this word or that, how slowly your hand falls to your lap, the shape of your hand when it lands, whether a character's thinking is precisely "soft" or "limpid" or "grave" on a certain line. In one rehearsal for *Springtime* we work at length on the quality of Greta's breathing during a particular scene. "How does one breathe when one is in love?" This is something I can see Irene has thought about. She herself tries out various ways of breathing, catching and holding her breath, letting it out with an audible sigh. In another rehearsal of a scene where Greta is happy she notes, "Oh! I like what your toes are doing!" I had been barely aware of my toes and might never have repeated their little gesture. It becomes my happiest moment in the play. Late in the run of *Springtime*, Irene gives me a small note that changes the tenor of the last moments of the play. I am alone onstage, my back to the audience, looking out the window. The front row is twenty-five feet away and I face upstage so I let my feelings out a bit, quietly. At this point in the play it's a relief to cry. After weeks of seeing the play end in this way, Irene one night says "Oh, no, Molly. We shouldn't see your shoulders move or feel that you're crying. Someone who can cry is someone who is alive, who we can feel hope for. You must be absolutely still and quiet." I have a eureka moment and think, "Of course!" She's right. This stillness says more about Greta's state and the loss at the end of the play. Detail by detail, Irene is building up an extremely specific world that is very much of the senses, a world where even someone's still shoulders seen from afar or the precise energy of their thinking can become a telling and sensorial moment.

Another element of Irene's ineffable Ireneness is the sheer force of her imagination, which viscerally brings the world of the play into the rehearsal room and onto the stage. Of course all theater artists attempt this, but Irene does so with a complexity and mystery definitely all her own. I understood this only recently when I was thinking about the difference in rehearsing *Springtime* and *The Summer in Gossensass*. We rehearsed *Springtime* during the Spring, in fact. The room had large windows that let in luscious Spring breezes and sunshine. We'd often linger a little too long on breaks, Gordana Rashovich sneaking a ciga-rette out the window, Irene telling stories. There was a sense of deli-ciousness and frivolity and peace, with room for silence and contentment. In rehearsing scenes I remember a feeling of wind and light and time enough. We explored long silences. The rehearsal room felt like a pro-tected space but also porous to the elements because of the large win-dows. It seemed this lovely time might stretch on forever. Of course what I'm also describing is the world of the play. "Don't you love your little house?" she would ask us, referring to the set. It was a tiny, bleached wood, warm-weather house, full of light and air that entered easily through the cracks and windows, a small shared space full of love and silliness, trust and time. Irene and Donald Eastman, her longtime designer, surprised us late in tech by putting flowers outside the back window, flowers only we could see. It was a private idyll.

*The Summer in Gossensass*, a play Irene was still rewriting while in rehearsals, dramatizes Elizabeth Robins' and Marion Lea's attempt to mount the first English-language production of *Hedda Gabler* in 1891. The two women faced enormous obstacles: Lily Langtry's rival production (which never opened), difficulty getting legal rights, a poor translation and Ibsen's scandalous reputation from earlier productions that had received bad press elsewhere in Europe. In Irene's play the two women piece Hedda together one stolen fragment at a time. Theirs is a desperate and dramatic struggle to pull off the premiere, to understand the character of Hedda and who this Ibsen is who created her. Their world is full of flurry and bustle and intermittent flashes of despair and inspiration. Needless to say, our rehearsals for *Gossensass* echo this: days of searching, many animated discussions, worry and time pressure, scenes tried countless different ways, chronologically rearranged, cut altogether, new scenes added or spliced in, tears, epiphanies, and occasional ebullience. Irene is so sharply attuned to the moment exactly in front of her, that she can become agitated or disappointed if all the detailed work we mapped out in rehearsal loses vibrancy. Here we go! No beautifully detailed, dead character edifices for her! Perhaps more than any other director I've known, Irene values theater as a living, breathing event. No matter where we are in rehearsal or even in the run, it's time to let it go, change her mind, start from scratch, focus on something else. This can certainly be frustrating, but I have rarely been so aware of loving the theater, with all its Sturm und Drang. And this, of course, is precisely what *The Summer in Gossensass* is about, honoring the absurd and sublime and sometimes difficult world of the theater and those who devote themselves to it. ("And most importantly…the women among them" — E. Robins.)

Irene's process is subterranean and thoroughgoing, deeply sentient and alive to the specifics of each moment. I venture to say it's not a completely conscious method. Indeed, her focus is sometimes trance-like in intensity, which is not to say reverent or still. Even sitting in a chair, she is slightly aquiver with the energy of her observation. Her eyes flash, her toes bob and tap. She is paying deep attention. To one detail at a time. When she is in this mode it's hard for me not to imagine her as some very alert and not unfriendly beast, keenly intent on something extremely specific just a little to the side of most people's perception. She's somehow plugged in and humming along. The sparks that she throws off unleash the emotional energies of the play, and we are drawn along with her in ways that we don't completely understand. She is working to allow us to be truly alive on stage. For all its beautiful and subtle language, hers is a theater of viscera, I think — full of breath and life and wonderful, inimitable, queenly…Ireneness.

# ✣ JOHN SEITZ
*Actor*

I WAS ACTING AT THE O'NEILL CENTER'S playwright's conference when I was sent an unfinished manuscript of *Abingdon Square*. Unfortunately auditions were one day only and I was unable to make it back to NYC. However, some weeks later a meeting was scheduled; the actor cast as Juster hadn't worked out. I met Irene and Julia Miles (the producer). I was floored by Irene; I don't think I'd ever met anyone quite like her. The sticking point quickly became about the rehearsal period. I argued for a delay of the scheduled opening; I wanted a full rehearsal even though I was coming aboard late. This idea was troublesome to the producers though I think Irene didn't care one way or the other. It was actually emotional when I declined, but I felt the alternative was a compromise of my artistic needs and process.

The next day I got a call from the casting director. Irene wanted to see me. I was also assured that the producer was giving serious consideration to a delay. So I left home in a pouring rain for the rehearsal space in Chelsea. I met the cast and spoke for some time with Irene, telling her I was eager to commit as soon as the decision on opening was made. As I got ready to leave, I discovered my umbrella was missing. Irene suggested that I might as well read a little with the cast till the rain slacked. I started work and never stopped (eventually she returned the umbrella). It became one of the most fulfilling experiences of my life. I can only compare it to working with Richard Foreman or Robert Wilson. But then she's also the writer and that's happening, too. She wouldn't give us one scene, said she'd written it in her mind but hadn't transcribed it. It made me crazy but I never stopped trusting her. What a trip it was. The play got an Obie, Irene got an Obie, and I got one too.

I last saw her at an invited dress for NY Theater Workshop's *More Stately Mansions* in October 1997. It was wonderful to share that challenging four to five hours with her. An original and a supreme artist.

# ✹ MICHAEL CERVERIS
*Actor*

I HAD THE PRIVILEGE AND GREAT FORTUNE to work with Irene Fornes twice as an actor, once in the premiere of *Abingdon Square* in 1987 and once in a play called *Dogs*, written by one of her students, which she directed in LA in 1990. Both occasions were full of wonderful frustrations and difficult comforts. That's what working with Irene was like for me. In many ways, she is a supremely motherly presence, nurturing and utterly loving. It is her love for you as an artist and craftsperson and for the work that you are creating together. And it is that compassion that precedes the sometimes stern and rigorous quality of her direction, providing an atmosphere that, even in the most trying rehearsals, makes you explore even deeper, rather than giving up. Her writing and directing have tended to draw the best work from me, in spite of — or probably because of — my not always feeling sure what I was doing.

Irene has an uncanny ability to reveal the most mysterious things by focussing on the most specific. My favorite memory is of rehearsing with Madeleine Potter a scene for *Abingdon Square* in which she was asking me a series of seemingly superfluous questions ("Have you ever stolen anything?…etc." ). We'd gone through it over and over and weren't finding the scene. The questions seemed silly, random, and hard to play. Irene wanted the exchange to make a tangible bond between our characters, a private world that we were creating. All we were coming up with were a string of questions and answers. Madeleine asked Irene what she was meant to be doing with these questions, why was she interrogating me like this? Irene thought for a moment, then said, "It's not that you care what he says. You don't care what his answers are. You just love his teeth. He has the most beautiful teeth in the world and you ask him these questions so that you can see them. You want to make him smile so you can see them even better, and so you ask him silly questions. You just love his beautiful teeth." It was a simple, minutely specific task. And for the rest of the rehearsals and performances, Madeleine asked me those questions and got me to open my mouth and to smile so she could see my teeth. And we were connected in an exact and private way. The audience would never have any idea what we were doing, but what I'm sure they felt was the uncommon bond between these characters. The little task Irene gave us translated into all the depth and mystery of the feelings between these two. That, to me, is the essential magic of Irene's work and her art. It is as simple and direct as our human needs are, and at the same time as mysterious and unfathomable as our minds and hearts.

Michael Cerveris (Frank) and Madeleine Potter (Marion)

*ABINGDON SQUARE*
The Women's Project and Productions, the American Place Theatre,
New York City, 1987

Photo by Martha Holmes

# ✸ MADELEINE POTTER
*Actor*

I PLAYED MARION IN THE 1987 PREMIERE of *Abingdon Square* written and directed by Irene Fornes. It is difficult to write about the experiences that form you; they remain behind the eyes and within the senses, and become the mechanism through which you understand and measure other experiences, all the ones that come afterwards.

I have hardly seen or spoken to Irene since I did *Abingdon Square,* but the love I developed for her during that time remains as strong, and my admiration simply grows with time. She is full of beautiful contradictions, or perhaps she is just a very complete artist. She is a great writer, a poet, but as a director she has a profound interest in the physical, in gesture, in the distances between people in a given moment of communication, in subtle shifts of focus that transform and illuminate a moment. She is a poet with a powerful interest in silence. Rehearsal was full of possibility and a creative energy that continually pushed me beyond self-consciousness because Irene is herself is so open, so curious, so filled with humor and an endless empathy for human beings and their ways. She was the writer, but in rehearsal she was in a state of complete discovery, often cutting, rewriting, reshaping the play as we went along based upon what was being found, a very equal partnership of discovery between herself and the actors; and this allowed a fusion between the actor and the words. She created an atmosphere of faith in the rehearsal room; and somehow in that atmosphere the unconscious, the subliminal, flourished, as if finally, both personally and collectively we were dreaming the same dream. And Irene never speaks in general terms. She has a genius for addressing a particular person in a way they can understand. Her ideas are always specific, and always fertile, a doorway, an adventure, a beginning.

A couple of scenes into *Abingdon Square* two fifteen-year-olds have a playful fight. Out of the hilarity and the scuffle, the girl begins to speak an aria — I say aria because the sense in the speech if it is done correctly feels transporting, almost more like music than words.[1] The aria is about her love for the house in which she stands, and which she will shortly enter as a married woman. We had played with this speech and worked it in many ways, and I had never experienced any self-consciousness. At the technical rehearsal I began to speak and became completely paralysed. Irene came down to the stage from the back of the theater and asked what was wrong. I said, "I'm sorry, I can't do it. I don't want to make myself. I'm afraid of breaking it, I'm afraid." I am sure that most directors would have said to me: "Never mind, it's a new space, do it, it will get better," or "Never mind, it's a technical rehearsal, it's not for you anyway." Irene said, "Imagine you are walking through the Alhambra." I had never been in the Alhambra (and I still have not), but it did not matter. I was transported to a place of archways and infinite space, of certain and uncertain light, of the faintly dusty light of cathedrals, and I was completely released. Instead of chastising me, or ignoring my fear, Irene spoke to me particularly, addressing my imagination and my soul. I will never forget it because she taught me two great things for my work and for my life: that the only road for the artist is to forge further into the imagination, and that imagination is the only refuge from fear.

1. Maria Irene Fornes, *Abingdon Square* in *Womens Work: Five New Plays from the Women's Project,* ed. Julia Miles (New York and Tonbridge: Applause, 1989), pp. 4–5.

# ✸ DONALD EASTMAN
*Set Designer*

EVERY SET I DESIGN WITH IRENE IS AN opportunity to design a heaven room. They are always interiors. No matter what the theater, we design and build our own walls to cover the existing walls. When I say heaven, I'm speaking of a purity. It's all based on reality and research, but captured in a golden moment. There is a purity and honesty of materials. The woodwork is well oiled like a church pew or left alone like vermeer stripped of color or stained a pure red.

A warehouse space will have a fresh coat of whitewash. An unpainted plaster wall can have the texture of a Monet. If we think of marble, it's alabaster.

In everything there is a spirit of housekeeping. I will always remember Irene's big note when I was designing *Abingdon Square*. "In this house there is always fresh cream to feed the cat."

When we're in the theater together it's all about work. We're so serious and so butch and we laugh a lot. At any moment Irene will lean over and say *sotto vocce* "I tell you, we are gorgeous."

If you're being as "artistic" as we are, the idea of recognizing it is a secret pleasure. Because, before all, Irene has taught me that hard work is our duty and our first pleasure.

# ✾ ANNE MILITELLO
*Lighting Designer*

TO ME, IRENE FORNES IS ONE OF THE greatest visual artists in the theater today, as well as being one of the greatest playwrights. She is an expert on visual language. She knows exactly how to integrate all the design elements so that her plays can exist in a perfect space.

My work with Irene began soon after I moved to New York in 1980. I designed thirteen productions for her and I consider that work to be the most inspired of my theater career. From her, I learned how to extract and express emotion with lighting. She always encouraged me to go further, darker, dimmer using focus and respecting every visible detail.

She taught me that simple images, such as a figure as a black silhouette speaking against a dim background, or a half-lit face in the distance can add serious emotional depth. The subtle shift of a single shadow in conjunction with precise timing by an actor could create intense beauty. Her timing is exquisite. My ideas expand greatly every time I work with her.

When she directs, she choreographs every movement of the actors and the light together with focused precision. Somehow, she gets the actors to respond to the movement of light, and every night, they remember and use it for great effect. I've never seen any other director be able to achieve such support from a cast. I am constantly in awe of her generosity and wisdom as a teacher.

We have had to defend ourselves to several production managers, to convince them why we need another day of tech time in the beginning of rehearsals. There have been arguments, but she has always made converts after a brief drop-in to our rehearsals by those same people. Sometimes, at the beginning of tech rehearsals, the uninitiated actor is puzzled why an inch of movement or scenery placement could be that important until they see and feel the difference. Her results are breathtaking.

My work with her has influenced all of my subsequent designs. I feel extremely lucky to know her.

# ✸ SCOTT T. CUMMINGS
*Professor, Theatre Department,*
*Boston College*


## AMBER BEER
## AN OCCASIONAL PIECE IN CELEBRATION
## OF IRENE FORNES

IRENE FORNES IS THE FIRST PERSON I EVER
knew who ordered beer by the color.

We were at a bar in Pittsburgh in 1986, where she was directing a production of *Lovers and Keepers* at City Theatre, and a bunch of us went out after rehearsals one night to get a drink. When the waitress came to take our order, Irene asked her, "Do you have any amber beer?" Thinking this was a brand name, the waitress started to rattle off different labels — Iron City, IC Lite, Rolling Rock, Budweiser, and so on — until Irene interrupted and said something like, "No, no, amber, you know, golden brown."

When the drinks came, Irene's beer had the warm glow of a medium ale and she smiled at the sight of it. Even though I knew that the color simply indicated the type of beer that Irene liked the taste of, I could not help but think that she preferred it in part because of its reddish-gold translucence. A pilsner would be too clear, a stout too opaque. I remembered something Irene had said to me in an interview a year or two earlier about being in a bar with a friend talking about the unabashedly romantic aspects of her play *Molly's Dream*. She was insisting that love alters perception, that being in love makes everything different, and that light, for example, streaming through a glass of beer shines with a new radiance. "It *is* more beautiful," she said, "It isn't that you want it to be more beautiful or that you are lying to yourself. It *is*. Your senses are sharpened."

When I watch a Fornes play, my senses are sharpened. The love that imbues every moment onstage makes things more beautiful and I see and hear and feel in a new way. Irene has added much beauty to the world, not only through her plays but in the passion, principles, and inspiration she has imparted to countless colleagues and students. Her compassion is balanced by an almost ruthless honesty and an insatiable pursuit of truth and understanding. Even the most casual conversation with Irene is peppered with questions — about how something works, why something is done a certain way, what your perception is of a given subject or situation. I don't think I've ever said "I don't know" to any one person more than I have to Irene. She wants to know.

What emerges over a period of time of knowing Irene is that in her theater light, love, and learning are all conduits for a single, basic, irrepressible joy of life. It can be found in the discipline of her work and the meticulous care she brings to every word, gesture, and image onstage. It manifests itself in the playfulness of her creativity and her courting of the found and the accidental.

As sure as that joy lives in her heart and in her art, I think it must be in her genes as well. I remember a summer's day in 1991 at the Storm King Center in the Hudson River Valley where an early version of Irene's *Terra Incognita* was being showcased in a small workshop production. Her mother Carmen, small and spry and nearly 100 years old, was there. After the midday performance, the three of us, her mother in the middle, were strolling toward the reception across a huge lawn that stretched between two buildings. All of a sudden, Carmen leapt into the air. She just jumped, straight up, assuming that we would catch her, which we did, and carried her forward for about ten steps as she laughed and laughed and kicked her feet. When we put her down, I thought I saw Irene shoot her a look of disapproval, as if to say "What are you doing, you crazy? You could get hurt!" But then, as I recall, she smiled and rolled her eyes. She knew that her mother was jumping for joy.

✸ JANET NEIPRIS
*Tisch School of the Arts*
*New York University*

STAR GAZING
(for Irene Fornes)

At night
In the meadow
The fireflies waltz
On toes of thin silver
Who knows what they whisper
Who knows what
Strings of sounds
Slip from their lips
Their lean lips
Spilling onto the pond
Where I float
Eyes skyward
Star gazing
Catching words
Like butterflies.

# ✺ PEGGY PHELAN
*Professor, Department of Performance Studies, Tisch School of the Arts, New York University*

## MARIA IRENE FORNES'
## *SPRINGTIME:* A RESPONSE

CHARACTERS:
> A woman dreamer, in her late thirties.
> Maria Irene Fornes, as herself.
> A woman psychoanalyst, late 50s. Wears intellectual-black throughout.

SETTING:
> New York, 1999.

Scene One: *Dreamer's bedroom. A small room. Above the bed, a big print of Mark Rothko's squares, salmon and yellow; one on the right wall Andy Warhol's Flowers (any color). To the left of the bed is a night table. On it, there is a large radio with a digital clock. A glass of water. Several books and art catalogs. Downstage of the bed there is a small window. A woman in a bed, sleeping. Blue nightgown visible. Low lights.*

VOICE FROM RADIO: *(Read in manner of prose poem.)*
> Sometimes I dream I am a woman
> playwright. I wear a big hat like Lady Di
> and I have a Cuban accent like Fornes.
> I am famous because I made love
> between women on the stage commonplace.
> In my dream I am out
> for the first time with a woman I want to keep
> going out with. She is smoking.

*(Lights fade, button-like cigarette end, then black.)*

Scene Two: *Same as scene one.*

VOICE FROM RADIO:
Later I dream Fefu is giving a prize to Fornes.
Fornes takes the award and says I called her
from a pay phone to tell her I was in a vertical
coffin, and that after death there is still electricity,
lights, and telephones. The smoking woman
from the other dream says Fornes is making it up
and that the only person I call from pay phones is her.

*(Lights fade, button-like cigarette end, then black.)*

Scene Three: *Fornes stands at bottom of bed. Dreamer sitting up in bed, still in blue nightgown. Fornes lights a big cigar. She laughs somewhat largely, like a bark. After silence (three beats) she begins, gravely:*

FORNES: Can you paint? *(Gesturing at Rothko's print.)*
DREAMER: A little.
FORNES: Only women who paint can understand theater. It's all color
you know.
DREAMER: I think it's character too, and dialogue.
FORNES: No. It's mixing colors. The characters are like different col-
ored paints; the dialogue mixes the hues. But if you don't know
that I'm not telling you.

*(Laughs again, as above. Lights out abruptly.)*

Scene Four: *Still the same room. But now the dreamer's bed is made and she lies on top of it with her feet where head was in scene one. Fully dressed. Head is raised on pillows, back to audience, eyes facing her feet. Next to her bed, a large overstuffed chair, in which the analyst seats. Soft light.*

PSYCHOANALYST: What do you make of this dream?

DREAMER: Well, when I first recorded it in my diary, I made a big fuss about Fornes' use of "hues" and the two uses of "you" in the next sentence. Double-you. Women. Waiting. Words. Wonder. But now when I tell you the dream, rather than writing it down for myself, I am not so interested in the linguistic puns. Now I think what's remarkable about it, is that my dream is refusing to give me "advice." The way Fornes says "I'm not telling you" was really powerful for me. It's such a dramatic way to tell myself to recognize what I do know.

PSYCHOANALYST: What do you know that you would prefer to ascribe to Fornes rather than to claim yourself?

DREAMER: Well. Before I answer that let me say this: I think if I ever took a class from Fornes it would be just like this dream. No advice, but a lot of mixing of colors.

PSYCHOANALYST: Were you thinking of taking a class from Fornes?

DREAMER: No, but I feel like I am taking one from you.

PSYCHOANALYST: What link do you make between me and Fornes?

DREAMER: Well, you know. You both are — well, you know — more established.

PSYCHOANALYST: Established as what?

DREAMER: Well, maybe as paintings. Not so much as painters, but as images I carry around in my consciousness.

PSYCHOANALYST: Images?

DREAMER: Well, yes. I know I talk to you. Or rather I know that we talk. I don't talk to Fornes.

PSYCHOANALYST: Would you like to talk to her?

DREAMER: No. Reading her is enough. But I guess I should tell you, I know you write, but I have no desire to read you. I think it would make me self-conscious.

ANALYST: Yes, that makes sense. But I have noticed your apparent disinclination to show me any of your writing.

DREAMER: I have been very tempted to, of course. But I think I like keeping it a little fictional. It must be the way patients must feel about having analysts meet their lovers. I like that I can say anything I want about my writing, without you comparing it to the real sheets of paper. Do you understand?

ANALYST: I think it's worth pursuing a little more. But time's up for today. I want to return to the question of what you think Fornes knows that you prefer to ascribe to her, rather than to yourself. Until next time then.

*(Both characters rise, lights fall slowly.)*

Scene Five: *Dreamer, sitting up in bed. Lights on brightly. Holds book on her lap as lights up. Takes letter from book and reads:*

DREAMER: "My beloved, I'm sometimes obliged to do things that are dangerous — and to do things that I hate. To befriend people and then betray them. Someday I may be hurt. If this happens, and I'm not able to tell you this, I hope one day you'll open this book and find this note. I love you more than anything else in the world and it is to you that I owe my happiness. I always felt I didn't want to love only halfway, that I wanted to love with all my heart or not at all, and that I wanted to be loved the same way or not at all. With you, I had this and if anything happens to me I wanted you to remember this: That you are my angel and I will always love you. Even after death. Forever yours, Rainbow."[1]

*(Reader looks at Warhol's Flowers. Three beats. Then carefully folds letter as lights out.)*

Scene Six: *Same as Four.*

ANALYST: We were approaching the question of why your psyche would be attributing your own knowledge of certain things to Fornes.
DREAMER: I don't know.
ANALYST: What is your relationship with her?
DREAMER: My actual one or my psychic one?
ANALYST: I do not appreciate the distinction. Tell me how you relate to her.
DREAMER: Well I've met her a few times, but know her only slightly. But her work has meant a great deal to me.

ANALYST: What aspect of her work?

DREAMER: Fragments. Lines. Scenes between women especially. Her use of light as a director is extraordinary. She goes at the lightboard like a typist stroking the keys. There's a kind of punchiness to it. But really a fragment called "Springtime," part of a larger play called *What of the Night?* is the play I feel closest to. I wish I had written it.

ANALYST: Why?

DREAMER: Oh, it ends with a letter. I always wanted to write back.

ANALYST: You wanted to write the letter or you wanted to respond to it? You wished you had written the play or you wished you responded to the letter in the play?

DREAMER: Well, I guess, uhm…*(Silence, two beats)* Yes. All of that. And more too. There's a bit in the play where one of the characters, Rainbow, the one who writes the letter, says one of my favorite lines in contemporary theater: "Why should I try to love someone I don't love when I already love someone I love?" I just love that last part: "I already love someone I love." I sometimes whisper it under my breath when I'm anxious.

ANALYST: Why?

DREAMER: It's all the trying in love and all the achievement in love, all in the same sentence.

ANALYST: I'm not sure I follow. The sentence isn't "I will try to love the one I love" is it?

DREAMER: No. It's not at the level of the words I guess, it's more the grammar. It's as if I said to you, "I already wrote the book I am writing." I already love the one I am loving. But what's so great about Fornes' sentence is that the "I love" is not a present participle at all, it's more like a condition of being, an "I am already the one I am because I love the one I am loving already." Obviously, her sentence is more elegant. But that's what I hear in it I guess.

ANALYST: But do you attribute the sentence to Fornes? Or to the character who wrote the letter? I forgot her name.

DREAMER: Rainbow. Rainbow is the one who says the sentence Fornes wrote. Rainbow is the one who wrote the letter that Fornes left for someone else. Someone in another language, by which I mean another art form, maybe a painter. Or maybe I mean in a language that was neither Spanish, English, or French. I think Fornes had to write Rainbow in order to have her write the letter she wished she had written, or maybe, the letter she wished she had left, whenever it was she left. Or maybe it was a letter she wished she had received when someone left her. Or did receive...

ANALYST: Are you speculating? Or are you referring to Fornes' own autobiography?

DREAMER: Speculating of course. Projecting I guess you would call it. I have no idea what dramas Fornes has survived, or not survived, in her own life. There's just something about this letter that Rainbow leaves for Greta that has a different kind of resonance than the other writing.

ANALYST: A different resonance for you? Or do you mean it stands out in Fornes' work?

DREAMER: I do not appreciate the distinction. I can only tell you that the letter stands out for me. It's written in a different field, has a different auditor than her other writing. For me.

ANALYST: Is there a letter you failed to write? failed to send? that bothers you now?

DREAMER: Yes, many. And not only the ones I have not written or sent, but also the ones I will not write or send.

ANALYST: Well, we will have the begin there next time. There is more to say about all of this. Good day.

*(Analyst and dreamer slowly rise as lights fall slowly.)*

Scene Seven: *Same as Scene Five, except Dreamer now has notebook, paper, and pen, on lap.*

DREAMER:
Dearest My Own:
I loved your letter. I've written you back a thousand times. For me, it was never halfway. I know why you left. At first, I was so devastated. I've gone over it all so often in my mind. I try to see it from your point of view. I try to think of ways to help you see it from mine. I was jealous of course. Maybe also I was competitive.

I wasn't aware of that then… You know I was sick. But there was another thing beneath the illness. We each had our own wars I know, the scars to survive, before we even met.

But sometimes now I think our silence about all that was a mistake. It was partly English darling. Some of it I just could not translate.

And you? Your letter sounds so precise, almost formal. As if you rewrote it several times, or as if you thought about it so long it just came out with a clarity your speech did not often convey. Although you were always very precise in your language about sex and love.

I've painted you almost as often as I've written to you. I took the photographs as models. When I put my hand on the outline of your face I can sometimes still feel how it felt when you kissed me. Do you ever remember kissing me?

I know you wanted to save me. And in so many ways you did. Can you, will you, save me again? I'm seeing an analyst. Mainly we talk about my dreams. I am better than I was, I promise. Please come back. I'll teach you German. I love you always, even now while I'm still alive and every day plunged again into the bracing waves of your absence. Greta. P.S. Where are you?

Scene Eight: *Same as Scene Four.*

DREAMER: Well I did write a letter back.
PSYCHOANALYST: To Fornes?
DREAMER: No, to Rainbow.
ANALYST: Within the fiction, to whom did Rainbow write her letter?
DREAMER: Well to me I suppose.
ANALYST: Within the fiction?
DREAMER: You mean within Fornes' fiction?
ANALYST: Within the play. Yes.
DREAMER: A character called Greta.
ANALYST: Do you identify with Greta? Is she a writer?
DREAMER: No. She's a patient.
ANALYST: What's wrong with her?

DREAMER: It's unclear. Although she's German.

ANALYST: Is she sick because she's German?

DREAMER: Well, I would put it a little bit differently, she's sick to be German.

ANALYST: What nationality is Fornes?

DREAMER: Cuban. But she lived in Paris. Saw Beckett's original *Godot* there. God, can you imagine?

ANALYST: Is she Beckettian?

DREAMER: At times. But she's really a woman, and he, well, he wasn't in the end.

ANALYST: What do you mean?

DREAMER: Well Beckett tried really hard I think. But his heart just wasn't in it. There's a famous story

*(Analyst begins speaking now and the two are overlapping:)*

ANALYST: I don't like to interrupt you, but as you know, time is short and

DREAMER: about him performing Winnie in *Happy Days*, as he wrote it, you know, taking things out of his purse and measuring the time it takes…

ANALYST: I want to return to your dream. I am trying to follow the connections. Why do you think she makes the remark about theater being painting in your dream?

DREAMER: Well, she says theater is about "mixing colors." There's nothing pure. Everything is mixed up. Even love. It's stained with betrayal, no matter how much you already love someone you already love.

ANALYST: And how does that relate to your relationship to writing?

DREAMER: My motives are mixed, my genres are muddled. I can't seem to tell if I am in love with writing, or the person to whom I am writing. Maybe it doesn't really matter. Maybe the point is just to write and to love and worry about who receives the letter, the love, some other time, some other way.

ANALYST: Do you write for a specific person?

DREAMER: When I write a letter, I do.

ANALYST: And when you write other things?

DREAMER: Well I can see where this is going, and as you say, time is short. I'd rather talk about the other part of the dream that I can't decipher very well. Fornes says when I called her I said a pay phone was a vertical coffin, and that after death electricity and telephones still work.

ANALYST: What do you make of that?

DREAMER: Something about connections that endure after the call is cut off.

ANALYST: But your call went through to Fornes, didn't it?

DREAMER: Well yes I suppose. And perhaps hers went through to me. But that doesn't mean those are the calls we were trying to make.

ANALYST: Who were you trying to call if not Fornes?

(Silence. Six beats)

ANALYST: There was something else you said that survives death. Electricity and telephones and there was a third thing. Do you remember what it was?

DREAMER: Yes. Light.

ANALYST: What do you make of that?

DREAMER: I think it is an elaboration of the sending/receiving thing. We're all groping in the dark trying to find something before death, before darkness, but maybe we should not bother. Maybe there is more time, more light, than we think.

ANALYST: Perhaps. But our own time here is very short. As you know, I will be returning to Zurich to continue my training. I will be back in New York in three to five years, as I've told you. Have you given any more thought to continuing our conversation in writing, by letters, and FAX?

DREAMER: Thank you very much. Good luck. No, I will not be writing.

(*They remain in their respective places. Lights out.*)

---

1. Maria Irene Fornes, last scene of "Springtime," from *What of the Night?* in *Women on the Verge*, ed. Rosette C. Lamont (New York: Applause Books, 1993), p. 191.

# ✸ PAULA CIZMAR
*Playwright*

MAYBE THERE'S JUST SOMETHING ABOUT
sitting in the darkness — maybe it's just so close to dreaming, or maybe
it's just the prime and obvious location for a bolt out of the blue —
but the most vivid of the images that have haunted me for years (in all
the best ways) have arrived in the darkness, across the lip of a stage.
There's one in particular I can never shake. Imagine sitting in the Inter-
art, innocently processing the information that you're merely about to
see a play, never for one minute expecting that your life is about to change.
And then it does. Stage pictures, voices, costumes, colors — and words,
amazing words — you're watching *Eyes on the Harem!* And you had always
hoped and prayed that the imagination was limitless, boundless, unfet-
tered, open, but you never had proof before. And now you do. Now
in this theatre, in the darkness, you know, watching the work of Maria
Irene Fornes — now you know as a writer, as an artist, that you really
do work in a field of endless possibilities. You're free to take any dare,
free to explore any idea, in your own way, in your own voice. No nasty
borders. No rule book. You're just free. And you carry an image from
that play — the colors, a character's face, a gesture — with you wherever you go. To remind you that you that someone has opened the gates,
someone has parted the darkness, and made it easier for you to see your
way through.

# ✵ LISA PETERSON
*Resident Director*
*Mark Taper Forum Theatre, Los Angeles*

MARIA IRENE FORNES IS RESPONSIBLE FOR showing an entire generation of American playwrights that freedom as a writer is not only possible but necessary. I can't even count the number of writers that have been encouraged by Irene to break the rules, forge their own structure, write from the place of mystery. I first became aware of Irene as a playwriting teacher and muse for most of the interesting young writers of the late twentieth century. I still believe she's had more influence on contemporary American theater than any other single theorist or writer.

I remember that when I was directing *Fefu and Her Friends* at Yale Rep during the 1991–92 season, Irene was very generous with her time, both in person and over the phone. Her generosity is boundless. Like Caryl Churchill, Irene resisted all high-concept interpretations of her play, and was interested only in the simple situation, the reality of the play and this surprised me, since I thought I was working on one of the avant-garde classics. I remember talking a lot about rabbits, since a dead rabbit enters at the end of the action, and Irene had a lot of good advice about how to make it look real. I was impressed by the practical bent of our conversations and was made to understand that Irene, like all the greats, was a theater artist, not just a writer. She infected me with the pure thrill of giving the audience an experience, putting on a show.

# ✱ JONATHAN MOSCONE
*Associate Director*
*Dallas Theater Center, Texas*


## ENCOUNTERING IRENE


I FIRST MET IRENE FORNES DURING A VISIT she made to Yale in 1992 to see Lisa Peterson's production of *Fefu and Her Friends* as part of Yale Rep's Winterfest. Irene gave a writing workshop and talked about masturbation as a way to get the creative juices going. Later that summer, three classmates and I were treated to an excursion to Italy to document the 1st annual Dionysia Festival of International Playwrights. Irene was there, along with her mother Carmen, who would announce proudly, and often, that she was 101 years old as the actors rehearsed a fascinating piece called *Terra Incognita*, in which the myth of Columbus was contemplated by a group of tourists on vacation in Spain. Irene's actors adored and revered her, and they listened to every single thing she had to say. Irene stressed the non-exclamatory, the non-tense, and the non-"dramatic" in the actors' work. Quiet thoughts were more interesting to her than Sturm and Drang. Not every moment is in tension, she would state emphatically. Kind of Zen-like, I thought, but is it good theater?

Later that year I took on the challenge of further developing *Terra Incognita*, collaborating with Kim Sherman on an original score, and talking to Irene (and Carmen, who was now 102 years old) about the piece. To go into that process now would require reams and reams, but suffice to say, my feelings for Irene can be summed up in a phone conversation from the Yale Cabaret building. I was in the middle of trying to decode this extremely difficult piece, and I needed her help. I asked her about the last section of the play and whether it was ironic or not, and she answered quite definitely that she did not believe in irony in the theater. Irony bored her in life, so she did away with it in her plays. "In my plays," she told me, "people say what they mean." It's a simple thought, but it was the key. Like Chekhov, Fornes' characters speak as much from their hearts as they do their minds. The barrier between thought/feeling and word does not exist.

In Fornes, grace is the ultimate goal, the highest standard. And her characters are either in search of grace or are running from it. But it does exist.

Irene Fornes is a great and rare playwright. In striving for the pureness of thought and feeling, her work redefines what is dramatic. For Irene, tension only matters when juxtaposed with ease. In moments of eloquent contemplation, Irene's characters can fathom the profound, and they can see the spiritual. It is the ultimate sadness in the acknowledgment of a world that tramples grace at every turn that makes Irene's work so fully human. Her love of, disappointment in, and concern for humanity place her in the ranks of Chekhov and Brecht. And her mom was pretty fabulous too.

# ❁ CAREY PERLOFF
*Artistic Director*
*American Conservatory Theatre, California*

## PERSONAL KEYS

I REMEMBER VIVIDLY THE FIRST TIME I read *The Conduct of Life*, on an airplane flying to California. The tension and inexorability of the piece left me completely stunned; I don't think I breathed during the entire second half of the play, and I got off the plane thinking that somewhere in the hills of Padua, actors were at that very moment bringing the play to life, and wishing desperately that I was there.

Years later I began to work with Irene; in fact, she was the first director I hired when I became Artistic Director of The Classic Stage Company (CSC Repertory) theater in New York in 1987. It struck many people as odd that I began my tenure at this classical theater with a visionary avant-garde Cuban playwright, but there was a specific impetus that propelled my decision, namely my experience of watching Irene work on *Hedda Gabler* at Milwaukee Repertory Theater the year before. I remember wondering why on earth Irene had been drawn to that play; her work is so elliptical, mysterious, and painterly, and Ibsen's work (forgive me) is often so schematic and so freighted with exposition, that I wondered where these seemingly opposite and equally strong-willed artists would meet. I arrived at the first preview on a freezing evening in downtown Milwaukee and was greeted by a breathtaking, enormous white room (designed by long-time Fornes collaborator Donald Eastman) with strangely angled walls and surprising levels and undulations, absolutely spare, entirely covered in flowers that had been scattered exuberantly all over the floor. Not a single Victorian ornament or overstuffed couch for Irene: Her vision of Gabler's house was a light-filled wonderland with no furniture and endless possibilities.

Indeed, every single choice Irene made about the play was unlike anything I had seen in reference to *Hedda* before, and yet the whole thing worked in a vivid and wonderful way. One of the most startling moments was the entrance of Lovborg: usually cast quite literally as a Romantic blond hero with vine-leaves in his long locks, Irene's Lovborg was Richard Riehle, a large and slightly ungainly actor of immense talent and equally immense threat, who burst into this quiet white world like a violent and over-grown child desperate for love and attention. I was reminded over and over again of how unsentimental Irene is, and of how radical her notion of love is: images of upturned chairs and stained walls from the passionate affair in *Sarita* kept floating in my mind as I watched this mad man-child attempt to make love to the lady in the white room. The lady was both horrified and mesmerized; he left tracks on her floor.

Finally I understood Irene's personal key to the play. She chose to emphasize neither Hedda's likely pregnancy nor the unhappiness of her marriage to Tesman. Rather, she understood Hedda's dilemma to be agoraphobia. As long as she was within the beautifully arranged walls of her home, Hedda could be gracious and in control of her destiny; whenever she was asked to leave those walls, either for her honeymoon or to go visit the perpetual aunts, she became horrified, irrational, terrified. This is why Fornes chose to make the home such a welcoming and open ship of possibilities, and why the outside world was kept so violently at bay. Fornes' interpretation gave Hedda's behavior an envelope in which to explode; her Hedda played off the eroticism of the enclosed room just as the heroine of *Abingdon Square* finds the whole world of forbidden possibilities in a single space. This lent real poignancy to the negative sniping Hedda indulges in much of the play. And it reminded me of Irene's extraordinary ability, as a playwright as well as a director, to create rules for herself and her characters that are very precise, and then to watch as that precision raises the stakes to an almost unbearable intensity. Only Harold Pinter has ever matched Fornes in making four walls the most dangerous and alluring environment ever invented. And so *Hedda* via Fornes felt utterly new to me, which is perhaps the greatest gift a director/adapter can give to a classical play. It was perfectly Ibsen, but it was profoundly Irene. An artist who can make that kind of marriage work is an artist to be treasured.

# ❀ RICHARD RIEHLE
*Actor*

MY LOVE AFFAIR WITH IRENE FORNES began in the late 1960s as a college student stuck in the Midwest, reading about her work in New York and imagining what it would be like to see it, or even to read it. (I am amazed how little of her work is in print even now.)

At last, in Seattle in the late 1970s, I got to see *Fefu and Her Friends*. I returned several times, following the story through each of its different routes to the truth. Now I had to find some way to work with her.

The opportunity came a few years later, in Milwaukee, with a production of Ibsen's *Hedda Gabler* during the 1986-87 season. I believe it was her first time directing a play she hadn't also written, but that certainly didn't prevent her from making it her own. I had played Judge Brac twice before, and thought I knew the play pretty well. Was I in for a surprise, beginning with my casting as Lovborg. The traditionally romantic writer became more bloated and dissolute and the vine leaves from the start were dead and brown, covering the floor of the sitting room in General Gabler's house, having blown in while the Tesmans' were away on their honeymoon. From Irene's adaptation of the text and her direction, I found myself continually exploring the story and the characters in new and previously unimaginable ways.

And during the rehearsal period, I had the incredible opportunity to take part in a playwriting workshop she taught for the company. I have never considered myself a writer but was amazed by what developed through her exercises, guidance, and enthusiastic presentation. And she wholeheartedly participated in these exercises right along with us — such as when she produced a 1950s paperback mystery from her bag and arbitrarily picked first and last lines for a scene from it, or when she took us on a mental journey to find some long-forgotten special place, write a detailed description of it, draw it, and create a scene around the first person who wandered into it. This perhaps took some of the mystery out of the process for us non-writers, but without losing any of the magic. For even knowing what the task was and performing it yourself, the ranges of imagination and technique were evident. And as with her directing, Irene provided the most exciting, as well as, the safest environment for creation. For her it was always first and foremost about the writing — not judging, just doing.

Philip Voss (Juster), Annabelle Apsion (Marion),
and Pearce Quigley (Michael, background)

*ABINGDON SQUARE*
Shared Experience, The Soho Laundry, London, England
Directed by Nancy Meckler, Designed by Lucy Weller, 1989

Photo by Sarah Ainslie

# ✺ AUSTIN PENDLETON
*Actor*

## WORKING WITH IRENE

I HAD HAD THE PLEASURE OF KNOWING
Maria Irene Fornes slightly, and of course her work more than slightly,
for over twenty years, when in 1987 she called me in to talk about playing the title role in a production of *Uncle Vanya* she was about to do
at the CSC Repertory theater in New York.

Maria looked at me with her infinitely soulful eyes and told me
how she saw the part of Vanya. She said she thought he was having a
nervous breakdown.

I was just that week in the process of being fired from a musical
that I had directed and for which I had written the book, and on which
I had worked fairly steadily for two years. This musical had just had a
tryout at a nonprofit theater in Philadelphia.

I told Maria I was pretty sure I could commit to her vision. There
are very few people I'd have said that to at that moment. It is a strange
and silly thing to commit to the idea of expressing a nervous breakdown in a play when you are in fact, for all you know, on the verge of
having a nervous breakdown. But one look at Maria's eyes, one moment
of listening to her soft, melodious, intelligent voice convinced me that
I would be safe, and who knows, perhaps even productive.

There followed one of the richest trips I've ever been on as an actor.
Maria's love for the play was as deep and healing as the ocean that of
course comes nowhere near the country house in which the beleaguered
characters in that play are stranded. They are landlocked and
unhealed, but Maria and her intelligence and her kindness and her craft
made it possible to trust the idea that one could inhabit them. It was
an irreplaceable experience and — somehow the most heartfelt trib-
utes in this business inevitably end up as a request for a job — I would
work with her again tomorrow.

# ❋ JEFFREY M. JONES
*Playwright*

## PRAISE OF *MUD*

UNTIL I SAW *MUD*, I THOUGHT I KNEW ALL about Irene Fornes. I didn't, of course, know anything about Irene Fornes, but until I saw *Mud* I could assume with perfect confidence that her plays were all kind of…oh, let's say, whimsical. Not that "whimsical" is the right word either, but the right word would have to convey what I thought Irene *looked like*, and if you couldn't immediately conjure up the impression I had of an exquisite, reticent, emigreé grace, well — you'd simply have no idea how wrong I was. *Mud,* after all, is about as whimsical as a curbside execution.

*Mud* also taught me just how good a writer Irene Fornes is, because it's the reinvention of a kind of play I thought everyone else had pretty much gummed to death by then — the kind of play about Little People and their Hopes and Dreams and so forth; their sad, dull, wretched and pathetic Lives and tender Feelings and so forth — Irene Fornes as the legatee of (what a concept!) *Marty* and *Of Mice and Men* — *that* kind of play. Which she does, incidentally, by the numbers, with breathtaking economy — although I'm guessing that's probably not the first thing you notice. The first thing you notice, I'm guessing — oh, around the time Lloyd starts going off about "doing it with Betty" — is that this play is a little bit, how to say, *twisted?* I mean, there's not a lot of bestiality on the America stage these days, but such as there is rarely constitutes the author's joke at her characters' expense. The author, after all, is as God to her characters. And what kind of cruel and savage god is manifest in *Mud?* A god of methodical, coldhearted devastation, a god who maims and betrays her characters, breaking their hearts, dashing their dreams with feral symmetry. The Book of Job has nothing on *Mud.* Except, of course, for the thunderings of YHWH.

So this is kind of *bracing*... And another thing I'm guessing you noticed early on (say, as Lloyd heads off for the drugstore with his axe) is that these folks are all a bit...what? Simple? Primitive? Stupid??? Because it's more than a matter of literacy and counting to ten, though illiteracy and the arduous processes of reading and learning to read do make up a prominent motif in the play. These guys are missing more than a high school education. They're *dim*, they just don't seem to get it, their lives and thoughts and motives and even the nature of their feelings are baffling to them. But not for lack of insight, oh no — not for want of trying. They look inward all the time and — this is what's wonderful — they even understand their thoughts and motives and feelings quite perfectly. And yet they still remain baffled.

What I find revelatory about Irene's play is the clarity with which she examines this particular problem of character: the relationship (such as it is) between behavior and intent, between a character's outward actions and their inner life, their hopes and dreams, and so forth. It's among the most profound investigations of which literature is capable; profound of course, because it lies at the heart of our actual experience of people. What are they thinking, these other people? What will they do next, and why will the do it? For that matter, why do *I* do the things I do? Bear with me on this.

A lazy writer, an easy writer, will take care that his characters eventually explain themselves. He will take care that nothing of significance goes unexplained because of course this tidiness is reassuring in the theater and constitutes, in fact, one of the principal satisfactions of a certain kind of theater — knowing and seeing that, however things turn out, there will be at the end no questions left unanswered about the *reasons* for the doing of things. Satisfying, of course, because the reasons real people have for doing things are typically less than transparent.

So the more thoughtful and skillful writer will take up the problem as she finds it in real people — who do all manner of things, to be sure, yet whose thoughts and feelings are forever hidden from us... except through their actions and words, but words are so notoriously unreliable, so easily uttered, so readily twisted, so false. The thoughtful and skillful writer will address, in myriad ways, the myriad ways in which words and deeds fail to correspond in real people. The degree to which words and deeds not only go their separate ways but also are allowed to go their separate ways, and must be forgiven their divergence as "the way people are." The skillful and thoughtful writer, surely, will start from the understanding that people are fundamentally unknowable to each other and themselves. This is the fundamental *stupidity* of being a real person that Mae comes closest to articulating:

MAE: I feel I am hollow…and offensive.
HENRY: Why is that?
MAE: I think most people are.
HENRY: What do you mean? Explain what you mean.
MAE: I don't think I can.
HENRY: I am not offensive. I don't think I am offensive. I think I am a decent man.
MAE: You are decent, Henry, I know you are, and so is Lloyd in his own way.
HENRY: Then what do you mean when you say we are offensive?
MAE: I mean that we are base, and that we spend our lives with small things.
HENRY: I don't feel I do that.
MAE: Don't be offended, Henry. You are not base. Of all the people I know, you are the finest. You are the person I respect and I feel most proud to know. — I have no one to talk to. And sometimes I feel hollow and base. And I feel I don't have a mind. But when I talk to you I do. I feel I have a mind. Why is that?[1]

Mae of course is quite wrong about Henry, as she will finally learn as he stands before her, masturbating:

HENRY: …I can satisfy you. I am potent. — I can make you happy. Kiss me, Mae. — Tell me you still love me. Kiss me. Let me feel you close to me. — You think a cripple has no feelings. — I'm not crippled in my parts. — It gets hard. Mae, I love you. I'm coming…I'm coming…I'm coming…I'm coming…
MAE: You can walk, Henry. You took my money… (p. 37)

Ah, yes — and is it any accident that parallel lies form the pivot points of Irene's story, for lies are the clearest case of words and deeds diverging, and the unmasking of a lie — and look how it comes about: When Lloyd finally musters up the (sense?) to get his prescription filled, when Henry finally declares his (love?) — in the moment of unmasking comes the realization that all along, you had absolutely no idea what the other person was really thinking. What you had taken to be their inner life was just a screen thrown up to deceive you. And the moment of this understanding is the moment when you feel the full measure of your own existential stupidity.

*Mud*, then, is a profoundly stupid world because the people in it are profoundly stupid. And here is the cruel barb that threads the bait of their existence. They have been given self-awareness. They understand that they are stupid — know that everyone else is stupid, too — because they are capable of understanding almost everything about themselves and the people around them…and yet nothing makes sense.

What can one possibly learn in the theater, after all? What can one possibly learn from the contrived spectacle of imagined characters, except that a person can understand everything about another person and yet nothing will make sense.

1. Maria Irene Fornes, *Mud* in *Plays* (New York: Performing Arts Journal Publications, 1986), p. 24. Subsequent references are parenthesized. Stage directions have been omitted by Jeffrey M. Jones.

Patricia Mattick (Mae) and Alan Belbelthau (Henry)

*MUD*
Theater for the New City, New York City, 1983

Photo by Anne Militello

# ❋ BONNIE MARRANCA
*Critic, Editor*

## FORNES, AN ALPHABET

A, acquaintance
B, body
C, catholicism
D, desire
E, education
F, film
G, grace
H, home
I, intimacy
J, justice
K, knowledge
L, labor
M, mother
N, numbers
O, ontology
P, pain
Q, quotations
R, reading
S, sexuality
T, texts
U, usefulness
V, voice
W, women
X, xanadu
Y, ying and yang
Z, zigzag

## ❋ MAGGIE MACKAY
*Post-graduate Student, School of English and Drama, Queen Mary & Westfield College, University of London*

## KISSING THE LEPER

DARKNESS AND THE SOUND OF SOMEONE earthbound, leaping in the dark,[1] gives at once an image that is deeply prophetic as are Orlando's first words "Thirty-three and I'm still a lieutenant" (p. 68). He reveals a consciousness of time but, crucially for this play, a consciousness devoid of a spiritual understanding of time passing, devoid of any sense of eternity. Fornes immediately gives Orlando the conventions of a soliloquy to supposedly reveal aloud his innermost secrets but his truth telling reveals the opposite of Fornes' illuminating self-knowledge: the murky shade of egotistical self-deception. The circle is completed because we the audience see this truth. Saying "Man must have an ideal, mine is to achieve maximum power. That is my destiny" (p. 68), Orlando seeks to master his life and the lives of others. He is not a dispassionate Faust locked away in his study pursuing knowledge and earnestly dissecting himself. Rather, in his dining room, Orlando repeatedly uses "I" as a modern emotional, self-absorbed, already mired man desperate to get beyond his present rank and break social constraints to fulfil his ambitions. Orlando is Faust-like in that he too finds power an irresistible temptation, is willing to be utterly ruthless and, like Marlowe's protagonist, he opens the play by making a contract feeling that time is against him and running out. Like Faust he is an over-ambitious character with energy for change yet set upon a dark, anti-pilgrimage. This tragedy of self-destruction brings a descent into hell.

If this opening staging and soliloquy can call to mind Marlowe's fallen Doctor Faustus,[2] its issues around the sin of nonbelievers or the hopelessness of being subject to fate, and its Elizabethan staging of hell, earth, and heaven become here multi-horizontal spaces of tests and sufferings to be what Marranca has identified as giving "stations of a life."[3] Here Fornes has rapidly set out her stage to carry the spiritual dimension of characters struggling between darkness and light, moving perhaps toward increasing brightness in a play that is a meditation upon the conduct of life.[4] Such deep reflections might no longer be made from a Christian viewpoint that includes the acceptance of absolute Biblical truth. Instead, one might regard religion as a fanciful notion best left behind, looking instead toward a belief in the primacy of the individual conscience. Wherever one stands, the Bible is for many of us, part of our cultural conversations, a religious work of powerful literary resource in a largely secular culture. *The Conduct of Life* contemplates issues around the creation of the self and how to live one's life: a life where ethics are essential and redemption just might happen. Indeed the play is framed by the Biblical Temptation of Christ in the Wilderness and the lessons of the Sermon on the Mount.[5]

The first scene raised the image of a falling man's internal temptations with a coexistent lack of spiritual awareness. The second scene links this to the destruction wrought on relationships by the need to dominate. It gives views of the spaces between characters, their movements as they reach out, attempt to seize another, or fade into isolation. Whilst Leticia, speaks with feeling and rejects hunting "the most beautiful animal in the world" (p. 68), the military, opinionated Orlando is bound to the hunt. Whilst Leticia tries to incorporate love into marriage and their present life, Orlando now sees marriage as a legal manoeuvre to control property, to control money even beyond death, and to ensure that his wife will not bring humiliation upon him by giving money to the poor. His repeated use of "foolish" (p. 69) in rejecting her philosophy strongly links her to the long history of fools who, paradoxically, whilst being licensed to tell the truth, have low status but superior knowledge and sight that others lack or have lost. The contemptuous "foolish" plus the content of what Leticia says links her to the famous Fool of Christ, Saint Francis of Assisi (1181–1226) who, in preaching poverty and identifying with his "brothers" and "sisters" of the natural world, was a holy fool. Typically such fools get abuse for "the foolishness of the holy is quite a different matter from the folly of the knowing."[6] One could say that Leticia is indeed a fool for love. Leticia is that bruised and bandaged Fornes character who recognises the transcendental in life and could be moving toward self-creation. She turned to Alejo for help on this quest into the future (pp. 70, 75), but he is a modern John the Baptist (Saint Matthew, 3:1-2) and a failing one. He is a prophet within his own wilderness, unable to teach others, unable now to believe in change or a future of hope, and unable to convince his loved friend that it is time to repent (pp. 70, 75, 76).

Central to this approach to the play is Nena. Like Orlando she also has to make a choice in the wilderness but she is the antithesis of Orlando. She is representative of older societies violently robbed of so much, often in the name of Christianity, and sorrowing before a bloodied crucifix. She is also representative of the victims of this present century, victims of generals who have sought power to enforce political utopias. They have used the language of certainty and, as the warehouse here implies (pp. 70, 73, 76), let market needs dominate. Brute force and scapegoating have been their response to the growth of disparity between rich and poor. It is a force that Orlando demonstrates makes such regimes unstable and that his death makes him a victim of.

First performed in 1985 as set in "A Latin American country. The present" (p. 66), one of the beauties, and simultaneously a sadness of the play, is the fact that it evokes present events. Nena's history — her extended imprisonment in the temporary cellar-home below ground and her repeated rape, as a symbol of both the control and silencing of women — suggests a grim future without choice. Yet within this literal descent, within this nocturnal place of daily darkness, a wilderness of hunger and thirst (pp. 76, 84), a place of enforced solitude and fever, this descent into hell, Nena makes a choice. In the face of the profane she finds spiritual strength. Living a nightmare she dreams of transcendental love and so moves toward light and freedom. She illustrates the paradox that even from evil we can bring forth goodness.

Nena is indeed a figure of contradictions reflecting verse after verse of the Sermon on the Mount that employs paradox to look at the individual, at the very foundations of organized religion, at how society might erupt from the bottom. The Sermon on the Mount is not about religion to make life "Sunday safe." Those counted as amongst the least — the poor in spirit, those who mourn, who are meek, who seek a spiritual life, who are merciful, who are pure of heart, who are peacemakers, who love their enemies (Saint Matthew, 5:3–9) — all, in their suffering, can be transformed on their quest for identity. Identifying with the suffering perhaps we, the audience, might also change. We might also, in a sense, "ask," "seek," "knock," (Saint Matthew, 7:7-8). It's interesting to note that the first production of *The Conduct of Life* had lepers "who walked slowly and looked up at the audience and asked for money"7 because leaving the Mount after His Sermon, a leper approached Jesus saying, "Lord, if thou wilt, thou canst make me clean" and the response was "I will: Be thou clean" (Saint Matthew, 8:2–3). Unlike the modern leper seeking money the Biblical leper journeyed with faith that he could change. Sadistic-state-torturer Orlando is also a man of shocking wounds, and refusing to take responsibility for his acts, not looking toward repentance or change, he is altogether deeply repellent. Like Odysseus we could leave this Philoctetes alone upon his island and sail away. But such characters confront us with questions: What is to be done? Can Orlando be forgiven if he does not acknowledge guilt? What *should* we do when the likes of Pinochet come calling for English tea?

As Olimpia and Nena work "separating stones and other matter from beans" (p. 83), Nena speaks of lovingly caring for her demented grandfather. She alludes to the sacrificed Christ and speaks of her kidnapping, of her rapes and torture. This torture includes the crucifixion imagery of her suffering hung upon a wall (p. 84), highlighting the human miracle of her continuing effort to defeat her suffering at the hands of others, and a desire not to be deflected from her chosen course. She ends the scene with a passage beginning "I want to conduct each day of my life in the best possible way. I should…" (pp. 84–85).

This "I should" repeatedly takes her further toward another teaching in the Sermon on the Mount, "Be ye therefore perfect, even as your Father which is in Heaven is perfect" (Saint Matthew, 5:48). Nena gives us the reign of terror she endures and the spiritual base from which come the conscious choices she makes to find her identity and live life her chosen way. Yet, separating beans from the stones gives the play a twist and reminds one of pages of scorn Dostoevsky, a believer, wrote against organized religion in *The Karamazov Brothers*. His Grand Inquisitor denounces Christ's "Man shall not live by bread alone, but by every word that proceedeth out of the mouth of God" (Saint Matthew, 4:4) — it being Christ's response to the temptation to turn stones into bread. The Grand Inquisitor says "But You did not want to deprive man of his freedom, so you rejected the suggestion, for what sort of freedom would it be, You judged, if obedience were bought with bread?"[8] He argues that people would always seize the bread, take happiness and so forgo the struggles that a freedom of choice between good and evil would present. Whilst Orlando uses his freedom to chase external power, perhaps with the expectation it will bring happiness, Leticia seeks freedom via formal education. She wants to be listened to rather than be judged unimportant and ignored, just as she indeed ignores her servant (p. 71): just as she ignored torture (p. 85) until it was brought home.

Yet Olimpia is not the subservient servant as victim but a person whose freedom is handicapped by lack of choice. Her voice may be less powerful but she too dreams of change. Despite her difficulties she is the only character who responds appropriately to Nena. Amongst these characters only Olimpia and Nena can be happy in the here and now, in their shared and authentic friendship, in their childlike play (p. 80). At the end of *The Conduct of Life* Nena raises her eyes heavenward (p. 88) seeming to have a choice that could be seen as a possible attempt by a child in shock to deny the self or a Christ-like fulfilment, a kind of Gethsemane of suffering as she prepares to give herself up, betrayed by others.

Fornes is that most wonderful of teachers, one who lets us see old questions with new resonance. We are to consider the spiritual quest for self-knowledge, consider reward and punishment, confession and forgiveness. It is an emotionally charged play that speaks out for the individual. It denies the commonplace mitigating plea that individuals are insignificant, and that therefore individual actions are insignificant. Every action here has a consequence for, like it or not, all are interconnected. *The Conduct of Life* is a play about piety, empathy, compassion, coaxing us to rethink both beliefs and behavior. It is a play that utterly rejects cynicism and all hedging of bets. Fornes doesn't give us saints or heroes. She doesn't make it easy. She refuses us answers.

1. Maria Irene Fornes, *The Conduct of Life* in *Plays* (New York: Performing Arts Journal Publications, 1986), p. 68. Subsequent references are parenthesized.

2. See *The Oxford Anthology of English Literature: The Literature of Renaissance England*, eds. John Hollander and Frank Kermode (Oxford: Oxford University Press, 1973). pp. 348–99.

3. Bonnie Marranca, *Ecologies of Theater: Essays at the Century Turning* (Baltimore and London: John Hopkins University Press, 1996), p. 82.

4. Pier Paolo Pasolini's *The Gospel According To Saint Matthew* (1964) gives a highly political Jesus as a revolutionary in a black-and-white film that uses largely unknown performers. As Pasolini's camera focuses attention in silence upon the individual so Fornes uses darkness and light to make things visible. She also gets her audience to meditate upon the importance of the individual solitary temperament from which change comes.

5. *The Bible*, Saint Matthew, Chapters 3–8. By giving his age as "Thirty-three" (p. 68) Orlando has become linked, by paradox, as fallen man to Christ who is thought to have been around this age when He was tempted in the Wilderness not long before His death. All future references within the text will be from the King James Authorised Version.

6. Robert Alter and Frank Kermode, *The Literary Guide to the Bible* (London: Fontana Press, 1997), pp. 391–2.

7. Maria Irene Fornes in *On New Ground: Contemporary Hispanic American Plays*, ed. M. Elizabeth Osborn (New York: Theatre Communications Group, 1987). pp. 48–9.

8. Fyodor Dostoevsky, *The Karamazov Brothers*, trans. Ignat Avsey (Oxford: Oxford University Press, 1994), p. 317.

# ❁ CRAIG LUCAS
*Playwright*


## WHILE BEING PHOTOGRAPHED
## STRANGLING MARIA IRENE FORNES*


SETTING:

Photo shoot for a Sunday supplement

CHARACTERS:

Maria

Craig

*(Lights up. Maria and Craig are standing around, waiting to pose for a magazine photograph.)*

CRAIG: Maria, do you remember our first exchange?

MARIA: What?

CRAIG: I wrote you a note and passed it to you across a table: "You are my favorite playwright." And you wrote back, "Who are you?"

MARIA: Oh yes. Well, I knew who you were.

CRAIG: You did?

MARIA: Yes, I just didn't know what you looked like.

CRAIG: Well, I liked it my way better. Do you know the story about W.H. Auden riding the train out to teach at Swarthmore?

MARIA: No, tell me.

---

* September 1998. Playwrights Craig Lucas, Han Ong, Suzan-Lori Parks, and Tony Kushner sat down for an photo with Maria Irene Fornes for the *New York Times* Sunday magazine for an issue devoted to television. An accompanying article by Tony Kushner was entitled "The Twentieth Century: Good or Bad."

CRAIG: He was being stared at and stared at and whispered about by these two very attractive young male students, and they passed him a note and he opened it and read, "Are you Carl Sandburg?" And he wrote back, "You have spoiled mother's day."

*(Loud, long, shared laughter. Pause.)*

MARIA: But tell me… Was it really Mother's Day?

*(Curtain.)*

While being photographed strangling Maria Irene Fornes for the *New York Times*.
Han Ong, Suzan-Lori Parks, Maria Irene Fornes, Tony Kushner, Craig Lucas with
Jan Leighton as FDR and Carla Johnstone as Monica Lewinsky.
Commerce Street, New York City, 1998.

Photo by Jake Chessum

# EXERCISES

# ⊛ LISSETTE CAMACHO
# AND PHYLLIS ZATLIN
*Department of Spanish and Portuguese*
*Rutgers, The State University*

MARÍA IRENE FORNÉS,[1] FREQUENT WINNER
of Obies, holds a position of unique distinction on the American stage:
She is a Latina playwright who is so completely integrated into the English-language theater world that her Cuban roots tend to be forgotten.
Her distinguished career and close identification with the Off-Broadway
stage have transcended the limitations all too often associated with Hispanic authors in the theater world of their host countries. In this respect,
one might compare her to Fernando Arrabal: a Spanish-born author
who has become such a significant figure in French theater that many
people forget that he is Spanish. Among playwrights of Cuban origin,
her assimilation may be compared only to that of Eduardo Manet's on
the French stage. But Manet, despite the international acclaim his works
have received in performance, has been long overlooked by scholars,
both of French and of Latin American theater. Fornés, on the other
hand, has received the kind of critical attention that her plays so richly
deserve.

The integration of María Irene Fornés into the American stage has
not been at the expense of her bilingual, bicultural heritage. Although
she came to New York when she was fifteen and has on occasion stated
that the relatively short amount of time she lived in Cuba has not been
an important influence on her work, she also admits that life in Cuba
had a strong effect on her. Through the writers' workshop she founded
at INTAR Hispanic American Arts Center, she has effectively served
as mentor to younger playwrights, primarily Latinos. In 1995, when Ollantay Press published *Teatro: 5 autores cubanos*, an anthology of plays by
Cuban writers in exile, her Spanish translation of *Fefu and Her Friends*

fittingly appeared along with works by Manet, Pedro R. Monge-Rafuls, Héctor Santiago, and José Triana.

Fornés' plays in general are noted for "their zany, whimsical humour and the use of innovative, cinematic techniques."[2] These salient traits are also typical of the theater of Manet and of many other Cuban and Latin American authors. Fornés' work, which resonates as well with characters and themes that are connected to Hispanic experience, serves as a point of departure for the US Latina playwrights who have followed her.

While not reflective of her comic bent, *The Conduct of Life* (1984) is both one of her best-known works and one that is overtly Latin American in setting and theme. Orlando, a military officer who tortures political prisoners for the state, kidnaps Nena, a twelve-year-old homeless girl, then keeps her locked in the basement of his house where he repeatedly rapes her. Reluctant to acknowledge her husband as a torturer, his wife, Leticia, reacts only when personally interrogated and abused by her husband. She shoots Orlando and hands the gun to Nena, hoping the child will take the blame.

Fornés locates herself within the Hispanic historical tradition in which the artist and the intellectual are privileged as spokesperson or critic. She lures her audience into focusing on the individual Nena while subversively providing a social critique of US–Latin American relations. Orlando's abuse of Nena and his interrogation of his wife are extensions of his role as military torturer that effectively blur the boundary between the military state and domestic violence. By placing torture within a domestic setting, Fornés is able to draw upon her North American audience's familiarity with issues of violence in the home and military regimes abroad. Her skillful domestication of violence, which entices the audience into a sympathetic reading of the play, also indirectly locates the spectator within the politics — including US foreign policy — that make the violence possible. In this sense, a young, but not so innocent United States of America is left, like Nena, holding the gun.

Whereas the English language of the play is a sign of María Irene Fornés' more than fifty years of residence in the United States, clearly the content of the play shows that she is not willing to compromise her social consciousness or Latina identity to achieve artistic success.

1. Thoughout this piece we use the Hispanic accented spelling of her name.

2. Frances Bzowski, "Maria Irene Fornes," *The Cambridge Guide to Theatre*, ed. Martin Banham (Cambridge: Cambridge University Press, 1992), p. 357.

# ❀ TIFFANY ANA LÓPEZ
*Assistant Professor, Department of English*
*University of California, Riverside*


## READING FORNES AS A LATINA DRAMATIST


PREPARING FOR MY FIRST INTERVIEW meeting with Maria Irene Fornes at a small cafe on New York City's Bleecker Street one late summer's day in 1994, I was very aware of her opinions about ethnicity and identity politics. In published interviews she resists any attempts to definitively label her as a feminist, Cuban American, or even as a role model. If she were to be placed in any category at all, she preferred the avant-garde.

Before our meeting, I'd been thinking about the evolution of contemporary Latina drama and had begun to interview playwrights. It seemed contradictory that Fornes was named consistently by those who freely categorized themselves as Latina/o dramatists — voices as diverse in cultural identity and politics as Cherríe Moraga, Migdalia Cruz, Caridad Svich, and Luis Alfaro — as the person most influencing their sense of vision and craft. Including Fornes and her self identification with the avant-garde within the descriptive category "Latina drama" completely sabotaged the ways Latina/o plays had been discussed as inextricably linked to identity politics with Latina/o dramatists read as definitively speaking for an entire community. What was one to do with the fact that the artistic mentor of over a generation of Latina/o dramatists is a Cuban born playwright who refuses to identify herself *as* a Latina dramatist and, in over thirty years of playwriting, has written only a handful of works dealing with things popularly understood as directly linked to Latino culture? i.e., *Sarita*'s treatment of a Puerto Rican immigrant family; *The Conduct of Life*'s focus on the impact of fascism on family relations in an unspecified Latin American country; *Tango Palace*'s exploration of gender and power exemplified in that dance; *Terra Incognita*'s response to the Columbus quincentenary. Placing Fornes at the very heart of a discussion of the development of contemporary Latina drama challenged me to completely rethink how I'd been trained to read plays by Latina/o dramatists.

According to the Latina/o playwrights who have attended her workshops, Fornes has taught them most to think about telling stories as a form of painting with words. Many dramatists and practitioners have argued that in contrast to television and film that rely on visual images to tell their tales, plays are a distinctly literary art because they privilege spoken conversations and capture them in the written word. As a formally trained painter turned dramatist, Fornes creates plays whose language and images clearly depend upon one another. Think about the integral relationship between theatrical images and utterances in so many of her plays: the endlessly flipping cards and verbal jousting in *Tango Palace*; the huge dirt mound and Mae's frustrated words in *Mud*; *Fefu and Her Friends*'s physically shifting audience and Fefu's outrageous attempts to emotionally move her guests; a boat sailing across the stage following the cafe conversations of tourists visiting Spain in *Terra Incognita*. Might Fornes prefer to direct her own work because she can make explicit on stage the interdependence between words and images that so clearly comes across on the written page?

Listening again to the interview tapes of my conversation with Fornes, I'm struck by the number of times we stop our chat to turn attention to several small theatrical scenes that seem to unfold just for the occasion of our interview: a barefoot street person singing an ethereal melody; an elderly woman wearing what we think is an amazing hat but upon further inspection discover to be flowers carefully rolled in newspapers and artfully balanced on her head; fashionable men parading designer dogs to the cafe's repeated play of the greatest hits of Patsy Cline. I hear myself say more than once, "that's an amazing image." This word — image — then naturally opened up a space for me to ask Fornes about the chosen details for a specific work and her larger vision as a playwright and director.

Earlier that summer I'd had the fortunate opportunity to see the Padua Hills production of Fornes' *Terra Incognita*. In talking to Fornes about my impression of the work, I found myself remembering the play through the images more than the dialogue. I recalled a huge wooden cross dragged about by one of the play's fringe characters; a boat on casters wafting across the stage; and the final closing scene of tourists/actors actually getting into a red car and driving away from Spain/Padua Hills. All of these were the product of Fornes' efforts as a director to work with the available props and the outdoor landscape at Padua Hills, things that necessarily shaped her revisions of the play. She confirmed for me that most of her plays do begin with an exercise of some sort.

A typical workshop exercise, as Fornes described it, consists of putting people in pairs and having them make a drawing of each other. Her goal here is to force the writer to concentrate on mapping the most important details: "It's about being able to have a second perspective beyond the words being said by someone." Fornes also demands that students refuse to be apologetic for how the drawing comes out: "You're not making a drawing of the person to portray them exactly; rather, you want to put down the kinds of details that allow you to recollect." But most importantly, she pushes the participants in her workshops to, above all else, be true to the vision they see before them, especially if the writer's initial response is that the result feels visually jarring, uncomfortably unexpected, or completely out of character.

It was this discussion of the centrality of images and the importance of workshop exercises that shifted my thinking about Fornes' role in the evolution of contemporary US Latina/o drama. Fornes lies at the center of a discussion of Latina drama not because she is Cuban-born, but because she played a central role in the establishment of an institutional space for the development of Latina/o playwrights. She began The Hispanic Playwrights Lab at INTAR in New York City with the intent of fostering new voices that would revitalize the American theater across its various genres: avant-garde, musical, realist. Significantly, Fornes created writers' workshops that she, herself, would want to attend and ran them in such a way that participating dramatists were expected to take themselves seriously as professional playwrights: They were paid a stipend, given a space in which to write and required to do so for a designated amount of time per day; they were also offered detailed comments on written drafts by Fornes and given the opportunity to revise the work and later hear it read. And never did Fornes ask dramatists to write "as" a Hispanic, female, homosexual, or whomever because in her opinion to do so would forever cripple the playwright and make him dependent on the expectations or acceptances of others. Likewise, Fornes resists the use of identity categories because in her words, "just as you go to McDonald's and expect a certain kind of meal, you come to expect a certain kind of writing from a chosen category of writers." Rather than ideologically or politically validate her students's work, Fornes demanded that they take themselves seriously as dramatists and concentrated on giving writers the tools they needed to more forcefully direct their own creative vision. By doing so, she artistically validated their existence not merely as Latina/o playwrights but as playwrights, period. Perhaps the greatest testament to her impact as a mentor is that so many of her students — Caridad Svich, Luis Alfaro, Cherríe Moraga, Migdalia Cruz, Carmen Rivera — are currently working as dramatists full-time and conducting workshops of their own in nationally recognized theaters.

I pass on Fornes' vision to my students at the university by teaching her plays and interviews and by unraveling the brilliant contradictions within that challenge us to grow as both critical thinkers and human beings. The anecdote I find myself sharing the most comes from a phone conversation where Fornes succinctly illustrated how, while categories can be initially useful, they can also be blinding, such as when critics who saw *Mud* expecting a feminist portrait of Mae expressed anger and disappointment with the portrait actually painted. Because they were prisoners to their expectations, they'd completely refused to see the work on its own terms. The way Fornes so eloquently expressed this and how I say it to my students: They were presented with a chair and rather than talk about the intricacies of this singular chair, they complained about how it wasn't a table.

A graduate student with whom I work closely recently read the works of the writer, journalist, and performance artist Sandra Tsing Loh whose father is Chinese-born and whose mother is German. When initially asked to describe Loh's work, she could only rail against her for not writing as an artist facing the hardships of being a person of color. My response was to talk about my encounters with Fornes' work and the absolute centrality of it to my thinking about Latina drama and to share the Fornesian chair/table analogy. I told this student before she could complain about what a writer wasn't doing, she had to first tell me what she was doing. Weeks later the student returned with a much richer exploration of Loh's work and a theoretically sophisticated discussion about the pitfalls of reading people of color with assumptions about the relationship between identity and art. Working with students is ultimately about getting them to independently engage in the process of revision — seeing something twice in an entirely fresh way. Fornes deserves tribute as a most extraordinary teacher whose lessons continue to echo beyond the classroom walls, as all art should.

# ✤ KAT AVILA
*Professor of Spanish and Latino Studies*
*University of California, Irvine*


## A THOUSAND WORDS MORE.

> Cold as it was,
> we felt secure
> sleeping together
> in the same room.

> Matsuo Basho, haiku poet


IN CHICANO THEATER I OFTEN FOUND THE sanctuary I needed for creative and intellectual expression amongst the playwrights, actors, and directors I interviewed for my "Buscando California" newsletter, a project I undertook to gather material for my graduate thesis on Chicano theater as political communication. I never completed the paper, but my interest in the theater continued, tumbling and leaping forward as a loose pebble in a fast-flowing river, an interest almost bordering on obsession as I drove for hours to watch this and that little production, just to sit in a sports bar as a production competed with a VERY LOUD basketball game on television, or in a centro cultural as planes constantly took off overhead, or with an audience so rude the lead actress stormed off the stage as the cast was taking its bows. A few attractions of the theater.

What I also found attractive about our theater was that the virility/radicalness of the Chicano is reestablished and central, the diversity of the Chicano experience knocking down our own culturally constructed bloody fences, to include the story collages of Chicanas, regionally identified (by US state) Chicanos, and lesbians and gays.

Maria Irene Fornes, even though she is not Chicana, has a connection to our theater, one that I have followed through Jorge Huerta's lectures, productions of Fornes' work by local Chicano theater groups, and the playwrights I interviewed who listed her New York writing workshop in their resumes with great pride.

She is part of the tapestry. She has given a thousand words more to the next Belinda Acosta, the next Josefina López, the next Edit Villarreal. She has given us and them a thousand more words about freedom, about human dignity, about respect, and she has given me a few words more to write about the theater I love.

# ❀ EDIT VILLAREAL
*Vice Chair, Department of Theater*
*UCLA School of Theater,*
*Film and Television*

I FIRST MET MARIA IRENE AT INTAR IN NYC. I was selected to be in one of her first playwriting labs and I traveled from California to New York to study with her. It was a crucial time for me. After years of thinking about writing, I knew it was time to stop talking about it. And to actually do it. I arrived in September and waited, scared to death, for my first New York winter to arrive. I had never lived where snow fell. I had never lived where it got colder than freezing. The winter came, of course, and I remember one morning when Maria Irene and I walked together to the lab space. The streets were covered with ice and snow and just when we got to the lab, I looked down and saw a crisp, clean, dry ten dollar bill on the ground laying daintily above the snow, undamaged in any way. How lucky! How unusual! That experience, in many ways, foretold my time learning about writing with Irene. She taught me to trust my subconscious. To let it open up to my conscious self. She taught me to be playful with my writing and be ready to consider a crazy idea when it hit me. She taught me to search for material everywhere: in pictures, drawings, paintings, newspaper articles, magazine ads. She taught me to overhear conversations on buses and art galleries and theaters and remember, remember, remember. She taught me to be serious about my writing. To not shy away from emotions. To this day, eighteen years later, I use her exercises when I'm stuck somewhere in a play. What would Maria Irene suggest I do? Which one of her exercises will help me break this block? How do I loosen up here? What am I REALLY trying to say? I should tune in with my subconscious. I should be bold. I should be silly. I should be feminine. I should be human. But also, I should work. I should define a place where I work. And work there. I remember the little wooden desks we were given to write on. The desks were smaller than my desks in Catholic school. Every morning, we would sit at our desks and try to write. If we didn't feel like it, we waited and did exercises until we did. I learned all this from Maria Irene that snowy winter of 1981 in New York City.

 MARTIN EPSTEIN
*Playwright, Teacher of Playwriting and Dramatic Literature, Tisch School of the Arts, New York University*

## THREE FOR MARIA IRENE FORNES

### I. ANOTHER LIFE

It seems like I never stop reading Irene's plays. One of the reasons for my obsession with her work is practical. I teach playwriting and dramatic literature at The Tisch School of the Arts, and Irene's plays can be counted on to shock and inspire in ways that make young writers engage themselves and the theater on deeper and more courageous levels. After her first encounter with *Fefu and Her Friends*, one of my students wrote: "I read the play twice in one sitting. I read it again a day later. I wanted to think about it, mull it over, and take it in. I read the play again this morning. What does that mean?"

Like the opening scene in *Fefu*, Irene's plays excavate those impacted rocks in the psyche, beneath which all kinds of crawling things have established their mysterious and awe-full existence. "It is another life that is parallel to the one we manifest," says Fefu. "It's there. The way worms are underneath the stone. If you don't recognize it…(Whispering.) it eats you. That is my opinion. Well, who is ready for lunch?"[1]

That we could stop for lunch, or have a water fight, or gather in small communities of shared urgencies while this other cannibal life *pursues*, demanding we come up with a language that will unashamedly tell us who we are — this is the physical and metaphysical stuff out of which Irene makes a world.

## II. ENDURANCE

In *The Conduct of Life*, the lights come up on a half-uniformed Orlando who "does jumping jacks as long as can be endured."[2] I love this stage direction. Because it gives so much difficult freedom to the director and actor who have to stage "endurance." Twenty-five to fifty jumping jacks would define, to my mind, a wimp production of this play. Seventy-five to a hundred, and the audience would have to endure Orlando's endurance. But what if the actor/Orlando could come up with two to three hundred jumping jacks? How then to approach this ritualized suspension of time, not to mention the potential hilarity of such a relentless and seemingly never-ending moment? And how, in turn, are we to endure our own voyeuristic complicity when we are subsequently allowed to watch as Orlando kidnaps and repeatedly rapes the twelve-year-old Nena in the basement of his house, before returning to his public life as a torturer for the military junta that runs his country?

If "endurance" implies the grandeur of how much we can take before we fold, it also implies a lastingness that goes on and on and on. In the realm of art, or in Irene's case, theater, we call this kind of endurance classic — made for all time.

## III. PARABLE OF THE ONE-FINGERED HELPER

Some years ago, I saw a film called *Pumping Iron*. It was a documentary about muscle builders and starred a relatively unknown Arnold Schwarzenneger. Though fascinated by the grease embalmed rituals of pumping up, I was also taken by the idea of "weight lifting" as a metaphor for the writing life. At one point the camera introduced us to Arnold's chief rival, Lou Ferrigno, who would later become TV's The Incredible Hulk. At this moment in his life, however, the slightly deaf and good-hearted Lou wanted one thing only. To wrest the Mr. Universe title away from Arnold, the reigning King, who was also his idol. A series of bench presses were called for to build that extra bit of muscle. Lou, on his back, both hands chalked, gripping the bar, was lifting and counting, lifting and counting. His goal was ten. He had just completed four. The iron bar, with its double sets of weights, was suspended an inch off Lou's chest. And it was obvious from the strain on his face that he was finished. He simply did not have the physical or mental energy to continue. And then something amazing happened. Lou's Father/ Coach, a retired cop, straddled the bench. Looking down at his Son/ Protégé, he put one finger under the center of the bar and growled: Get serious! Shouting Arnold's name with each successive thrust— "Arnold! Arnold! Arnold!"— Lou pumped, pushed, pressed another six.

Would we all had access to a one-fingered helper when we needed one.

Meanwhile, the American theater and all of us who share the weight of its wonders and complexities, have Maria Irene Fornes. May she continue to make and direct the kind of plays that urge us to get serious—! And may we continue to applaud her for the pleasure, wit, and theatrical exuberance she has given us over the years.

Bravo, Irene.

1. Maria Irene Fornes, *Fefu and Her Friends* (New York: Performing Arts Journal Publications, 1990), p. 10.

2. Maria Irene Fornes, *The Conduct of Life* in *Plays* (New York: Performing Arts Journal Publications, 1986), p. 68.

# ✹ ALAN MACVEY
*Professor and Chair of the Theatre Arts Department, The University of Iowa*

## IRENE FORNES, TEACHER

DRAW A PICTURE OF YOUR STOMACH. THIS was the first thing I heard about Irene Fornes' approach to teaching playwriting to Princeton students. As Director of the Program in Theatre and Dance at Princeton University I had looked up Irene's phone number, called her out of the blue, and invited her to teach a course. She said yes. What a simple, pleasant surprise from someone as distinguished as Irene. Her direct, open manner on the phone told me a lot about what was to come.

Draw a picture of your stomach. This littler assignment was a surprise to the Princeton students. It was also as direct as it could be, although they didn't think so. "What does your stomach have to do with playwriting?" one of them asked. I didn't know exactly what Irene had in mind, but it sounded like she was aiming directly at the viscera of students who spent most of their lives in intellectual pursuits. That's where her plays aim, right where the stomach churns. It was the perfect place for those students to begin.

I don't know how much the Princeton students thought about their stomach drawings after their term with Irene, but I've never forgotten the assignment. It was a great teacher's surprising way to stimulate a young artist's imagination. It was absolutely direct, yet open to interpretation; it was mysterious, strange, simple, yet very peculiar. It invited an idiosyncratic response

In all these ways it was like her plays.

At Iowa, Irene's approach was different. By the time I came to the University in 1991 she had been a guest of the Theatre Arts Department several times. On one of her visits, while working with MFA playwriting students, she told them: Build a model. Create a world, and build a version of it out of cardboard, metal, paper, wood, whatever you want.

In a program where language and emotions are never undervalued, Irene reminded her students that theater is about more than words and viscera. It is about the creation of an entire world; it's about the way space works on characters and on an audience. It's what an audience sees as well as what it hears. She reminded her students they are not writing poetry or fiction but are filling a real space with real life. Her assignment was difficult — the students said so: They weren't model builders, they were writers. But when they arrived with their models, they had already entered the world of their new plays by a surprising door.

A great teacher understands what her students need. That may be a picture of a stomach or a model of a world. She surprises them; they surprise themselves. Eventually, they may surprise us.

Irene continues to surprise, in the theater and in the classroom.

# ✿ MATTHEW GOULISH
*Collaborative Member of Goat Island performance group, Chicago*


## MICROLECTURE: EVERYTHING ABOUT LIFE


IT IS THE SUMMER OF 1984. SEVENTEEN of us sit in a classroom on a campus outside of Los Angeles. The room is silent and full of light. Lin Hixson is there, Karen Christopher is there, and I am there. Everyone is writing. We are students in a playwriting class taught by Maria Irene Fornes. The birth of Goat Island remains three years in the future. The idea exists unarticulated. For now, we each write a dialogue of our own invention. Irene picks up a book from the small pile of books she has brought to the workshop, and she instructs us, "Now one of your characters says to the other..." She opens the book at random and reads:

"Do you really imagine you know everything about life?"

Later many of us read our dialogues aloud. In all the variations of time, place, character, conflict, tone, theme — in each of them at one point, unexpectedly, one character says to another:

"Do you really imagine you know everything about life?"

And in each dialogue, the line fits perfectly.

I cannot imagine teaching, either alone or collaboratively, without my experience as a student of Irene Fornes. In a book of interviews with women playwrights, I recently found this passage in which she describes her approach.

My Lab is a place where we do many experiments on writing. Unlike most workshops and classes that exist in universities, where you go home and write, bring your writing to class, have it read and get criticism, the Lab is all about inducing inspiration. I have never felt that criticism was the way to teach writing. In painting classes you paint together; you don't paint, bring your work to class and have it criticized. There is a model and everyone is working together. The important thing is to teach how to work, not how to criticize a finished piece. There is something about the atmosphere in a room full of people working. Each person's concentration is giving you something. Once you've experienced this phenomenon in the practice of another art form, you have a knowledge that it exists. If you've been exclusively a writer, I don't think this way of working would ever occur to you. In fact, most writers say, "I have to be alone to work." That's nonsense! They usually need to be completely alone because the other people around them are not writing. But if you experience working in a room with people who are also writing, there is no distraction. There is an exchange of energy and you know the other writers are not there for you to chat with. Even if you wanted to talk, you would be interrupting, so there is no temptation. No one is waiting for you, distracting you, and yet others are there. It has all the advantages of being alone, without the isolation.

People who come to visit The Lab are always amazed by its peacefulness and the beautiful quality of the light.[1]

It is the spring of 1994. I am reading Albert Camus' novel *The Plague* in my living room in Chicago. Goat Island is seven years old. We are in the process of our fourth performance work, *It's Shifting, Hank*. I reach the bottom of page 129. "I've little left to learn," says Mr. Tarrou, and the doctor replies:

"Do you really imagine you know everything about life?"[2]

1. Kathleen Betsko and Rachel Koenig, *Interviews with Contemporary Women Playwrights* (New York: Beech Tree Books/Quill Edition, 1987), p. 156.

2. Albert Camus, *The Plague*, trans. S. Gilbert (New York: Vintage, 1991) p. 129.

# ❂ PAUL BERNSTEIN
*Writer, Director, Performer, Faculty Member, University of Amsterdam, Lincoln Center Institute, New York City*

## A RECKONING WITH MARIA IRENE FORNES

THE SUMMER OF 1987 WAS NOTABLY HOT in Marin County. By 9:00 A.M. one might already be starting to perspire. It was the day before the opening of the eighth Bay Area Playwrights' Festival and I was a young artist-in-residence with the honor of serving as teaching assistant to a well-known Cuban-born playwright. Apparently she had invented a series of highly progressive writing exercises. Everyone seemed to know all about her except me. If asked I'd have to say, "I don't know your work or why they made me your assistant." Maybe it was because I had a car. Someone had to pick up Irene Fornes at a certain time every morning and deliver her back to her housing at the end of the day. There was some speculation that her mother might also be there.

In exchange for my upcoming work as an assistant they allowed me to live above an auto shop where I stayed up most of that night reading Fornes plays amid the smell of motor oil and fuming gases. At a table covered in race-car decals, speaking some of the lines out loud, there was a clear sense of being challenged by her sensibility before I'd even met her.

Fornes' work opened a new dimension of sub-colorful possibility for me at the time. The work appeared at times to be sparse and simple while in fact it was tremendously suggestive of another unspoken layer. "You can lead a horse to water…," and she does this masterfully, audience members have no alternative but to arrive at many conclusions for themselves. Dramatic tension is at times created in the theater through sheer multiplicity of contextual options. We are unsure how to receive the work. In the case of *The Danube*, Fornes' nuclear play that was being premiered that summer at the festival, her writing compelled us to project into vital information that seemed hidden or missing; this is part of the friction that allows this play to be so active/performative. We are kept continuously off-balance. The language offers just enough ground for the characters to move forward but they must do so on a precarious slant, in this case one of imposed artificiality. The speech of the characters, though at times conversational if not commonplace, has the potential to submerge into abrupt monologic extensions of thought. With an economy of English language that I would liken to a good drill delivering screws into wood, the sharpness of the words embedded themselves into my brain. Irene Fornes' plays made another kind of sense to me, like the realization of a parallel universe of options; murky at times yet having existed out there all along.

I woke up to the alarm of a faulty borrowed clock. It went off thirty-five minutes late next to *Mud*, the Fornes play I'd been reading when I fell asleep. Roger Nieboer was there on a cot in the grease-tracked corridor to the auto shop. He was in no better shape than I but we had to put on shoes and go with no coffee or grooming procedures, to pick up Irene Fornes. Once outside in the bright light and all of our typical haste, we lightened up. Ah. The dashboard clock said that it wasn't as late as we'd thought and there'd be time for strong tall coffees-to-go and a sit-down on our usual perch by the steep ravine. At the base of the slope was a trickle of a stream that I stared at while telling Roger about Fornes' harsh treatment of dominant male tendencies in *The Conduct of Life;* the graphic portrayal of sexual savageries, the impact the writing had on me. All seemed like it was coming together, I was filled with a great sense of well-being although our fate with Irene Fornes was about to be sealed. A procession of three boys on weird bicycles rolled over the ridge and downward in a diagonal line toward the first man-made jump, a ramp consisting of propped-up boards. The first boy had on a black shirt and he landed well over the stream, but the second boy in the striped shirt was large and he landed hard on his side, screaming amid wet rocks. We abandoned our coffees and ran down to where the other two boys were still inactive with shock, their friend's arm bent way out of shape between the wrist and the elbow. Roger knelt and dabbed his handkerchief into the stream and wiped away the blood that had begun to seep out of a gash in his eyebrow. I told the third boy to ride up to a house to call an ambulance. Roger made sure the boy who'd been downed didn't squirm around too much. "Best to stay still for now," he told him along with other words of encouragement. "You're going to be just fine," while my mind turned again to the image of Irene Fornes waiting, the exact time she was to be picked up, the extra money I'd already been paid to take care of this. When the ambulance arrived we scurried up the hill like criminals, grabbed our coffees and took off. Still wet, we blurred the ink on the directions that we pored over at each red light. Surely she would be understanding about fifteen or twenty minutes. Twenty-five minutes late, across the shadeless suburban streets of Larkspur, California, we searched, soon to learn a good deal about the woman.

She stood in the driveway to the left of her ancient mother, both wearing black for the heat wave. The presence of the mother did not cause her to spare us. We stepped out next to the car mumbling in unison, removing our sunglasses. Then she lit into us, first about the incompetence of the festival in general, then about the twelve people who were going to have to sit and wait for her because of us, whoever we were. Thirdly she did not believe that we were sorry. We apologized more emphatically but she did not accept so we gave up. Fornes looked powerful, immovable in the torn blue backseat of the white Nova. Me and Roger Nieboer looked terribly shabby, unkempt beyond what the reader might imagine. I kept wanting to talk about the boys who came suddenly over the ridge, the blood on the handkerchief, but it seemed too obvious that we were at the core of the problem. Actually we were rather forthright playwrights ourselves, now both sweating, I through a white tee-shirt and Roger through a yellow one. The mother of Irene Fornes sat contentedly in the rear-view mirror and seemed to enjoy the ride next to her seething daughter.

Then of course there came an awful silence. In the swelling of the pause I interjected that Roger was innocent, it had been my responsibility. Irene Fornes didn't want to hear that either. I began again to tell about the…but couldn't speak. The mother didn't add one word either, I thought because of all the trouble. Later I found that she spoke no English. She continued to sit calmly as people usually did during the domino-effect delays of the Bay Area Playwrights' Festival. It was common and indeed quite Californian to allow time to move partially of its own accord. Not for the rest of that summer.

I became impeccably prompt in picking her up, out of respect and also some degree of fear. Enough to incur the wrath but once, yes, but the lesson extended beyond the playwriting arena. We became accustomed to riding in the car together twice a day. Sometimes we barely needed to speak. The silence reminded me of how the mother of Irene Fornes would take a ride. Nothing extra was needed in terms of communication.

As her assistant I learned to pay careful attention to what Fornes would and wouldn't put up with. The list grew and I learned to protect people, to warn them, and to keep them on their toes which was the way it absolutely had to be. It was with this uphill climb that the three-week writing workshop took shape. Not a passive molecule in the air.

Later that summer, inside the Larkspur house, Irene's mother Carmen had chicken claws floating on the top of her boiling red soups. She was over one hundred years old with magical smiling eyes that danced from side to side, up and down. We had unexpected soup at a small table and while eating, through translation from Irene, the mother enjoyed hearing why our clothes smelled like motor oil. Carmen leaned over and sniffed my shirt-sleeve and then nodded to Roger who laughed suddenly, wildly as he sometimes tended to do. To this rash openness Irene and her mother responded visibly, instantly! Then I thought I had a realization about how these California theater festival folks must appear to them. Each day they had plenty of contact with people but all arts-related, nothing real. Roger and I had become fairly real to them. The mother looked directly at us with a joy that was unusual to me. She liked us best because we'd gotten yelled at by her daughter on the first day, chuckling to herself whenever she saw us, then laughing continuously in the front row while watching us perform at the end. Somehow this created a full circle.

It was through Carmen with whom we had little contact that I was able to feel the warmth behind our teacher's behavior. From up close people were often in awe of Irene's timeless wave-length with her mother from whom she appeared to be completely independent. It seemed that they could never get in each other's way.

The in-class work became increasingly demanding and exhaustive. No laptops back then, you wrote and wrote. Irene's exercises were endless, multiple, exposing of our shortcomings and again, personally confrontational. At times the in-class truth seemed slightly biased to her way of thinking and writing, often hidden but shining slightly (if you looked hard for it) like silver in tall grass. The quality of work that emerged had a root in the collective unconscious, a core in the unknown with a use of language that was deeply attached to character yet not so easy for actors to motivate in the traditional sense. Irene's taste seemed to be for written voices that emanated from states of being as well as clear intention, from an open-endedness rather than a filling to the brim. We learned to look with a third eye for this something else, an edge, words seeming at times to represent the reverse side of the dramatic specter. This back door took a good deal longer to find but she offered her most unadulterated attention to the search for this separate entrance, so that we might come to know it too. The tone could be somber, more serious than we ever expected. One got hooked on the process of making and showing continually. It made us perspire onto the paper as if part of the relentless heat. Though sensitized we also became less wimpy. No longer just writing, we were now bringing in actors and making performance. The actors were showing up to help because Irene was there. Some of them stayed with the class the rest of the way. There was a clear sense of being challenged by someone whom you'd barely even gotten to know. She did not believe in compromise and you didn't have to believe in it either. Quietly charged, it was sometimes exciting as all hell.

Irene Fornes would go on to butt heads with others that summer, which relaxed Roger and me although it made everyone else a little tense. Eventually all those involved managed to learn what it was going to take in terms of commitment. We could feel how this gift of teaching was somehow firmly attached to Irene Fornes' own searching existence as a writer. Not that there was a shortage of fun, eventually, after the tone was set. There was something unspoken here as well. In a sense the class reminded me of her plays because we were led in mysterious ways with not much to go on. We followed but didn't get it, didn't get it, then an understanding took over nearly all at once. Irene backed off to write and to present as if she were one of us. We then learned mainly from her way of improvising with a sharply honed purpose. The relationship between internal monologue and dramatic action was what I found, and a dose of discipline. The lessons were difficult but in all the complexity of writing precisely from one's core, Irene Fornes could identify what of each playwright's work had intrinsic "value." "Value," pronounced with a *w* on the *v* like "walue." She must've used that word twenty times a day while teaching.

In writing workshops people often get caught in their heads and the writing sounds like caught-in-the-head writing. The experience of Maria Irene Fornes was much the opposite — a very physical one. There was something surrounding this woman that we could not identify and yet she also seemed quite normal. I feel that she was asking us to listen to that which is locked inside human nature. The revelation for her students was that this was not necessarily an issue of content but rather one of approach. These days nearly everybody talks about being based in process and yet to my experience very few teachers have been able to create such a full-scale march in that direction. Maria Irene Fornes is a woman who knows what she is insisting on.

INTAR Lab Members, 1991:
Lorenzo Mans, Caridad Svich, Leo Garcia, Oscar Colon, Maria Irene Fornes,
Migdalia Cruz, Nilo Cruz, Lorraine Llamas

Photo by Jim Kent

# ✸ MIGDALIA CRUZ
*Playwright, INTAR Hispanic-Playwrights-in-Residence Laboratory Member 1984–90 (with a year off for bad behavior)*

COFFEE BREAK:
A GROUNDED MEMORY IN THREE ACTS
FOR MARIA IRENE FORNES

CHARACTERS:
   SHE — a powerful woman and coffee mentor
   ME — a humble coffee novice

TIME:
   november 1984, february & may 1985

PLACE:
   an empty studio in the west 50s of Manhattan

ACT ONE *the fall*
Scene 1

SHE: You are in kindergarten. I am in fifth grade. *(Evil laugh; taking the last sip from a plain white mug)* You know nothing. I know a little something. We need coffee.
ME: I'll make some coffee.

Scene 2

SHE: Your coffee stinks. Where did you learn to make coffee? A gas
station? (*Takes out a gun.*) People who make bad coffee are often shot.
ME: I'll try to make better coffee tomorrow.
SHE: You're hiding from the strength of the coffee. You'll never make
good coffee until you honor your memories of coffee. Go back in
your mind's eye, to a time before your tenth birthday. Imagine coffee brewing. What is the texture of the coffee? The color? What
does the coffee smell like as it brews? Is it a mild bean or an espresso?
What is the quality of the light in the room where the coffee is
being made? Or is the pot being brewed outside — by a lake or a
river? What is the time of day? Don't try to control your mind, let
it drift into your memories, uncensored by previous thoughts. The
coffee pot itself — is it a percolator? Auto-drip? Colador? Does the
brewing require a filter — or a cloth? Is it instant? When you have
a clear picture of this coffee, of this day when the coffee was made —
I would like you to describe, either in words or in a drawing, that
coffee on that day. When you have finished your description, look
up so I know you are done.
(*ME looks up immediately*)
You can't be done.


Scene 3

ME: I can only see tea.
SHE: Then I can do nothing for you. Go.
ME: (*Exiting slowly, then turning back suddenly and tearing the gun out
of SHE's hands.*) Don't try to find me.

ACT TWO *the winter*
Scene 1

> *(ME enters covered with snow as SHE sips from her white mug, now covered with red lipstick kisses.)*

SHE: So… Good trip?
ME: It's snowing so much I couldn't see out of my eyes. My eyes let my nose lead me here. The roasted aroma of your small, delicate hands guided me. You did want me to come back?
SHE: Your choice. You have to be ready to grind.
ME: I am.
SHE: Where's my gun?

> *(ME reaches with one hand into her pocket, and then leans over to kiss SHE's mug and leave her lip prints there. As she is about to pull something out of her pocket, blackout.)*


Scene 2

SHE: Let me explain the nature of coffee. Some think it should be mild, sentimental — like the farina your mother once fed you before your mouth was sophisticated enough to handle more oral complexity. Like the taste of snowflakes that fall too quickly from a clear sky — they land without character, without dirt ever spoiling their whiteness. That is not good coffee. Good coffee has a rough, bitter edge. Good coffee must be tamed by the cream that covers it — and that cream cannot be taken from a carton or a bottle but must come from within you. That cream — the cream that fills the best cup with the right kind of light, cannot be poured into an already pale brew. It is your duty to add more grounds and prevent your creation from being an embarrassment. If you try to serve this "pap" to anyone, they'll know you are a fraud, a glib excuse for a brewmaster. You have to take responsibility for your drip. No one else can measure out your grounds for you. And if you do not follow my advice then for Godssake, don't ever tell anyone that you know me.

ME: How do you know if the brew will be too light until you make it?

SHE: You feel it — you let yourself feel it. If you begin the process, without feeling the rightness of the bean in your bones, you must stop and start again. To continue without this feeling is suicide.

ME: *(Pulling out the gun.)* Tell me about it. *(ME puts the gun on the floor between them, each staring as time passes.)*


Scene 3

*(SHE lunges for the gun. ME holds it out of SHE's reach.)*

ME: Teach me — don't tease me…unless you're going to please me. *(Blackout.)*


ACT THREE *the spring*
Scene 1

*(ME hands SHE a red mug filled with coffee. SHE sips it pensively.)*

ME: Is it…?

SHE: Hmmm. Not the worst. There's even something… *(Taking another, fuller sip.)* Intriguing…about this little cup.

ME: I was careful picking out my beans.

SHE: I could tell. And you ground them perfectly for this particular brew. But —

ME: What's wrong?

SHE: Did you feel it? I'm not sure you felt it — not fully.

ME: I did stop myself at some point — I mean, I was feeling so much — it scared me. I never felt anything that intense before.

SHE: How dare you?! You ask me to teach you what I know and then you deny yourself the chance to truly know it!

ME: I wasn't sure if I was feeling it or if I just had too much caffeine. They say that can make you very emotional.

SHE: You're a foolish child who doesn't belong here. Why do you stay?
ME: You're the only one who tells me the truth.

*(ME reaches out to kiss SHE's mug, SHE knocks it to the ground, shattering it into pieces.)*


Scene 2

*(ME repairs SHE's mug with Elmer's glue. SHE enters and watches.)*

SHE: That won't hold for long.
ME: Why do you hate me?
SHE: I don't know you well enough to love. And anyway, it's more disdain than anything else.
ME: I don't blame you. *(ME breaks the mug again against her head and sobs.)*
SHE: That's more like it.


Scene 3

*(SHE holds the white mug with a straw up to ME's heavily bandaged head.)*

SHE: This is from your best pot of coffee. You should be proud.
ME: I am — but — do you know when the bandages will come off?
SHE: Never. They'll just grow into your skin and stay there forever. Other people will stop seeing them, but you'll know they're there.

*(SHE puts the coffee down, then SHE pulls out the gun. SHE places her hand over ME's hand on the trigger. Together THEY shoot the mug. The light slowly narrows down to a spot on the shot mug — its spilled contents look like blood rather than coffee, then blackout.)*

END OF PLAY

# OCTAVIO SOLIS
*Playwright*

## DEBT
## (PARA MARIA IRENE FORNES)

When I lost in a circle of writers my larynx,
the story found its voice
and on her lips I saw the curl of satisfaction,
The toothy smile of yes.

Now, in the years that have passed, the smile persists
even as the stories do, and taking stock of my artistic capital,
I see my debits clearly.

To her I owe
this pen which bucks and jars at my control
and cuts its own furrows
on the page
toward fortunes
and mysteries unimaginable

I owe
these words from which vortices
are revealed worlds and faces, browned,
iron-cast and true, hitherto unrecorded,
yet familiar, bodies planked with the wood of my own house
and studded with the nails of my own life

I owe to her the elation,
pronounced in every language as a single uncolored sigh,
which is the prize of every writer
who knows when the work, like a long kiss,
is good

I am these many times indebted,
and would many times over be thralled in her instruction,
for the sake of knowing once again,
that the stories orbit not outside of me
but circulate like blood within
and, like blood, feed the heart with air and cadence and feeling

If all these debts I've paid to her
in thanks and in the quality of my craft,
if the slate is clean between us,
still
thrice in arrears I remain to her
for being muse, teacher, *curandera* to my inner ear.

INTAR Lab Members, 1988:
Above: Paul Durand, Maria Irene Fornes, Octavio Solis, Roberto
Bedoya, Caridad Svich, and Dennis Ferguson-Acosta (seated)

Below: Maria Irene Fornes, Ela Troyano, Roberto Bedoya, Ana Maria Simo,
Lorraine Llamas, Paul Durand, Lynette Serrano-Bonaparte, Caridad Svich, and
Lorenzo Mans (seated)

Photo by Dennis Ferguson-Acosta

# ❀ LUIS ALFARO
*Poet, Playwright, Co-director of the*
*Latino Theatre Initiative*
*Mark Taper Forum, Los Angeles*


## MAKING IRENE LAUGH: A MEMORY


IN 1991 I MADE MARIA IRENE FORNES
laugh. She probably doesn't remember it, but I do, as if it was yesterday. Consequently, I also made Irene's mother, Carmen, laugh.

As one the original members of the Mark Taper Forum's Mentor Writers Workshop, Irene was one of the first instructors we studied with. The Taper provided us with an extraordinary cross section of writers like Mac Wellman, Sybille Pearson, Paula Vogel, Eric Overmyer, and John Steppling. They turned our playwriting worlds inside out.

It was an amazing time for us, mostly because we were a rowdy bunch. The group of writers that were involved in the program, which included, among others, Han Ong, Kelly Stuart, Leon Martell, Oliver Mayer, Lynn Manning, Alice Tuan, and David Lee Lindsay, have emerged as some of the best playwrights working in Los Angeles today. It's hard to imagine how we contained enough energy to sit and do the yoga, the exercises, the reading, *and* Irene's thoughts for the day for three hours, six days a week. But somehow we did.

Studying with Irene was the walk through fire for me. It was the place where I jumped over the cliff and stopped being a hobby artist and dedicated myself to full-time truth telling.

It was in Irene's workshops that I discovered what the *electricity* of playwriting was. I had already been working as a poet and in the performance world. But Irene showed me that theater was the *alchemy* part of writing. It was the place where my passion and craft met. The beginning of mixing desire with technique.

And she was hard on me. Which is one of the many reasons why I am happy I made her laugh.

One of the first meetings we had, she asked people what kind of play they wanted to write. Well, I had been active in local politics for awhile. Everything from tracing my body with paint on a sidewalk for a protest group against the war in El Salvador to marching and getting arrested at the Federal Building when the attacks on the National Endowment for the Arts were beginning.

So, I immediately spoke up and arrogantly stated that I wanted to write a political play. "Ugh," was what I heard her say. I'm not so sure anymore but I think she said that she hated people who wrote political plays.

I was, of course, young and devastated.

She told me that if I wanted to write a political play, I should write no play at all. I should go off and do politics. I should go be political, live and breathe politics. Then I should come back and write a play about nothing, a rock, and it would be political.

Well, it sounds like a cliché now, but back then I took that advice quite seriously. I went off and worked for a local of the Service Employees International Union. Later, I went to work at The Gathering Place a center for people with HIV and AIDS. I demonstrated with ACT-UP, I did a million benefits and at one point I even helped people organize *how* to get arrested.

Irene, of course, was right.

I just lived and breathed for awhile. And then I started to write. And after that I started to live and breathe art. The country of playwriting became a great, extraordinary place that I never have gotten tired of.

So, there is this thing about making her laugh.

The truth is that I did love writing my politics out on the page. Mostly because I was trying to get a hold of what my politics were.

One day, Irene gave us one of her infamous exercises, probably something to do with a picture or photo. These were especially hard for me because they were something that I could not possibly attach my politics to. So I started to write about the only other thing I had going for myself and that was my body. This odd burly sexy *Rubenesque* body.

What I began to write was deeply emotional to me. And what was unusual for me was that the mother tongue took over. My Chicano tongue. And it was trying real hard to straddle both sides of the border. And somewhere in the middle of that struggle I started to describe a strange, kind of surreal world. A world where the painful poverty and violence of the downtown Los Angeles that I was raised in, emerged as language that was wicked, dark, sexy, and most of all, the *beautiful ugly* of that street corner in downtown. And to my surprise, the tongue was funny.

So, I started to read aloud in the workshop from this new voice.

And Irene laughed.

She laughed out loud.

And Carmen, Irene's 100 year-old mother, who we lined up chairs for to make a bed, laughed out loud too.

And the other playwrights smiled and laughed too. And I joined a community, a place where I could counter the silence of my pad and pen. The lonely solitary aspect of writing was made bearable with a group of writers that I was inspired by.

And now, here I am, almost ten years later. It's midnight in the hills of Echo Park. The dogs are barking and the graffiti is fresh. Little gang boys dream of moist cakes and innocence. And I am remembering some pretty good spaghetti and writing nights with Kelly Stuart, Han Ong, Roxanne Rogers, and Alice Tuan. And I'm thinking, "Wow, a laugh made that."

Not any old laugh, mind you.

Irene's laugh.

# ❀ CHERRÍE MORAGA
*Playwright*
*Oakland, California*

## THE ZEN MASTER

(The) play is a riddle. A riddle that's in the head of the author…
Something that intrigues the author but doesn't have a shape yet. He
doesn't even have a question… (I)n the beginning all the author has
is that there is something to be discovered…the writing of the play
is the discovery. By the time the author gets halfway through, she
knows what the question is. Then, answering the question begins to
shape the play.

> *Theater Magazine*
> Fornes, of course

           I SIT IN AN OVERSTUFFED ARM CHAIR IN
the library-sitting room with five other women playwrights. The theater company has put us on an island in Washington. We are in retreat.
The group, overwhelmingly heterosexual, I am the only lesbian, keeps
making jokes about what will happen without men around for ten days.
I keep thinking, that's how I live most days of my life. But they're a
wonderful group of women — smart women — passionately committed
to playwriting. We debate. Race. Sex. Plastic Surgery. Class and the Classics. Does one have to teach Ibsen and Chekhov to teach playwriting
well? I remember María Irene's* love of Ibsen. And I remember I had
never actually seen a live piece of theater (Ibsen or not) on a real stage
until I began writing with Fornes in the mid-1980s. I say, "Had I not
begun writing plays with María Irene, I never would have become a
playwright. Had I had to start somewhere other than my own voice,
my own manner of telling story…" That's the point. We turn later to
reading the classics. Or maybe not at all. The debate is unimportant

to me. What is important is the model of writing and teaching María Irene introduced me to that I have carried with me for the last fifteen years. You begin first with the heart of the matter you discover your play. Punto.

When I think of Fornes, I think always of playwright, Migdalia Cruz. Possibly because Migdalia and I were first students together under María Irene's tutelage at the Hispanic Playwrights Project in 1984. She and I, two of the three women in a ten-person workshop. Ana María Simo, the third. Possibly I think of Migdalia because I see the playwright she has become: all things I admire, because I believe Fornes was pivotal in the emergence of this (under-recognized) infinitely responsible writer of integrity and talent. The integrity and responsibility is now thoroughly Migdalia's, as is her talent and the journey her own voice has taken. But from the beginning, María Irene didn't let Migdalia lie. She asked her go to the hardest/ugliest truths (the writer's truths) of what it is to be Latina, hungry of body and sex and spirit in this pitiful country. She encouraged those journeys into the forbidden. I thank María Irene for this. For the writer she helped shape in Migdalia, in me.

In 1990, Fornes directed my play, *Shadow of a Man*. It was the most artistically rigorous experience of my life, forcing me to sift through the layers of lessons María Irene had to teach me. At the beginning of the rehearsal process, we sit down to table at a salvaoreño restaurant in San Francisco's Mission District. I believe my play is done. Fine-tuning is all that is required, I think. María Irene holds her hands in the air in front of my face. She leans into the table, closer to me. "A play is like an airplane," she tells me. She contains the shape of what is clearly a very rickety flying machine within her hands. "If all the pieces don't work together perfectly, it won't fly." And with that pronouncement, I envisioned my play nose-diving into the Pacific. Thus, began five weeks of the most intensive playwriting lessons of my life. Y más. Because it was not only play construction that María Irene had to teach me. She would also teach me how to appreciate my work (its poetry), defend my work, fight for my work, stand up to the master-teacher when I felt my vision was at risk of compromise. I was a student and what is hardest for the student to know is when resistance to the teacher's counsel is based on an intuitive faith in one's own original purpose and when it is pure arrogance. In my case, it was both. And María Irene suffered both in me. In the process, I learned a lot about power (María Irene had it) and respect (María Irene deserved it), and somewhere in that mix the young writer struggles to gain the tools of her art and her artistic survival.

I am sitting in the Eureka Theater watching María Irene rehearse my play. Manuel, a middle-aged man of thick softening muscle, sits at the morning kitchen table. He very laboriously writes a letter, ignoring the wife and two daughters that surround him. He determines the silence in the room. One daughter escapes into her homework over a bowl of cereal. The other, the youngest, watches her father for signs of distress. Nothing escapes her. Minutes later, the daughters exit for school in the habit of their mornings. The wife brings Manuel a cup of coffee. He is angry at the wife. For no good reason. For his reasons alone which are no good. She knows this, but dutifully brings him his cup of coffee. The husband presses the back of his hand against the bowl of the cup and pushes it very slowly and with full deliberation an entire arm's length away from him. We hear the cup slide across the table top. The wife watches. Line: "Why are you writing him?" And thus begins the final demise of their marriage and Manuel in Act Two.

I remember while watching María Irene rehearse this scene, I ignorantly questioned (to myself) why at least a full hour of rehearsal time was spent on this one simple physical action of moving a cup of coffee. I soon learned why. María Irene choreographed such moments in the play as if each were a moving painting. To the amazement and sometimes impatience of her actors, she produces emotionally riveting work. This is the best of collaboration: for a director to teach the playwright why we write plays, to remind the playwright of the promise of the body when it steps into the full meaning of the words we have written. It scared me a little, the gravity of my own words made flesh. It has kept me writing theater for fifteen years.

On opening night, the plane soared. The critics didn't think so, but they are usually of low opinion. But in the eye of the author's mind, the director had brought forth the dignity and indignity of my characters' orgullo and longing through the three-dimensional world of the Mestiza body, the painterly sensibility of the Mexican mural, and the bass beat of tuba and tambor found en los desfiles del pueblo on the cobblestoned streets of Indigenous México. My work was illuminated by Fornes' touch.

I must confess that months later, when I was to publish *Shadow of a Man*, I made changes to the work that María Irene would not have allowed. And allow is the operative word here, for I did, at times, make compromises my writer's-soul told me not to. Irene was too formidable a master-teacher to challenge. Like a Zen master, I say, whenever I'm asked what it was like working with María Irene Fornes. You bow your head and take the rap on the head as a lesson in humility. You learn through great discipline of spirit what is priceless to find out: a theater of economy, a theater that goes always first to the heart (broken and bitter) of the matter and the play emerges from there. There is no room for excess except if it brings you a delicate pleasure. And you only get to indulge such delicacies if you have earned your way, proven you are relentlessly committed to a theater of truth. As is María Irene Fornes.

I remain ever-grateful for that experience, the only time in my life where another artist of María Irene's calibre and power, fell in love with my work enough to realize it so beautifully on stage. "What's your favorite play," the interviewer inquires of Fornes during a promotional cable TV spot. "*Shadow of a Man*," she answers. Because *Shadow* was Fornes' play of the moment, the one requiring all of her artistic attention. I was honored and awestruck. A lesson in teaching. Such generosity of spirit ensures the continuance of art production in the emergent artist.

The art of Fornes' own plays hold hard truths. What on the surface appear to be such brutal portraits — the pitifulness of our human condition, our base hungers exposed and abandoned — are what finally forces us to confront ourselves and our own defilements. Hers remains an uncommodified art in an American theater of consumerism. No one is buying María Irene Fornes. She remains free to the rest of us who still garner hope from her renegade example.

---

* I call her María Irene pronounced in Spanish, because I'd like to believe we (Latinos) matter differently to this dramaturga extraordinaria, que somos familiar to her in a way distinct from all the others she has taught.

# ❁ PETER LITTLEFIELD
*Director, Writer, Stage Manager of several productions for New York Theatre Strategy*

I MET IRENE DURING THE MID-SEVENTIES when she was running New York Theatre Strategy, a playwrights' collective. The idea was to give playwrights the producer role and more power over their productions. Autonomy is important to Irene — defines her terms as accurately as possible. And it's something for which she's willing to pay the price. In the case of Theatre Strategy, she ended up with most of the work, and for seven years she struggled with every level of production. I remember standing with her in the old Gate Theatre on 2nd Avenue. There's wood and every other kind of thing piled up. The place is a wreck, and I'm thinking that we should give up and go home. But she set to work, so I did too. The Gate had a heating problem: When the heat went on, water rained down on the stage. The play was *He Wants Shih!* by Rochelle Owens. Every evening at the same moment, just as Princess Ling kills herself in a long poetic monologue, little pearl-like droplets floated through the lights and landed on her black velvet deathbed. To correct this, we devised a huge wood frame stretched with plastic, which — constructed by us and raised thirty feet to the ceiling — siphoned the water down a hose and into a garbage can. She had a preference for homemade solutions, and she seemed to operate in a realm of timelessness. Personally, I was intoxicated by this brilliant woman for whom no amount of exploration, conversation, attention, or calculation was too much to be lavished on the moment at hand. One night just before the play opened, I came to her apartment to find her sound asleep under her writing table. She had fallen where she worked.

During this time, Irene started leading a writers workshop at INTAR. I took it though it was in Spanish, which I don't speak. I don't know how Irene developed her writing exercises, but they demonstrate very clearly how to locate your source of creativity. Each member of the class drew a picture. Then you'd choose one that you liked and give it a name. Then Irene set all the pictures — with their names — out on a table. We each chose a drawing — using these two elements to write a story. This hit me like a vision. I had a little squiggle called Ernesto. I looked into his dark image as if I was looking down a deep hole — from which I simply pulled out the story. The fact that I couldn't understand what anybody was saying added to my sense of the Fornes magic. If creativity is about encountering life, she has an instinct for stripping everything else away.

Irene didn't do much writing during the Theatre Strategy years. I think she was looking for a more immediate stage language. One thing she did was interview people on tape and transcribe the words to explore the way people talk. There's a parallel here with her Theatre Strategy work — theatrical endeavors at the most earthly level. And the end result — in *Fefu and Her Friends, Evelyn Brown, Mud,* and what followed — was theatre that struck hard at the bedrock of experience. Her language showed the way people use words to struggle with reality. She used found texts and objects to bring the materials of life onto the stage. And she built a stage reality out of the materials of the stage — words, sound, movement, set, props, lights. Life made from life.

She told me that she doesn't think of herself as a writer when she isn't writing. And I don't think she hesitates for a moment to lay aside the lofty mantle of writer to explore some other side of life. Because Irene isn't afraid of life. She's not afraid to be a part of it.

# ✹ ELAINE ROMERO
*Playwright*

## TRIBUTE TO IRENE FORNES

IT SEEMED LIKE EVERY LATINO WRITER I knew had studied with Irene Fornes. I pictured her out there influencing every new voice that came along, shaping them into her own image. It bothered me: Why should one person have so much power?

So much for misguided preconceptions. I finally got the opportunity to study with Irene in Taxco, Mexico, over a two-week period in 1997. At this time, I had already written twenty or thirty plays, had a long list of credits, and a strong sense of what playwriting meant to me. Hell, I was a regularly produced, published playwright.

What immediately impressed me about Irene was that she took little interest in what we had written or what we were writing. We had all shown up to her workshop with our plays carefully tucked under our arms. I think most of us were expecting to receive notes from the master. It didn't take long for me to realize that Irene does absolutely nothing like other people.

Within minutes of starting the workshop, Irene had managed to make everything that had come before or had been written before seem irrelevant. We were there to rotate our ankles and to shake our wrists (writers torture themselves in their chairs, she told us), to learn her process, to uncover the stories and characters that dwelled deeply in the unconscious through visualization, sense memory, and a walk into a refreshing three-dimensionality that eludes many playwrights. We were there to confront our characters, wipe sweat off their brows, and to touch their skin if that was what was required. There would be nothing secret between playwright and character. All would be known.

Irene does not have a Latino-character or political-story mandate. Her techniques are more about her integrity to the artistic impulse, about facing what is inside us without passing judgment on it or censoring it. Each exercise is a new channel to creativity, a new way to access the inaccessible.

Her exercises took me to places I hadn't visited in a long time, to memories I had repressed, to the basic fears and loves that I kept guarded inside. The stories I was generating during the workshop seemed so different than "my writing." But they were my writing. Through the writing, the unconscious was becoming conscious. Well, that is what psychotherapy is all about, right?

I remember one exercise where she passed out old photographs. Mine was of three women sitting on a porch during the 1930s. Suddenly, a world sprung up around the edges of the photo and I could see what was inside the house, what hung on the walls, and the river that ran out front. I found myself writing about a time period I would have normally felt ill-prepared to cover. I felt as if I had stepped into a lucid dream where I could be volitional and force the dream to show me things that it had not planned on revealing. As Irene would prompt us, the story would flit through time, full of humor, pathos, and angst — all the things that make for good drama.

It seemed within minutes I was on my way to writing a new full-length play, featuring an Anglo couple during the 1930s. I never expected myself to write anything remotely like this piece and I found myself absolutely captured by these people and their petty little problems, which were merely human problems. So, how did Irene know how to get me there? What was she doing that other writing instructors had not done?

I've concluded that it is because Irene is "wired" differently. She was educated by her family and not in a school setting. She was not brought up with the educational misconceptions that many of us spend a lifetime overcoming. She has a basic faith in each human's ability to write. Irene is childlike without being childish. She has a generous heart and mind, and seems most comfortable in the cool realm of the unconscious. Irene does not feel the need to process every experience in life through her intellect, but through her heart.

Perhaps, Irene prefers to live in the unconscious world and is not as consumed by the conscious one. Those of us who have studied with her have had the pleasure of passing her on the way into her world and invited her into ours. One always gets the feeling that she would rather stay where she is.

# ✸ ANNE GARCIA-ROMERO
*Playwright*
*New York City*

ON A WARM JULY MORNING IN 1989, I
entered a room in a cinderblock building in the art department at Cal
State Northridge for a workshop at the Padua Hills Playwrights Festival. As the hour drew near, one by one, the writers solemnly arrived;
fellow students and visitors whom I did not recognize. Soon each long,
rectangular table was filled to capacity. A silent eagerness hung in the
air. Then in walked Irene Fornes.

As a young writer unfamiliar with Irene's work, I was struck by the
respect and reverence that this gathering of strangers gave to her. She
led us outside to a walkway where we lay on the cement floor as she
taught us physical warm-ups, legs and arms swaying in yoga-like movements. Then each person returned to her or his sacred space at the table
to await what would become a hallowed refrain, "Close your eyes, picture a character…"

Since that day, Irene has taught me to listen to the truth of my
characters as they forge paths through my plays. She has taught me to
always continue onward with my work, to speak up and contribute to
the collaborative process, to learn one new thing on each collaboration
and in doing so, to consider the experience useful. She has given me a
model for work that puts the writing process above all else. Irene's indefatigable optimism and spirit of generosity continue to guide me.

# ❋ SILVIA GONZALEZ S.
## *INTAR Lab Member 1989–90*

IN JUNE 1989, I WAS INVITED TO PARTICIPATE in Seattle's Group Theatre Multicultural Playwrights Festival. As part of the developmental experience, the winning playwrights received tickets to see Maria Irene Fornes' play, *Fefu and Her Friends*, directed by Fornes, at a local theater. The production took place in a Victorian house. The audience escorted to scenes in various rooms, with the final scene in the theater. At the discussion with Ms. Fornes after the play, I witness a passion for theater beyond belief. The power of the whole evening was electrifying.

Up to that point, I was tentative in classifying myself as a playwright. My blue-collar upbringing had pruned me to do something else. Images of *Fefu and Her Friends* kept coming back to me. Within two months Fornes invites me to participate in her Lab at INTAR in New York City.

The Lab included Migdalia Cruz, Nilo Cruz, Caridad Svich, Ezequiel Colon-Rivera, Lalo Cervantes, Chuck Gomez, Ela Troyano, Manuel Garcia Pereiras, Lorenzo Mans, and myself. Fornes' exercises were difficult for me.

"You are not letting what's inside out. You are hiding it." Fornes' stern remark catapulted me into self-examination. "You must learn to tap into the subconscious until what is inside comes out like vomit."

"How do you know when you have tapped the subconscious?" I asked.

She answered, "When you feel it coming out of a part of your body."

The writing method in the Lab was to have our writing tables situated in a circle, with the corners connected, so to acquire a collective energy. I felt there was a weakness in the circle from my end. Sometime in late October, I took a long weekend and went home. When I came back to the lab, Lorenzo said that Fornes kept asking where I was. He told her, but she kept asking every day. I gasped in surprise. Fornes hushed us and started the Lab. We wrote for hours, then read our work aloud. At class' end Fornes remarked how this was a very good writing day, that the previous work days were useless. Those were the days I was missing! So, maybe I contributed to the creative circle after all. Here I was thinking I was the kid in the class that needed to be on Ritalin.

Fornes cut us loose to finish our projects on our own. One day it happened. I was writing with incredible speed. I tried in vain to capture dialogue and images that pounded my brain. *I was a vehicle for the subconscious flow!* That's what Fornes was talking about. I called her. "I FEEL IT. IT'S EXPLODING THOUGH MY ARMS." She said, "Good, good." I memorized the feeling for the next time.

There were many "next times." A large number of plays, monologues, and prose sit in my hard drive. Some produced, some published, all inspired by a unique teaching method that promotes prolificness.

To this day, I wait for that "feeling" Fornes taught me before I write. I remember fondly her saying, "If you do this, you will be amazed with the results."

### ⊛ ALBERTO SANDOVAL
*Professor of Spanish*
*Mount Holyoke College*

### ⊛ NANCY SAPORTA STERNBACH
*Associate Professor of Spanish and*
*Portuguese, Smith College*

## MARIA IRENE FORNES AS MENTOR

WITH HER 1977 PLAY, *FEFU AND HER Friends*, Maria Irene Fornes initiates a theatrical paradigm that will become characteristic of almost an entire decade of Latina playwriting (1977–1986). Specifically, she stages a collectivity of women, Fefu and her friends, who de-center male protagonists and characters. Using the dis-ease of male/female relations as the unspoken agenda that under-scores her work, Fornes also hints at the possibility of a sexuality beyond compulsory heterosexuality in her suggestion of a possible lesbian rela-tionship between two of her characters, Cecelia and Paula. Sexuality also figures into the equation in that one of the characters has been sex-ually molested, a subject that later resonates in plays by other Latinas, such as in Cherríe Moraga's *Giving Up the Ghost.* Beginning with Fornes' innovative staging of four simultaneous scenes, to its shocking ending when Fefu shoots Julia, *Fefu and Her Friends* has generated a vast amount of speculation among critics. To begin with, the reader, who is clearly at a disadvantage compared to a spectator, may have trouble visualiz-ing the type of fragmentation that characterizes the play. Furthermore, there is virtually no plot. What little cohesion there is centers on the meeting of eight college-educated women who gather at the country home of Fefu to plan a fund-raising event.

The play's deep feminist underpinnings suggest the extent to which patriarchy has invaded the characters' lives. The fragmentation of the action and the lack of any kind of linearity parallels Fornes' message about women's position in a patriarchal system and underlies the deep structure of the play. Her technique results in a de-essentialization of women that serves as a counterpoint to their usual position in patriarchy. Although they have internalized their oppression and the misogyny from which it derives, they nevertheless attempt to resolve the contradictions in their lives.[1] In this sense, each character brings to the play one other instance of a woman's "dis-ease in society" (p. 121). From being molested by secret police, to spousal abuse, to actual paralysis, each one of them embodies in her female flesh one more outrage against women. Their confrontations of these ills form the corpus of the play: One is bound to a wheelchair, the other drinks too heavily, another is plagued by hallucinations.

All of these constructs, hints, symbolisms, and gender constructions highlight the issues of identification that Fornes faces, even while these are never ostensibly what her plays are about. What they do accomplish, however, is to lay the groundwork for full development in the 1980s by the playwrights that Fornes herself will mentor; and these Latina playwrights will emerge from collective theater groups ready to take on their own individual projects. In this context, Fornes' play does not represent an isolated example of a Latina writing theater, but rather forms part of a continuum that is constantly manifesting itself through the theater and its practitioners. Her own way of doing theater and her feminist practices are the seedbed for a new generation of Latinas who simultaneously incorporate her philosophy while learning her greatest lesson: that they cannot imitate her. Thus, she transforms the art of doing theater in that she gives them the tools to explore their own theater practices. In this regard, her contribution has been invaluable. Given that this new generation of Latinas is producing plays about subjectivities-in-process, it is of vital importance that they not lose sight of their audiences, who are either community-based or in regional theaters. These playwrights have no desire to marginalize or alienate those very communities or audiences on whom they rely. Thus, they negotiate and accommodate a Fornesian philosophy to a community-based way of doing theater, whose entire essence is transculturation itself. That the most produced playwrights to come out of Fornes' workshops (Josefina López, Caridad Svich, and Migdalia Cruz) are those who take her messages, but imbue them with their own stories, attests to the necessity of a theater that is hybrid and transcultural in its nature.

While Fornes remains the indisputable mentor and role model of Latina playwrights, her personal politics have generated as much contradiction as her characters display. For example, she says that although "there is a rich Spanish tradition of classic theater…there hasn't been a strong modern Hispanic theater — by that I mean since the turn of the century. The Hispanic-American doesn't have a model yet." Many playwrights and theater people from Teatro Campesino to the *teatro de protesta* on the East Coast (1960s) would take issue with such a remark. It is clear that Fornes speaks from a positionality of class privilege, whiteness, and Eurocentric dramatic models. That she relinquished these positions to some degree through her work as director, mentor, and role model is to her credit. New generations of Latino/a playwrights continually acknowledge the fact that she respects their autonomy and inspires them to find their own voice. For her, then, it is "very important to try to work with Hispanic playwrights at a level where they are just beginning to write, so that they do not dismiss possibilities of ways of writing that would be very original to them but ways they would not see models for in the active American or English or German theater."[2]

Considering how symbolic, fragmented, and postmodern Fornes' play is, our assertion that *Fefu* is a foundational piece of Latina playwriting may be questionable. After all, the play is noteworthy for its lack of ethnic markers. The women in the cast could easily be "everywoman." Nothing defines them or their creator as Latinas. Yet, once placed within the context of Latina theater as a genre in its own right, *Fefu and Her Friends* establishes links with both Estela Portillo and Cherríe Moraga. The play itself recognizes and decries the situation of women under patriarchy, even when the playwright can offer few solutions to their entrapment. Fornes presents a character whose final desperate, destructive act may be ascribed to madness. The expression of sexualities is both muted and articulated, both hetero- and homosexual. In its own embryonic form, Fornes' play anticipates the way Moraga's characters will audaciously accuse their sexual abusers. The entire play, then, underscores the playwright's outrage at the paralysis and even doom that seems to confront women in patriarchy. If the action of the play seems to stand still, this is intentional. There is no moving forward when women are trapped physically, sexually, and psychologically within the confines of the male-dominated world. Thus, the final shocking action, where Fefu allegedly shoots Julia, the "paralyzed" woman in the wheelchair, is tantamount to declaring that Fornes' theater has taken a social and political position, an exhortation to rebel.

1. Assunta Bartolomucci Kent, *Maria Irene Fornes and her Critics* (Westport: Greenwood Press, 1996), p. 120. Subsequent references are parenthesized.

2. "Maria Irene Fornes," in *Notable Hispanic American Women,* eds. Diane Telgem and Jim Kamp (Detroit: Gale Research Inc., 1993), p. 163.

WORKS CONSULTED

Fornes, Maria Irene, *Fefu and Her Friends* (New York: Performing Arts Journal Publications, 1978).

Fornes, Maria Irene, *Plays* (New York: Performing Arts Journal Publications, 1986).

Fornes, Maria Irene, "Interview," in *In their Own Words: Contemporary American Playwrights,* ed. David Savran (New York: Theatre Communications Group 1989), pp. 51–69.

Keyssar, Helene, "Drama and the Dialogic Imagination: The Heidi Chronicles and *Fefu and Her Friends,*" in *Feminist Theatre and Theory,* ed. Helene Keyssar (New York: St Martin's Press, 1996), pp. 109–36.

Lee, Josephine, "Pity and Terror as Public Acts: Reading Feminist Politics in the Plays of Maria Irene Fornes," in *Staging Resistance: Essays on Theatre and Politics,* eds. Jeanne Colleran and Jenny Spencer (Ann Arbor: University of Michigan Press, 1997), pp. 166–85.

Moroff, Diane Lynn, *Fornes: Theatre in the Present Tense* (Ann Arbor: University of Michigan Press, 1996).

Pevitts, Beverly Byers, "Review of *Fefu and Her Friends,*" in *Women in American Theatre,* eds. Helen Krich Chinoy and Linda Walsh Jenkins (New York: Theatre Communications Group, 1987), pp. 314–17.

Above: Mary Forcade (Lydia, seated) and Maria Irene Fornes in rehearsal.
Below: Suzanne Fletcher (Veronica), Jerry Jaffe (Tommy), Joe Goodrich (Chucky), Maria Irene Fornes, and Mary Forcade (Lydia, seated) in rehearsal.

*ANY PLACE BUT HERE*
by Caridad Svich, directed by Maria Irene Fornes
Theater for the New City, New York City, 1995

Photo by Maria M. Delgado

# ❀ JENNIFER MAISEL
*Playwright*

AFTER GETTING TO KNOW IRENE AT THE Padua Hills Playwrights Festival I took her seminar at NYU. Every Wednesday morning at 9 AM — unheard of for graduate students — we would gather in 721 Broadway's 7th floor black box theater whose curtains were, without a doubt, infused with a strange exhaustion-producing spore only theater curtains possess. Irene would lead us in forty-five minutes of yoga and then sit us down at the table near the curtains, always starting off one of her writing exercises with "Close your eyes…visualize…" Ten minutes later we'd open our eyes to write. Invariably one student would remain head crashed into notebook, deep in sleep. One day, when Irene commanded us to open our eyes, no one did. We had all fallen asleep. We woke up to Irene saying — "Sometimes you must write…and sometimes you must sleep."

# ✹ DENNIS FERGUSON-ACOSTA
*Executive Director*
*Teatro Municipal de Lima, Peru*

THE FRUSTRATION AT NOT PULLING UP from my insides dialogue and scenes was aggravated by Maria Irene's encouragement to write what I saw — and her frustration at my frustration. The images of the cosmos, deep space, and brilliant stars, sometimes with an overlay of characters from an unknown language running across the image like film credits, were beyond my capacity to describe in a way I felt appropriate to a playwriting workshop, the INTAR Playwrights-in-Residence Lab (HPRL) at that. Six years later in 1991 sitting with a group of colleagues in a circle under the full moon preparing to enter the narrow cave known as *Templo de la Luna* (Temple of the Moon) at Sacsayhuaman in Cusco for an Andean offering to Mother Earth, those images started appearing again. Surging golden light taking the shape of pyramids or moving across space and that deep infinity of stars. Only then did I begin to understand that the physical and meditative exercises that led into the writing exercises were connected to a profound inner self that fed creative thoughts and images. The HPRL experience in that neat, cozy, harmonious space on distant West 53rd Street was preparing me to enter the mystic world of Andean rituals.

After multiple collaborations over eight years at INTAR I had the MIF bug, actually I got it very early on. Hers is the single most important voice in forging my concept of what producing art should be and the referential — the vision — in the arts management seminars I have given in twenty-seven cities of Latin America.

While I was Managing Director at INTAR, Maria Irene saw me as the personification of unwelcome corporate authority, in her role as the Head of the HPRL, recipient of new work commissions and director of plays during the theatrical season. The complex eight-year relationship engendered some tense moments. The only time I have experienced an extensive barrage of screamed verbal abuse was at the corner of 10th Avenue and 50th Street in Manhattan after HPRL readings at the INTAR Stage Two. Irene was venting serious concerns but I do not remember about what, and I am sure she does not either. The lesson, I came to realize, is when you believe in an artist you develop a commitment to do whatever is necessary to make things work. Lots of compromising, negotiating, tolerance, looking for solutions in this vital pursuit of a vision — which in the case of Ms. Fornes is a constant transformation of her profound theatrical language.

Fortunately the confrontations did not dominate, and the process of working together in nurturing the HPRL to full bloom and her plays to the stage provided the context for the treasured memories of today. Another lesson in this process was that the solution to bringing a dramatic vision to life was not money. Even in the harshest economic times where budgets were shaved thinner than seemed possible, Maria Irene would come in under budget with a forcefully visual production, displaying inventive solutions that brought force and dimension to the work in ways that yet again surprised us.

Our contact post INTAR took on a different, definitely nonconfrontational, tenor focusing on exchanges regarding art — creating and communicating art. While I was Executive Director of the Latino Museum of History, Art, and Culture in Los Angeles, several gatherings with West Coast ex-HPRL participants kept us in touch and permitted the opportunity to share her vibrant Mama Carmen whose wit and *joie de vivre* had made her the focal point at openings and reunions. But I find myself missing the creative confrontations of the work relationship and particularly the camaraderie, the mystique of the HPRL. Maria Irene's innate ability to teach was complemented by her eloquent clarity about the integrity of the creative process. The truly connected process of creating is free and has its own structure, challenging the writer to get out of the way of the nascent play. Rewriting was an ongoing point of discussion in the Lab where some were satisfied too soon with their creation and others manipulated the work through erroneous preconceptions of what a play should be.

Curious that some fifteen years later I find myself discussing with concerned artist friends in Lima, Peru, the reality of a theater world controlled by the producer, *el hombre del maletín* (the man with the briefcase) as we have labeled him, and the aberrations it can engender in the creative process. I have quoted Maria Irene in these discussions as declaring that when everything falls apart, the institutional authorities will turn to the artists and they will fix the problem, because they can and because they will assume the responsibility. A dream come true would be to have Irene come to Peru to conduct playwriting workshops and plant the seed of her genius in this culturally rich country that is in the midst of rapid metamorphosis.

I still do not know the meaning of the cosmic visions I saw in the Lab, but I now understand that at some point intuition, creativity, and intellect will converge to provide a threshold to comprehending the meaning of me as a human being, a cultural hybrid, a bridge between worlds and options. Maria Irene Fornes, thanks for being a master guide in the process of life.

# ⊛ LEN BERKMAN
*Anne Hesseltine Hoyt Professor of Theatre*
*Smith College, Massachusetts*

THE FIRST TIME I EVER HEARD IRENE Fornes' voice I was half asleep. A late night phone ring; my wife, Joyce, and I in darkness in bed; I reach across Joyce to answer; Irene's magnificent high-wire tones leap into my ear. Irene needed to talk with Megan Terry, whose Omaha Magic Theatre company — brought by Joyce and me for a weeklong residency at U. Mass./Amherst and Smith College — was asleep in every available room of our home. A New York City performance, with Irene crucial in the arrangements, was next. And Irene was on top of each detail.

That was the 1970s. I'd long been enthralled by Irene's fascinating, inventive, dangerous, and evolving scripts and vision of theater. A year later, I would see the former Open Theatre actress K. Carney perform *Dr. Kheal*, one of my Fornes favorites, at the American Theatre Association convention in Chicago. I would literally be so rocked with laughter to the point of tears that I fell off my seat and saw half the play from the floor. When Irene gets to you, she really gets to you.

Our paths crossed numerous times in the decades since. Irene-the-teacher became as cherished a figure for me and my students as Irene-the-artist. Her methods, as we all know, are as pure Irene as her voice. One January, when I'd brought her to our Five College valley for a three-week, play-development residency, and she was incredibly putting up with an ill-heated campus guest room, Irene would enjoy making daily progress reports to me of each of the thirty-six student participants in our project. Of one newly matched Hampshire-Smith College playwright-director team, she would repeatedly announce, with infinite charm, "They are like sister and brother. They should get married." Wherever students kept plays confined to their black boxes and prosceniums, she opened their eyes to the universe.

With Irene's blessing, I succeeded her (from 1988 through 1990) as South Coast Rep's guest dramaturg for its annual Hispanic Playwrights Project and festival. There, and during my ten years with the Sundance Institute Playwrights Lab, I worked with one after another of Irene's devoted protégés, young playwrights who had studied and worked with her at INTAR, at South Coast Rep, at Padua Hills — playwrights to whom she had given vital self-confidence, and importantly the confidence to find their own voices, their own methods, separate from hers. Irresistibly, I launched a Latino/a Drama course at Smith, which I informally subtitled, "Irene Fornes and Her Children." My students read everything Irene had written to date, in print and in manuscript, alongside works of Eduardo Machado, Milcha Sanchez Scott, Migdalia Cruz, Bernardo Solano, Jose Rivera, Cherríe Moraga, Caridad Svich, and luminous others. The Theatre Communications Group Conferences of the 1980s would bring Irene back to Smith as well. I would hear Irene's voice call my name from across a street. I would look up and see her poised at a traffic crossing in bright sunlight looking lost — but knowing exactly where she was headed. It was nearly as though she'd forgotten she'd called out. I'd volley back to her, "Irene?" In a flash, that lost look, that alert and probing face, would burst into radiant smiles.

# ❋ JULIETTE CARRILLO
*Director*

I chose Fornes because she understands directors.
I chose Fornes because of her wickedly strange, funny, dark,
quirky, insightful imagination.
I chose Fornes because her struggles to understand the bizarre
interactions between the sexes very much reflect my own.
I chose Fornes because she surprises me.

WILLIAMSTOWN, SUMMER OF '93. I AM
working with the young Act II Company and I am supposed to choose
a play to direct that challenges all twelve of them equally. Something
that stretches them. I chose Fornes' *Molly's Dream*, a relatively unknown
musical with really only five roles. The rest of the company gets cast
as the chorus of "Hanging Women" and "musicians" (who "play" found
objects). They are furious at me.

They spend most of the rehearsal period furious at me. I make them
rehearse long hours in too-hot rooms, I don't give them long enough
breaks, I make them wear uncomfortable costumes. They were right
to be furious at me; I was being a bit martyrish. Looking back and seeing (how we all do at some point or another) how art reflects life, I can
see how I was processing the remnants of a lost relationship and using
Fornes' work to do so. In other words, I was healing a broken heart in
a very public way.

Fornes provided a wonderful canvas to investigate the ridiculousness of idealized love. It was cynical and whimsical at the same time.
It made us laugh at ourselves and cry at our foolishness and yet, in a
sweet naivete, celebrate our fantasies. It was very uncomfortable. Throughout the process, we sweated, argued, whimpered and pouted. But it was
also wonderfully creative. Cowboys did tangos with Vampire women
in candlelight. The Hanging Women (played by both sexes) drooped

with running mascara and old prom dresses. Shirley Temple tap-danced on the piano while our "musicians" played eggbeaters. We named the real parakeet in the play after the drink absinthe, a favorite request at the bar. Like in a relationship, we were simultaneously inspired and frustrated at the same time.

Of course, we tried too hard to understand the play. One day, I heard that Fornes was not too far away from us doing a residency at Dartmouth with New York Theatre Workshop. I jumped at the chance to visit and grabbed two cast members and drove down to see her (of course, the other cast members, true to the process, were furious at me). We sat in circle on a lawn, eager for answers. "What did you really mean by this?" "What does this say about men and women?" "How does it all connect?" Her, answers, big surprise, were just as enigmatic as her plays. "Did I write that? Oh, I really didn't mean that. I don't really know. I don't remember. Did I write that?" Although frustrated, I knew she was being provocative. She is an artist. Why would she want to provide answers? Instead she forced us to look deeper into our own interpretations, our own experiences and ideas. We returned to the rehearsal hall with even more questions, which seemed perfectly appropriate.

Despite the strange process, I loved wrestling with this play. It demanded utmost creativity, unusual approaches, trust, and a twisted sense of humor. Together, the group created a beautifully theatrical investigation into one of the most complex aspects of humanity, love. Fornes was our muse.

# ❂ NANCY MECKLER
*Artistic Director, Shared Experience Theatre Company, London*

I HAVE DIRECTED THREE FORNES PIECES, all in England: *The Successful Life of 3, The Danube,* and *Abingdon Square.* Irene was always available for chats, albeit mostly by phone.

My most impressive memory is a writers' workshop she ran at the National Theatre. I joined in just for the experience and was astonished to find myself pouring out reams of writing, so powerful were her exercises. To avoid the panic of facing a blank page, we began by closing our eyes and seeing a past memory, prompted by Irene. Next we drew the scene (for our eyes only), and then she gave us two simple phrases of dialogue to write under or in the picture. I should add that this was introduced by ten minutes of yoga breathing and physical exercises. Somehow this simple nonintellectual start of drawing from memory followed by Fornes' chosen words managed to stimulate the noncensorious, intuitive part of my brain and I, who usually abhor the thought of creative writing, was off and running.

I think all Fornes' work comes from that intuitive, nonjudgmental place. Afterwards, she applies all her great skills of shaping, editing, and storytelling. But the original material is intuitive. That's why I find her work so inspirational and engaging, both to perform and to watch.

# ❀ PETER LICHTENFELS
*Director, Tutor in Acting*
*Manchester Metropolitan University*

## MAKING NOISES QUIETLY

I FIRST CAME ACROSS A MARIA IRENE
Fornes play in the early 1990s when, as Granada Artist in Residence at
the University of California Davis, some students I was teaching decided
to do a scene from *Sarita*. I remember the moment as clear as a bell.
Hearing the writing, my ears immediately perked up. I remember asking myself why I hadn't heard of this work, kicking myself for my ignorance, given the shimmering quality of the dialogue? Especially I, who
had spent the previous twenty years working on new plays with new
playwrights, albeit in Britain.

What follows are thoughts on why Fornes hasn't been done in England to the extent that reflects the quality of her work. I'm going to
look at three different areas: the institutional ways that theater has worked
in Britain, the second is to do with cultural bridges that have to be built
between writers in one society and audiences in another, and the third
looks at Fornes' writing being quietly insistent, uncomfortable, the writing intrudes itself into your musculature, so that long after you read
it, or (I presume) see it, it keeps working its way in your memory.

For many years I was closely involved with new writing in the United
Kingdom. From 1981 to 1986 I was Artistic Director of the Traverse Theatre in Edinburgh, a theater specifically set up to produce new plays
by new writers. My involvement with new plays continued when I
became Executive Director of the Leicester Haymarket. My tenure in
running theaters coincided with Margaret Thatcher's years in power, a
byword for distrust of, and less government funding for, the arts. I made
the decision as an artistic director, to use the money that was available
for new British writing. It was important to introduce playwrights from

other countries, but I felt this could only be done during the Edinburgh Festival, or a Visiting Companies season.

The Traverse's remit was to produce the first two or three plays by new writers; as such, it's been the only theater in the United Kingdom to do exclusively new work. There are other theaters that do new work, the Royal Court, the Bush, Hampstead and Liverpool Everyman, but these theaters were as likely to do new plays by established writers. Nonetheless, they represent only a handful of theaters. The majority of publically funded theaters in this country are regional theaters that try to appeal to a large cross section of their community by producing a safe and conservative artistic policy. They do very few new plays, and then only those that have usually had commercial exposure elsewhere that their audiences might have heard of. If the Traverse then, which specializes in new plays, had trouble doing plays by writers outside this country, then the possibility of anyone else doing so became extremely limited.

Having said this, about the difficulty of non-UK writers being embraced here, there are some American playwrights from the non-commercial sector who have been taken up and perhaps even established by the commitment of individual British theaters to their work. There was Sam Shepard in the 1970s at the Royal Court, David Mamet at the Royal National Theatre and Richard Nelson at the Royal Shakespeare Company (RSC) in the 1980s. Shepard lived in England until the mid 1970s, and built up a network of contacts within the London theater world. Mamet and Nelson, on the other hand, write plays with strong narratives, which appeal to the traditional British theatergoer, or develop topics with immediate currency within the British community. And of course there are some playwrights such as August Wilson, whose work is already established and recognized, and therefore might make a more obvious case for being done here.

In all these examples the playwrights were directed by someone else, and championed by the artistic directors of those theaters. We have to remember that until the late 1980s and even in the 1990s there were few women directors and even fewer women artistic directors. It was mostly men who held positions of power within the British theater, and on the whole they reflected men's concerns. As is still the predominant case, we know from many walks of life that men share assumptions with other men, are responsive to them, therefore making it more difficult for women to gain recognition. Despite Caryl Churchill, who was championed by Max Stafford Clark at the Royal Court, there are still too few women involved in theater who might form their own networks of recognition.

I don't know whether Maria Irene Fornes chooses to direct her own plays, but the fact that she does so means that there is not that other person there to champion her, to bring her to a wider public. She develops her plays in the context of localized audiences, as both a writer and director, and as the writer she has to move on to the next challenge. What happens to her plays? In my experience artistic directors are more comfortable talking to other artistic directors, directors are more comfortable talking to other directors, than either of them are talking to the playwright. Without a director there, the writer will lose the normal bridge to mainstream theater. It may also be intimidating for a director if a writer directs their own play first. They may feel, despite the fact that we know this is naive, that the definitive production has been done. What is their creative input? Would they be transgressing the authorial voice?

It's also taken men a long time to deal with issues to do with women's relationships, the way men and women interact from a woman's point of view, despite British artistic teams, mainly of men, producing women writers like Caryl Churchill and Beth Henley. Some of that difficultly arises with women moving into central artistic spaces and how you handle those issues in terms of political correctness, or simply learning about them. But if people who are working within a conventional theater structure are to take on board plays from other voices then it has to be made advantageous to do so. On a superficial level exactly the same thing can be said for crosscultural theater, where the Arts Council has recently given some priority to work that is relevant to newly immigrant communities from Africa or Asia, the fallout from centuries of British imperialism. Art from other cultures, that doesn't have an immediate British context, simply has no visibility or is given no encouragement.

On a more profound level Maria Irene Fornes' plays belong in the tradition of Chekhov and resonate with other contemporary playwrights such as Franz Xavier Kroetz from Germany or Robert Holman in England, whose work I have produced. From my experience I would suggest that the main reason Maria Irene Fornes is not more widely known in the United Kingdom is that her work asks the audience to respond in ways that a British audience simply is not used to doing. I have spent most of my theater career trying to create a dialogue with an audience, rather than just feed people what they already know. To build a responsive audience takes consistent theater policy over an extended period of time. The most difficult work to introduce to an audience is the textually intense and lyric drama such as work from a writer like Fornes. For example something that each of these writers does in a different way is create texture in the script and on the stage. Kroetz slows you down so that time and place collapse. Fornes often does keep one space, but goes through many times, yet each change of time layers on top of the next, texturing, putting pressure on it, and getting a sense of density.

All of these writers write about ordinary people who would not usually think of putting themselves in a play. All three have a compassion for those characters that gives them an eloquence or language that they might not have if they were real. Although there's often an eloquence of words, there's also eloquence that points to their silences or their emptinesses. If theater is a middle-class pursuit in terms of audiences, which it is in the United Kingdom, then the middle classes never give themselves the space or time to be interested in people who don't share their values or their success — or perhaps they share the values but not the success. The middle class in England seems to be scared that if they don't keep priming society to work for them they will be vulnerable. They are so busy working the system for themselves they don't listen to other voices.

Maybe what's painful is that, even if the plays don't set out to remind us about it, because the writers are so caring about presenting the characters in their fullness, on some level middle-class audiences understand that they are middle class on the back of these characters. In these three writers, as in Chekhov, none of the writers seems to be judgmental, or overtly so, and that's what makes it difficult for any audience to dismiss the plays. The audience can't say "I disagree," it has to take it on board. What you learn has a way of infusing itself under your skin. Theater policies that try to encourage new ways of responding to different voices, do so by creating a dialogue over a period of time with the audience. There's an interdependency. You are asking people in the audience to learn and participate, to take the time to be involved so that they feel that they are doing something about the lives they see in front of them, rather than just feeling the pain. The plays ask the audience too not to be judgmental about the characters, and that's where you can get a dialogue.

Fornes, along with writers like Kroetz and Holman, are absolutely accessible. There's nothing weird or abstruse about the plays. They have great compassion and love for their characters — what's unfashionable about them is that they take their time, they get slowly to the moment, in the way that things are not sensationalist in life. Their plays are often placed in unassuming day-to-day settings; there's no escapism, it doesn't allow the audience into an obvious "good time," but it does makes important space for dialogue. There's a quietness in tone: making noises quietly.

# ❀ JILL DOLAN
*Theater Critic and Professor*
*University of Texas-Austin*

MUCH OF MY THINKING ABOUT FEMINIST performance theory and theater was formed as an awed spectator at productions of Irene Fornes' plays at Theater for the New City in the East Village of New York in the early 1980s.

In a small, narrow rectangle, spectators gathered to watch the magic we knew she would work in the even smaller stage space, directing her own plays with a simple, mesmerizing clarity of form and content, meaning and style. Watching the three characters in *Mud* move toward or against their inexorable destinies, I was moved, along with countless other feminist spectators, to contemplate the power of Fornes' dramaturgy to illuminate conditions of gender and class through the most compelling, clear theatrical gestures.

For me, Fornes' writing and directing has always proven the power of Brechtian theory when it's embodied in performance. Her characters demonstrate the illuminating social power of gestus, when their gestures on stage exemplify social relations as Fornes perceptively draws them. Her ability to historicize social relations, through her choices to place her characters in particular times or places (such as the unnamed Latin American country in *The Conduct of Life*, or the dislocated country estate in *Fefu and Her Friends)* allows her plays to resonate both universally and specifically in their call to real social relations.

Like many artists, Fornes is modest about the impact of her accomplishments. And like many female artists and artists of color, whose work hasn't received the wide recognition it deserves, I think Irene hasn't realized the lasting ways in which her writing and directing and teaching has influenced generations of theatergoers and students. My students hold her in great esteem and awe, since reading her plays opens worlds of dramatic interactions and compelling dramaturgy that their prior schooling in the conservative, traditionalist forms of American drama never revealed. These students are deeply affected by her work; they want to produce it, act in it, emulate it in their own writing and directing.

Although Irene sometimes stands back from feminist reclamations of her work, her plays and her thinking have been significant to feminist theater and performance criticism and theory for the last three decades. Very few women playwrights carve so viscerally, and sculpt so completely, the shape of gendered relations in contemporary American culture. Fornes' work tends to strike terror at the heart of patriarchy and bigotry, whenever spectators are smart enough to recognize the subtle but enormously influential meanings in her plays.

I know I speak for many, many feminist theater critics and students of feminist work when I say that Maria Irene Fornes has been one of the single most influential playwrights of our time. The way we imagine theater, and the great aesthetic and social things we expect from it, would be impoverished without her body of work.

# ✸ GAYLE AUSTIN
*Georgia State University*

## FEFU AND (ONE OF) HER (MANY) FRIENDS

IN THE SPRING OF 1977 I WENT TO A strange loft in downtown Manhattan to see a play. I didn't know that by the time I left, my life would be changed.

It was the first production of *Fefu and Her Friends*, produced and directed by Irene in that environmental, audience-moving-from-one-room-to-the-next style that would later be written about and analyzed, though rarely imitated by other playwrights. That night it was, for me, brand new. I knew of Irene, had even worked under her a few years earlier during another Theatre Strategy festival, but I knew nothing about the play except that I had been asked to go to it as part of my job, working at The American Place Theatre.

I was drawn into the play and the setting, sitting or standing in various rooms, watching eight women being together in a way I had never seen before on a stage. The play and the audience moved along, but there was no exposition, no rising action-crisis-climax structure, just women acting as women do, even though the costumes and the language made them seem at a distance in time from that day. I felt a growing excitement, an attraction to the women and their world. When it ended, I wanted to run onstage and call them all back, have tea in the living room, and tell them how much I liked them.

But the actors disappeared and I was left to find my way out. I couldn't walk — I started running, then skipping down the street. I passed the window of a Chinese restaurant and was not at all surprised to see my former theater history teacher from Hunter College having dinner with his wife. As if it were the most natural thing in the world, I waltzed in and began describing the play to him in great detail. At that moment

I realized I had fallen in love with the play, with the characters and its author.

I was assigned to Irene for the summer, to look into various uptown real estate options for transferring the play for another production by the American Place. Several sites were tempting, but too expensive or not up to code for public assembly. In the end, Irene designed the setting within the building of the American Place, and a somewhat different production opened that December.

In the two decades since then I've studied playwriting with Irene, interviewed her, written press releases for her, written articles about her work, watched rehearsals and held book on another play done by the Women's Project, and had many conversations. I've become an academic, written some plays of my own, and moved away from New York and Off-Off-Broadway theater. But the love remains. Something about *Fefu* is in most everything I do. Thank you Irene.

# ✸ LENORA CHAMPAGNE
*Playwright*

## NOTES ON ADMIRING FORNES

### I. MY FAVORITE FORNES WRITING EXERCISE

Those postcards. The only time I had the pleasure of doing an exercise led by Fornes herself was at St. Mark's Church. It was sponsored by the Ontological Theatre or the Poetry Project or maybe both, jointly, and she came in and talked to us about how every play should have a mystery in it (which hers always do). I knew something about it, because I'd directed *Fefu* at Trinity College in the mid 1980s and what did happen to that rabbit, anyway? (excuse me, I mean Julia). So she took out her postcards, which I'd heard about by then, and we each got one. (Mine had water and a tree and women and a man.) We had to write dialogue between two people in the postcard, and she gave us two lines to include in the scene. So we did, and some were read.

I'd heard about the exercise from Micki [Migdalia] Cruz or Holly Hughes, and I'd started using my own version in playwriting classes I taught. I'd bring in postcards from other times or places, or have the students bring them in, and you'd have to choose one and write a monologue. We'd read them out loud. Then you'd choose another one and write another monologue. We'd read that out loud. Then you had to put the two characters in a scene and have them talk to each other.

Now, maybe that is an exercise Fornes uses. It was what I thought she did, but when I actually got to do an exercise with her, the two people were on one postcard.

I've found either version to be terrific in teaching or writing, because it gets people to write about something elsewhere, something other, than yourself, and that's oddly freeing. Somebody else presents themselves to you, and all you have to do is let the character speak. It's a relief.

You're not starting with nothing. There's already somebody there. And from there, you see what happens.

Now.

## II. On Directing Fornes

What's frustrating about directing her work is that it's director proof. She's so specific, say, in a play like *Fefu* with a lot of entrances and exits, that it only works the way she's written it. Which testifies to how important it is that she directs her own work. She's said that she doesn't consider a play finished until she's directed it, and that's something I understand. That's when you know how it works in space, and a play is meant to exist there.

## III. The Figure

I love her plays and use them a lot in teaching (especially *Mud* and *Conduct of Life*). But what means so much to me as a writer is not only the plays, the work. It's Fornes the thinker, the worker, the personality, the character, if you will. The things she says and thinks about. Years ago, when I was first trying to write, I read an interview in which she said that, when she has to sit down to write, she decides to iron her blue jeans. (I believe it was starch and iron her blue jeans.) It was the perfect image of pointless activity, of desperate avoidance, and it helped me accept my own stategies and ambivalence. (I love to write, but you have to leave the world in order to do it, every time, and crossing that threshold is difficult.)

## IV. FORMAL STRATEGIES

Her formal devices are inventive and effective. And what she says about plot — *Fefu* being a plotless play, and all that — was crucial in reinforcing my desire to write for the stage using my own structures and forms.


## V. ELUSIVENESS OF KNOWING

Fornes' (or her characters') fascination with the desire to know (and frustration with the articulation of that desire, or the understanding of what they know) also makes her plays have a tremendous resonance for me. There is always, in each of her plays, tremendous desire, terrific restraint, and that tantalyzing mystery.

# ✹ BERNARDO SOLANO
*Playwright*

I SPENT TWO YEARS AT INTAR'S HISPANIC Playwrights Lab with Irene. She was my very first playwriting teacher and to this day I thank God I went to her before going to graduate school.

I remember one time a construction worker came to our door on 54th Street in the middle of a writing exercise with a sad story about losing his truck and needing money to get it out of the pound so he wouldn't get fired. Right away I gave him some money and convinced several others to kick in a few bucks. I was of course taken for a ride by this well-rehearsed con. And that's the kind of state being in Irene's lab put you in.

Irene taught me many things and here are a few of them: It's okay to write without knowing what or why or how; if you can see it in your mind and if you can hear the words, then it has value and you're a fool if you don't record it. It's okay to have a mission; that is, if you perceive a need and you think you can address it, then it's your sacred duty to try. It's okay to be naked. It's okay to impose structure at some point in the process, just don't wait too long. It's okay to write crap, because today's crap is tomorrow's fertilizer. It's okay to bleed, but please don't act it when you read. It's okay to use her exercises when you teach as long as you say where they came from. I'm sure that if I sat here a while I could come up with a bunch of other things, but in the spirit of an Irene exercise, my time is up and it's my turn to read.

# ✸ ELIZABETH WONG
*Playwright*

I STILL HAVE THEM, AND THEY STILL MAY have magical properties, despite their frayed/folded/torn/bent/neglected appearance. I am holding the homemade deck in my hand, the tired red rubberband stretched beyond endurance. I remember when I made these, lounging on a well-beloved/moth-eaten/hole-y baby blanket on the rooftop of a sixth-floor walkup, MacDougal Street below. The top card looks like this:

I made this deck of Tarot-like cards from standard index cards and a black felt-tip marker. The idea was sit down and let images and words and feelings arrange themselves on seventy-eight standard index cards, in whatever random manner, be they allegorical/mathematical/logical/nonsensical/cruel or kind or neutral. I thought it was a monumental waste of my time, and a childish exercise.

Back in the early 1990s, a marvelous playwright and professor Martin Epstein introduced a graduate school class at New York University to a play about an adolescent Cuban girl Sarita from the South Bronx. I was a new writer sitting up front per usual, the quiet one who took copious notes and rarely spoke, filled with facts and pyramidal thinking, scientific, tethered in clean logic, rooted to mental terra firma.

This day and that play *Sarita* was my first encounter with the work of Maria Irene Fornes, and the magical nature of ordinary objects. Until that day, I didn't understand the power of objects, how we imbue large meaning and heaping sentiment on a simple cup, or a fragment of cloth, or the pressed red rose in a Bible, how surprising mundane things can be transformed beyond their function or form. Both Epstein and Fornes suggested the transformative nature of objects, to put that into my writer's bag of tricks. Until *Sarita*, I was married to and happily fettered by pedestrian definitions and functionality. I trace my initial acceptance and experimentation with the sacred mystery of ordinary objects when Fornes' Sarita began telling fortunes with her cards.

I took my homemade cards and used them wherever I went for about one month, and like Sarita, I began to tell fortunes with them. Soon, I was constantly pestered with requests from friends to tell them their lives, past/present/future, with my Sarita insight and my Sarita cards. With this card:

I told Stacy she would meet and marry a man who didn't speak English as his first language. The next day, she met a war-torn Yugoslavian at a café we often frequented. With this card, I foretold imminent and unseen disaster:

I told Mark he needed to see a doctor. He did. The cancer was caught in its early stages.

Standard index cards with scribbles, wielding strange power and revealing strange coincidence. I put them away in a drawer, fearful of standard index cards with the power to compel a doctor's visit. Later, when I wrote my play *Kimchee & Chitlins*, a satire on American race relations, I remembered the Sarita cards and the power of imbued meaning to suggest/manipulate/force/cajole Change. I also took lessons from Fornes' *Drowning*, in which two potato-headed creatures Roe and Pea, celebrate and honor the lowly newspaper as if it were as monumental as the Dead Sea Scrolls.

Sacred objects. Ordinary objects. Sacred/ordinary.

Into the world of *Kimchee & Chitlins*, I placed such a sacred/ordinary thing in front of a Korean bodega for a Korean grocer to find. In the play, the grocer and the Black protesters, who are picketing the store, examine it — an innocuous basket. Look inside. Ordinary things — bird feathers, human hair, a girl's comb, a man's broken watch — but now transmuted, transformed by mutual Fear into a dangerous arsenal and agent of Hatred. It is a "wonga," a Haitian VooDoo practice, delivering its particular curse to the neighborhood of Flatbush, Brooklyn, with insidious intent to spread its hideous infection worldwide. In another play of mine, *China Doll*, there are Sarita-inspired objects — collected/coveted/adored objects — objects infused with unrequited love, namely, a napkin with a lipstick stain, and a half-smoked cigarette stained also by unattainable perfect lips. Sacred/Ordinary.

Favorite Fornes Exercise: Take any book. Open it. Wherever your finger lands, find a word. Use that word as the first of your first sentence. Begin writing. This exercise never fails to jumpstart or kickstart my writing.

# ❀ PAULA WESTON SOLANO
*Actor, Writer*


NEXT


WE WERE SITTING THERE, POST-EXERCISE,
listening to each other's work, trying not to think of our own, but just
trying to listen. Here we were with Irene. Irene, the woman who'd started
my husband, Bernardo Solano, as a playwright, a man whose work I
admire for the freewheeling images, the powerful emotion that hits you
from behind, the freedom, in general. Irene, who'd taught and influenced Caridad Svich, Lisa Loomer, Luis Alfaro, Leon Martell — friends
whose work I admire and countless others whom I'd never met, but
were all amazing and unique. Irene, who was largely responsible for the
Latino voice in theater today. Irene, who I'd been warned was tough.
I'd been told to prepare myself for harshness, up-front criticism... I'd
thought, "I can take it, I like directness. I'm just going to see for myself."
So I sat listening to the woman whose turn it was to read before me.
She had previously been an actress, so her reading was animated, she
just changed voices a bit to illustrate the difference in character. "Stop!"
Irene called. "Do not act. There is something that people do, which is
to act the writing, which intrudes on the listener's imagination, it imposes
the writer's interpretation. Just read it, without emotion, without acting." A blast of heat ran up my sides, shit, I am an actor first and a
writer second. I had written a character that I perform in my solo play.
How could I help but act her a little? That's what I do. It's how I think,
how I speak, for Christsakes! Shit. The poor woman whose work had
been interrupted by the small lecture had to continue. This time, without emotion. When she finished, another small discussion arose and
Irene went off on a couple other pet peeves. She started to talk about
how "some people these days try to be clever by writing in jargon, that
they consider to be cutting edge or street talk." That these people end

up writing all slang without substance. "They are so busy trying to show us how clever they are with their knowledge of this way of speaking, that they say nothing at all." I've stopped breathing, I can no longer control the squishing beneath my arm pits and I'm wondering if I should've just gone back to antiperspirant, fuck the aluminum or whatever is harmful about it. I, of course, have written this character who speaks in street slang. She is fifteen and part of the party crew scene in LA and says things like, "They are so down!" and "She was like, mad-dogging me." And I was thinking, oh shit, I am going to be skewered. I am going to be publically humiliated. I am going to be shamed for daring to call myself a writer, I should have just stuck to the humiliation and rejection I know as an actor. It's a fluke that I'm in here at all. I was amazed to be given the opportunity in the first place. Irene's casual, but focused gaze turns to me. Aren't we out of time for today? Isn't it time for a pee break? No, she is looking at me with this soft and expectant look, like she hardly knows who I am yet or maybe it means she has my number, has since day one. I take a breath, I've read writing exercises aloud so many times over the years, I can do this. I know you must not make excuses for your writing in advance, this is only a sign of self-consciousness or naivete, most people feel nervous, it's all stuff that's straight from inside you, without editing…just, I hear myself speaking, "I just have to say that I am completely intimidated" and I launch into explaining that everything that Irene has mentioned as bad in the last twenty minutes are things that I have done, probably. (Sure, I like directness.) With that, I say I will try not to act as I read, and I begin. I find that I am shaking under my words and that no matter how hard I try to suppress my emotion, I am caught up in the plight of the young girl I have just written and it is all I can do not to burst into tears. When I finish, there is silence. I turn, trying not to look straight into Irene's eyes. There is more silence. Finally, Irene says, "I usually don't say things like this, but I think because of what you said before, I should explain myself." Here it comes. She says, "I think what you wrote does not do what I said earlier. Even though I don't know people who talk like that, I think it sounded true and it wasn't just talking, to hear that way of speaking, she, the character, was really following her thoughts." I exhale. "Did you just write that all now?" Yes, I answer. "Well, good." Woa…I think I just escaped the horrible death of the writer in me. I think, maybe even, that was a compliment. Was it? Wow… "Next," she calls, and it is someone else's turn.

# ✸ TERESA MARRERO

*Assistant Professor of Latin American and Latino Literatures in the United States, University of North Texas*

## BEING IN A STATE OF MEMORY: NOTES FROM A FORNES WORKSHOP

I had the good fortune of attending a writing workshop with Maria Irene Fornes sponsored by ASK Theater Projects at UCLA, June 23–26, 1998. Thanks for this experience go primarily to Irene, Pedro Monge-Rafuls, Kym Eisner, Mead Hunter, and a grant from the University of North Texas. As primarily an academic (versus a creative) writer, I initially wanted to attend the workshop as research for a project that I had in mind. I asked Pedro and he gave me Irene's home number in NYC. I called Irene. She kindly agreed, but I had to speak to the people at the Audrey Skirball Kenis Foundation. Kym, executive director of the ASK Theater Projects (a private, not-for-profit outfit in Los Angeles) gave me one option: If I wanted to attend, I'd have to do it as a participant; send in a writing sample, and basically jump in the water! No safety net voyeurs allowed. OK, I said, great. This is the push I needed. I had been writing a novel for about a year. I had the hang of the narrative part, but needed a little help with the characters, especially one named Nenita, whom I had grown to dislike quite a bit in the course of my writing. I had come to the point where my personal aversion for Nenita was showing and part of me felt this was not fair to her. But, I had no idea what to do next. I stopped writing a few months before. So, I submitted a chapter of the novel and discussed my trouble with this particular character. It wasn't a play; but then again character development is character development, no matter the medium. Right? I had no idea what I was in for, except the intuition that this was something

I wanted very much. As a Latina/o theater researcher, I have been reading about Irene's famed workshops for years! I was too late for the long, leisurely ones at INTAR, but UCLA for the better part of a week sounded pretty good.

I arrived feeling like a spy: an academic in writer's clothing. There were about nineteen others there.[1] Mead Hunter, editor-in-chief of *Parabasis* and director of literary programs for ASK Projects was there to greet us. Actually he stayed during the entire workshop and proved to be a delightful person. After listening to the chatter in my head for many hours, I decided to relax into the whole thing. Then it got better. Nobody cared what kind of a writer I was. We each had our own personal goals. As an outsider from Los Angeles, I realized that I had fewer restraints in terms of "the work." I was out of the local "scene," which I came to realize was a blessing. There's a Buddhist saying that for the expert there are many limitations, but for the beginner, who knows less, also sees more possibilities. I fell into the beginner's category: This was my first writer's workshop, and it was with the person I had most admired. The rest was gravy. In this open state, I put most of my insecurities aside and relaxed, listened, visualized, and wrote. I wrote A LOT. The person next to me at one point commented on my constant scribbling. She couldn't fathom what all I was writing. I responded: "Everything. Everything that comes out of Irene's mouth, I am writing." Her reply was a rather soundless, "Oh."

So, the material for my contribution to this wonderful anthology that Caridad (my dear buddy and co-editor of *Out of the Fringe, Contemporary Latina/o Theater and Performance*) and the delightfully witty Maria Delgado have organized comes out of my notes from this encounter with Fornes. I have added a verb or subject here and there so that it makes sense as written text. They have an orality that is part of what they were originally: spoken words. Irene's way of speaking, the way she entonates her vowels, slightly open, makes me think of the renowned Mexican writer, Elena Poniatowska: the same melodic tone accompanied by vowels that linger in the air, suspended words that defy gravity, never wanting to land.

Irene's session with us focuses on her sense of the creative process. There are digressions as is natural of improvised speech. However, Irene's concentration on the subject in her mind's eye invariably brings the conversation back. The following are my notes from what transpired. Comments by students remain anonymous in order to protect everyone's privacy. My own visualization experience is written here in abbreviated form, again from my notes. My notes of Irene's comments are written in italics.

TUESDAY, JUNE 23, 1998, DAY ONE

*We are going to be looking at the exploration rather than the rules. You know, when something is so true, so right, when the thing pulls you. You want to get nearer to it; you want to get to know it better. Sometimes you push it away and a door opens, then you can just follow it. The ability to create is related to the state of dreaming. Even if you know it didn't happen, you can feel the impact. We feel frightened or hurt, or maybe it can be very simple. But we know that there is some truth there.*

*It is also important to learn to go into a peaceful, quiet place. In theater, we need to go into it, this place of peace and quiet, versus what we hear in the theater now: the negative, like tension, conflict, etc. It's easier [to go into the negative tension], because there is power in it. It's like the pot boiling, letting steam off. If it happens, then let it, but don't go looking for it. The writer should do real examination. Examine it with attention and patience. Understand how important it is when your character speaks a line, which by itself you'd think, so? But, it is so important [to pay attention to the character's speaking]. That is like the ground underneath, the foundation. The writer needs to recognize it.*

*I feel that the way to really concentrate is through visual imagery. Visual imagery is the passageway. Stanislavky started something very interesting, but he also started part of the problem. Stanislavky began the whole idea of the objective, and how attractive [this idea] has become to our materialist, structured world. The idea of purpose and final result is so overwhelming!*

*I grew up in a tropical, Latin country where the result is not the most important thing. In Cuba there was (at least when I lived there) a common activity of every citizen in the afternoon of just watching. In Havana*

*center, on the porch, you could see people coming and coming, for no pur-*
*pose. Not to gossip, just for no reason. Or from the balcony you could watch*
*them from the time they came around the corner and you watched until*
*the person disappeared from view. We were not consciously doing anything.*
*You know it's time to relax. I think the first time I noticed this was when*
*I did a piece with Hispanic actors in New York. And one of them said that*
*he liked to go to the Cloisters and sit there in the afternoon, "comiendo*
*mierda."* [2] *It means just wasting time, not doing anything. Here [in Cal-*
*ifornia] people may do it on the beach. But they do it because it's "good for*
*you." And I feel that the "purpose" or "objectives" have also come into the*
*theater, into the novel.*

    *Strasberg always spoke moment to moment. Then something happens*
*and you deal with that moment. I was invited to the Actor's Studio, the*
*playwriting unit, and he was always talking about moment to moment. I*
*don't know if Stanislavsky was misinterpreted on the "objectives"…maybe*
*it was more for the directors than the writers. For the writing has to have*
*vitality. That is the thing you have to have as a writer: vitality.*

    *Through the influence of the National Endowment for the Arts, the*
*theater has become an institution. The university also saw an opportunity*
*to have a new department, which brought in money. Imagine learning stage*
*management in the university! Before people learned by working and adjust-*
*ing themselves to the director, who used to be the boss! Now, the stage man-*
*ager is in charge of keeping the union rules, so sometimes it is the stage manager*
*that tells the director what to do!*

    *Douglas Baher Hill was the only person teaching playwriting at Yale.*
*(O'Neill took a class with him). But he was the only one. Now, because*
*the university has to set up curricula for playwriting, acting, stage man-*
*agement, directing, the whole thing becomes a structure. They are going to*
*teach the playwright how to structure. The playwright now serves the direc-*
*tor. What I object to is how boring the structure is! In that whole construct,*
*there is no allowance for art.*

    *The traditional formula is the exposition, development, conflict, cri-*
*sis, climax, and denouement. Can you imagine what would have happened*
*to painting if it had followed suit? Artists need one collector and a few peo-*
*ple to follow, whereas theater needs to have lots of people to pay a little bit.*
*For the playwright, she has to construct speech that sounds real, and structure*

*it like a painting, and then the whole thing has to have heart. The whole thing is very difficult for the playwright.*

*I do feel that the way to go about it is through visualization. Then you go very near the character, and you allow them to say things that have nothing to do with what you want to do, Maybe they'll start telling you things that you find interesting. It happens in dreams. Since Freud we know that our subconscious knows more than we do. If we can get closer, we can become more attentive. We have to learn to allow for the characters to speak. Take down what they see. Learn when the characters are blabbing. When they start doing this when you loose your concentration. Visualization is the way to learn to concentrate.*

Irene then passed out black-and-white photographs, from which we took two each. They all seemed to be from the turn of the century. She asked us to see which one spoke to us. I ended up looking at one that had a group of people, maybe five women, a man, a child, and a dog. There was a road off to one side of them, a prairie, and low hills in the background. The women wore ankle-length skirts. One wore a long apron. The dog lay at her feet. All the rest were nicely dressed. One younger woman leaned into the apron lady. On the other side stood a matronly, well-dressed lady. It was sunny, probably midday. Evidently this was a family with a reason to gather. The reason was not evident.

Irene led us through an exercise aimed at learning to see every detail possible. Afterwards, she asked us to close our eyes. She then began to ask us questions about what we had seen in the picture. This all seemed to take quite a while. When we opened our eyes, she had us draw every detail from the scene from memory. We then went back into our mind's eye. She led us through a number of questions, stimulating our observatory ability. She then spoke five sentences. They seemed arbitrary, such as: "I am going to tell them you came." She instructed us to listen to see if any of the people we were holding in our mind's eye wished to speak. We may or may not use the sentences she had given us. I had no problem with my set of people. Very quickly the lady with the long apron took over the conversation. She was very impatient to be standing still, wasting time as she said, on this photo session. Uncle Ned was coming by shortly and they would all have to eat soon. She had to get back to the kitchen. There was still a lot of baking to do. As I listened to these strangers come alive, I filled six pages worth of descriptions and dialogue between them. Somehow, they were old friends, although I had never seen them before.

Irene called time and we stopped writing. It was time to end the session.

I left feeling pretty high, like a new space had opened in my life. A space where anything is possible and many, many voices previously unheard live.

## WEDNESDAY, JUNE 23, DAY 2

I wrote in my diary that today's theme seemed to be "rattling, babbling and chatty." I was pretty impatient to get back to the visualization, but today, Irene felt like talking instead. We were trying to get through the whole room by way of introducing ourselves. I did not record all of that. It bored me. Instead, whenever Irene picked up on a particular point from a student's comments about their own work, I wrote those.

The introductions continued, and someone mentioned that her work is based on doing adaptations of other people's work. The word "explication" came in. Irene asked if it felt like an explanation of the importance of her work. The student replied yes.

*If there is a substance in you that is curious, that curiosity which prompts complete focus and attention, that is the most important thing. Once you think you know it, you have it, then you've lost something important as a writer and certainly as a human being. As long as you are curious, it means you are hungry for it. Then it will expand. The discovery. The hunger, the curiosity for the sweet things but also for the dark side. It is that hunger, that curiosity which will pull you to the interesting part of your work. When the hunger stops, it means it has died. It is just like to make pretend that you are in love with someone, when you are not. You don't fool anybody, not the other person, not yourself.*

*There is a very thin line between following your rhythm, your curiosity, and the thing that the machine does when it goes on and on, not getting anywhere. You have to know when to stop. How do you know that? You have to pay attention. If you stop a moment, you can really tell what part of you is really engaged. Well, that's not true. I don't know which part. But you can tell if you stop and consider. It's like making love, you know when you are really present. Let's think of a conversation rather than lovemaking. It's taking an interest. You know when you've had a real conversation because you were moved. Look for that experience when you are reading what you've written. The material takes you back. It makes you want more. Let a little time pass. I feel that my way of playwriting is not conducive to a great career (scattered laughter). But it is conducive to art. Don't even think that anyone will want to produce your work (nervous giggling). It's a sort of madness. You might as well enjoy it (burst of laughter)!*

Someone else commented that she was looking for a connection between herself and what she wrote, the source of which is usually outside of herself. But she wanted to make sure that she is on the page also. Irene commented on the outside stimulus:

*Make sure to pay attention to what grabs you not because it's a good character for a play or whatever, but because you want to know more about it. You are interested "because." You should not go there "because." There should no "because," but rather the thing should draw you. Following the very direct route is not necessarily the best way to get there.*

Someone spoke about the "earned pause" when nothing needs to be said or done. So much in acting there's a pause between the lines that is dead. It's important to follow emotional rhythms.

*In creative acting we should never be sure of where we are going. Strasberg's moment by moment. There should be no objectives. If you know where you are going, then the walking gets duller. Look at moment by moment as a form of investigation, not at all as in "follow the line." We know in acting the value of improvising, but the writer has to figure out from day to day where the whole thing is going — from day one.*

Someone else commented that he wants to create characters that are idiosyncratic on an emotional level. It could be by means of the language the character uses or because of the passions that are unusual or perverse.

*Rather than shifting the work to a middle ground, write two plays. Think of it as having different types of conversation like, the kind you'd have with an older person versus the conversation you'd have with your fiancée. Write another version, rather than censor yourself! (Most emphatic).*

Another person says that their work is often criticized for being "too wordy."

*See if the character is out of connection with the person that he/she is supposed to be speaking with. See if you, as a writer, are disconnected, if your emotions are not engaged. Rattling happens when we've lost the contact with the other person. Other times we are disconnected with the thing we are talking about. Intimacy is related by demeanor, by the tone of the voice, by body positioning. Intimacy is the opposite of chatter.*

After lunch we continued on the theme of objectives.

*Objectives lead to the future; they take you away from the moment. If every moment is alive, then you have dramatic action.*

Question: If you are not aware of objectives, how do you know when the piece is over?

*There is a "natural" end; one needs to be aware of the possible conclusion. It could very well be that the play does not have an interesting ending. It's not when; it's how it ends. If you relax with it, it will end for you. You cannot really invent an end. If you let it run itself out, it will end for you. You have to have objectivity. Leave it alone and get back to it later. Let the play end.*
*When the characters are listening to each other really well, they are explaining themselves to each other. Because real conversation is like a ping-*

*pong game where you don't know where the ball is coming back. The most difficult thing is the shifting back and forth of the characters. You have to be psychotic almost. When the character speaks you have to have the patience to shift mentally to the other characters.*

*In rereading my own material, I find sometimes that I am favoring one character over the other. The other is just a springboard. Then you go back and rewrite the springboard, just a better springboard. This doesn't work either. Then what happens? Well, the conversation ends. You have to go back and rewrite the conversation. The load of the conversation usually falls to one person, as it happens in real life. Keep responding. Try to see to it that the responding character is not an echo.*

A participant asks a question about how to hear the characters through a reading. She commented that sometimes the feedback she gets in staged readings doesn't work for her.

*The whole idea of feedback is the most preposterous and asinine thing in the world! Mamet is a great one for dialogue, if his stuff were work-shopped…(laughter)…they [the commentators] don't know what they are talking about. I think it came from the movies, where they show a movie to teenagers to see if they like it. The feedback needs to be focused on the writing, asking questions, not rewriting your play. At INTAR, all of the feedback to the readings were given to the playwrights in writing, instead of being spoken. It is more serious. Writing gives people the chance to think things through.*

Personally, I felt disconnected from today's session at the time. Too much talking. No creative writing. I hope tomorrow we write!

## Thursday, June 25, Day 3

I guess Irene read my mind. Today we began with visualization. No more lecture. Yes! We began with a place, any place that came to us. She led us with a series of questions: Where were we? Inside? Outside?

Was it cold? What did the place smell like? Where were the shadows? Was there anyone else present? What did they look like? Did they have fillings in their teeth? The details of her questioning lead me to the forest, a highland wilderness area. There were two men, who did not speak, a girl, and older man and a fully grown elk. Yes, an elk. The two young men did not speak to each other. The girl asked the older man why. He said they were waiting for her permission. She thought it amusing. "If they need my permission to speak, then let them wait. Let them figure out that they need to break the rules in order to gain the right to speak!" The girl went off down a path with the older man. The elk disappeared between the tall evergreens. The two men followed silently. After looking at the older man more closely, I realized that it is Armando, a character from my novel, the one I had stopped writing because of Nenita, his daughter. He does not know why he is here, in this strange landscape. The last time I saw Armando was in Mexico, where I left him for several months. He wondered what's happened. Now, he was confused. However he is aware that I called him here, now. I have wished it. His mind does not go beyond this idea. He doesn't know what role he is playing now, if he is a stranger, a lover, the father, a friend, a priest, a figment of my imagination. He does not know if he is "real." It doesn't matter. He is here. They began to walk and the girl told him her dream: "I had a terrible dream where all of the voices were muffled and it was night and a woman was being beaten by a man. Actually whipped by a man with a leather belt. It was her husband. She fought back, but her long white gown got in the way. She had him nearly pinned down to the ground in the middle of the street. He told her: Here, let me help you take off your dress. That way you can fight better and won't trip. He did help her take off the gown, lifting it over her head. Then, seeing the advantage, he took the belt and began to whip her bare skin. I ran for help. I was afraid he'd kill her. The 911 number did not work. I was desperate and did not know what to do where to find the right number. There were others gathered around, waiting to see what I'd say to the police. I said 'Hurry, they're in the seventy block of La Verne Street. Dial 811.' The 811 worked. I explained fast. In seconds the police arrived and cordoned off the area."

The scene went on, shifting back to the wilderness, the older man and the two silent young men. The girl said: "I am tired of knowing which way things will go. I am tired of knowing all the angles." Irene called time.

*The moment the writer tries to deliver the lines, the connection is lost. Particularly the speech. The further away you are from what you want to say to the audience, the better. The distance from your goal. We have to be careful in writing as in acting: forget the intention in a scene. Just concentrate on the moment. The minute you feel that the actor knows where she is going, it becomes flat. Go to an acting school and learn to write there! [Samuel] Beckett's lines have a sense of reality, of truth, even the characters say a strange line, and it's repeated because it is real to the character. Sense memory includes visualization, among other things, such as sounds, temperature, and smells. If the writer really, really visualizes when she writes, then when we read it, we can tell. Being in a state of memory.*

## FRIDAY, JUNE 26, DAY 4

Yesterday at lunch I finally had the opportunity to ask Irene my question: What does one do with a character that one grows to dislike, not fully aware why? The first thing Irene asked me was if I really knew this character. I thought I did. After mulling it over, I realized that a pivotal part of Nenita's background was missing. The novel began with her father, Armando. He had been widowed for some time. Nenita was fully grown. Even though her mother had been dead for years, the fact remained: I did not know Nenita's mother. Neither did I know Armando's life as a husband. On day four we began with visualization. Nena, Nenita's mother came in full force. The whole thing took me back to Cuba, in the '50s (although the novel was taking place in the present, in New York and in English). Nena appeared youthful, in a spaghetti-strap summer dress, with a black ponytail, red lips and no other makeup. She had on little gold hoop earrings. Nenita was about five years old. They were together on a beautiful, breezy day near the Malecón, by the boardwalk downtown. Mother and daughter were dressed alike, headed toward

Copelia, an outdoor ice cream parlor in Havana. I followed them all afternoon. I wrote everything I saw. Nena had a lover. Armando had known. Nenita used to see everything. By the end I understood Nenita. The whole thing was written in Spanish, as I heard them speak. I realized that without knowing the mother, I could never know the daughter. Nena will never appear in the novel. However, the time I spent knowing her became essential. A roundabout way of getting "there." Irene called time.

*We deceive ourselves when we think that certain phrases peculiar to a place make the character. It is not. It happens when the speech comes from the organism of the person versus those modes or identifiable place or class.*

*It happened in* Mud. *The characters there are American, the kind of Appalachian speech. But it's a prejudice to think that poverty comes from Appalachia. I thought: Later I'll find out how these people speak. But I never did. There was a technical person there from Appalachia, who later came to tell me he liked my play. The only place people had to work was in an Army base. The only way to get anywhere was for the guys to join the army or the girls to marry a soldier. I asked the technical person: Does it seem real the way these characters speak? He said, Yes, it's very accurate. This is how they talk. And I thought, This is impossible. The only knowledge I have of the way these people talk is from the movies in the '30s from Hollywood. Bette Davis movies. And I said, It's impossible. And he said, It is possible that it's not about how the person talks, but how they think. And I said, Yes, you are right.*

*If we are very confident that we know the language or social class of these people, and we know how they talk, then we create clichés. When you are closer to the character's feelings, what is in their heart, then you are closer to creating a real character. What I'm talking about is not relying on the formula or the cliché. By feeling and experiencing the character more carnally, their physical presence, the way the person breathes, the temperature of the person, then you experience the character not a cliché.*

*The moment you look for something "good," you don't pay attention to something little, something amorphous, the juice and liquids of things. I think writers need to learn to feel naked, to expose themselves. Constantly.*

*It has to be visceral. You can tell when an actor does it. You can tell when the writer writes it.*

It's taken me a year to get back to these notes. Today, as I reread them, the wisdom of the madness feels as real as it did a year ago. Which reminds me of how much I love to sit at my computer and see, hear, smell, suffer with these people that come to me. The slightly psychotic state. At this point, I am enjoying the ride. I returned home and finished the novel. Nenita and I made our peace. I had changed and so had she. Unexpectedly, without a visible goal in sight, the novel ended. I knew when it was time.

1. Actually, the participants were: Wendy Belden, Irene Borger, Norma Bowles, Ricardo Bracho, David Burton, Michelle Carter, Jorge Cortiñas, Leo Garcia, Steve Morgan Haskell, Peg Healy, Hallie Hobson, Brenda Krantz, Lisa Kron, Mona Mansour, myself, Susan Sabel, Nancy Sackett, Paula Weston Solano, Erica Paley Stevens, and Mark Van Wye.

2. *Comer mierda* literally means to "eat shit." It is a very Cuban way of saying not doing anything in particular, just "spacing out," being distracted.

# ✹ CANDIDO TIRADO
*Playwright*

IN 1982 I WAS LIVING IN A ROOMING HOUSE on 51st street. Most of the residents were alcoholics. I was under the impression that a true artist had to live under these conditions to earn the title artist. I was working at NYU Medical Building in the records department. For anyone who has been spared the records department of any institution, I can help you visualize it by just saying "Dante's Inferno." That spring I had gone to see the reading series INTAR was having for their alumni of the Playwriting workshop. I was determined to become a member the next year. Besides being in a group of professional playwrights led by Maria Irene Fornes, I'd be getting paid. At the time I had written one play, *Some People Have All the Luck*. It was my college thesis play. The deadline was approaching while I was making some final changes. As I made my way to INTAR's office the sky opened up and the rain came down in buckets. I put the script inside my shirt but it still got wet. I saw this as a good sign instead of being distraught. Somehow I knew I would be selected. Perhaps I needed to be selected because I couldn't continue working in Dante's Inferno. A few months later I received the call. I'd been selected for the coming year workshop. I immediately quit my job. A week before the workshop there was a getting-to-know-you party for the lucky playwrights asked to participate. I was wearing a cool black jacket that Fornes liked a lot. I turned out to be the youngest playwright in the group.

Like many writers who have been in the workshop, I feel the workshop saved my life. It legitimized me at a time when I was just beginning my adventure in the theater. It wasn't always a smooth ride. Sometimes it would get bumpy. Fornes and I sometimes would clash over seeming insignificant details. In thinking back, I'd like to blame myself for these tiffs, but an artist has to be stubborn while yet possessing a flexible mind, so perhaps it was my conation taking over. As the years passed, I've thought Fornes was right on many of the clashes. Ah, we live and learn.

I was having a lot of trouble with many of her exercises in the earlier part of the residency. It was a new way of thinking for me and I was a bit too rigid. I didn't like these free-association kind of exercises where the writing was totally intuitive. I liked the structured kind of writing where one plus one equals two not three. Then one day she gave an exercise that had a great impact on me and opened me up, allowing me to think differently about the craft. Fornes asked us to envision ourselves walking up to a stranger. After a brief description she told us to hug them. Now write what the stranger said. At that time I was supplementing my playwrights salary with hustling chess on 50th Street and Broadway. A street magician, after doing his act would come and play me and lose a few dollars. He was a curmudgeon, bitter and cutting. I imagined hugging him. He reacted by pushing me away and asking me what the hell was I doing? Then he told me if I did that again, he'd kick my ass. I told him it was a writing exercise; that he wasn't even real. I'd conjured him up from my imagination. He demanded that I let him go. I told him I couldn't until I finished the exercise. He gave me to three or he was going to make me disappear. I asked him how could he make me disappear if he was in my mind. I wasn't in his. He was stumped. He then told me to hurry up and finish the exercise so he could leave my mind. I finished writing and promised him that the next time I wanted to summon him up I'd ask permission first. He was cool with that. As I said good-bye I went to hug him, but he moved quickly away from me and began doing his magic act for the lunch crowd.

Fornes liked what I wrote a lot. I also thought I'd broken through my inability to allow the situation to just happen rather than to control it with plot. The value of that writing exercise was such that I've never forgotten it.

When I think of the kind of influence Maria Irene Fornes has had in the American theater, it is mind-boggling. For Fornes is a Latina Woman and the American theater doesn't even think that Latinos are part of the American theatrical equation. Two years ago, for the first time, they began to have a dialogue with the African American community. Our omittance is true absurd theater. That is why the respect Fornes invokes in white artists, who would never go to a Latino theater, is astonishing. I'd like to thank Maria Irene Fornes for all she's accomplished in the theater and may she write for another hundred years.

# ❋ HEATHER DUNDAS
*Playwright*

## MEETING IRENE

IT FEELS A BIT SHADY FOR ME TO BE CONTRIBUTING to a book about Irene Fornes, as I am one of the few writers I know who has never taken a class from her. I don't know why this is, exactly. Certainly it's not a plan or a statement on my part. I've just never been in the right circumstance to study with her.

Which is not to say that I've never run into her. In my fifteen years in the theater, I've run into her many times — at plays, at readings, at a reception or two. Though I of course recognize her, and have come to enjoy watching her take in, with owl-like intensity, any number of theatrical experiences, I doubt she has any idea who I am, even though we have been introduced at least half a dozen times. Every time I am introduced to her she never reveals any inkling that we have met before, a fact I've always attributed to the volume of people she must meet, to my unmemorable small talk, to absentmindedness, to shyness. Lately, though, I've started to wonder: Is this seeming ignorance a deliberate tactic with her? A game? A strategy? Is it possible that she's maintaining a distance because she's enjoying watching me — not me in particular, of course, but me as part of the collective — as much as I'm enjoying watching her?

Because watching Irene can be fascinating. A couple of years ago I sat next to her during the opening night of a production of one of her plays. The director, who was an acquaintance of mine, had invited me, but I hadn't known I was going to serve as escort for Irene until I walked in that night. I was daunted at the prospect of having to entertain a theatrical legend, and I'm timid by nature, but having been strictly brought up to fulfill a certain standard of southern hospitality I did my best to sit and make small talk with her until the play began. Though we were continually interrupted by people Irene did know stopping to say hello, Irene was gracious and kept up her end of the stilted conversation, much to my relief.

Unfortunately, almost as soon as the lights — actually, now that I think of it, before the lights went down — Irene began to object to the production. The opening moment was wrong. The staging deviated unforgiveably from her stage directions. Irene carefully pointed these errors in a loudish stage whisper. Oh no, I thought, what to do now? "Oh," I murmured back, "it will get better…" But it didn't, and in fact, Irene muttered complaints to me throughout the play. She truly despised one actor's approach to her character. Another actor was okay but misinterpreted certain crucial scenes. Since the director was obviously expecting me to act as her ambassador, I didn't feel I could respond with anything but diplomatic platitudes. "Hmmm," I kept whispering, "Really?" As the play dragged on and Irene's outrage continued, my attempts at soothing her grew more and more desperate and ever more banal. Irene eventually gave me this puzzled, "Are you really such an idiot?" look — I was hideously uncomfortable the whole time and so sorry that I couldn't really communicate with her at all. (And now that I think about it I've probably discovered why Irene can't remember me — I gave her nothing but smokescreen and who would want to remember that?)

Eventually, as the horrible night wore on, I gave up trying to soothe her and just watched her watch her play. The piece being presented was more than ten years old — surely she must have seen it dozens of times before. She sat rigid in her seat, leaning forward, glaring at the stage. When a moment worked she would nod involuntarily, and when it didn't she'd shudder and glance over at me to make sure I knew. Her intensity, her absolute focus, her ability to be elated by a line well-delivered, and the next moment truly wounded by a botched delivery…this was something to note, something to admire. Hospitality and graciousness were comfortable, but this, this complete uninhibited engagement with the work — this was something alive, something worth watching, something to remember. This was magnificence.

Since that opening I have reread and enjoyed that particular play, and have seen several other moving productions of Irene Fornes work.

And as I grow older I find myself more comfortable with her language, her passion, the same way I feel ever more familiar with that of her predecessor, Virginia Woolf. Since that night I have also had several more in-person Fornes encounters. We've been introduced a few more times, said hello, shaken hands. I have not, however, been asked to chaperone her again, nor have I repeated my attempts at small talk. Instead I have come to enjoy watching her from a distance as she takes in with owl-like intensity, any number of theatrical experiences. And I suppose you could say I've learned from studying Maria Irene Fornes, though not from taking her class. Indeed by watching her watch so intensely — by witnessing her full surrender to the experience of her own work — I believe I've deepened my understanding of what it is to be an artist.

And I still look forward to meeting her. Again.

@ LAWRENCE KORNFELD
*directed* Promenade *at Judson Poets
Theatre & The Promenade Theatre, NYC;
also* Successful Life of 3 *at Judson;
friend since 1963*

A SONNET FOR MARIA IRENE FORNES

Irene, dusting the corners of reality picks up
fragments of everyday: turning words in her hands,
she looks life in the eye and sees an ear — surely
she knows the ear is not an eye, but it doesn't

matter: she goes on listening in your mouth and
sees a mother. So, then is when she laughs: (she's
short on tears and laughing takes their place) Her
laughter is an opinion on life: get on with it! Over

many centuries she sifts the ruins of perception
for oddities of reality: pieces of life that dropped
from birds in transit, or rose from the earth as
seedlings left alone by snakes or larger little things.
That's it: her big things are born out of small eyes.
Reality is the life she travels lived in total surprise.

Ed Shea (Greta)

*WHAT OF THE NIGHT?*
Trinity Rep., Rhode Island, 1989

Photo by Anne Militello

# ❀ MARIA IRENE FORNES
## DISCUSSES FORTY YEARS IN THEATRE
## WITH MARIA M. DELGADO*

DELGADO: Rather than start at the beginning I want to begin by asking you about your most recent works like *The Summer in Gossensass.*
How did that play come about?

FORNES: I used to find reading plays difficult. The descriptions of
the characters, their actions and moods were so minimal that I frequently
found myself lost as to what they were doing or what was the significance of what they said. *Hedda Gabler* was the first play I read from
start to finish without stopping. The dialogue was so clear that it immediately invoked living images in my mind. When John Dillon asked
me to direct a play at the Milwaukee Repertory Theatre for the 1986–87
season, I immediately chose *Hedda Gabler.* While discussing the play
with the cast I discovered that my impressions of Hedda and of the
whole play were different from the impressions they had. They believed
that Lovborg was Hedda's love, (I thought the start of his name Lov
contributes to that belief) that he is handsome and romantic. And that
Hedda was forced to marry Tesman for the sake of stability and financial security. I was amazed. I wondered if they had seen a Hollywood
version of the play. I read the play over trying to see if I had misinterpreted everything. My views didn't change. I didn't think Ibsen intended
for Lovborg to be a poetic, dissolute leading man. I thought the photo
album scene makes it quite clear that she is not attracted to him while
it is clear that he is quite attracted to her.

I also thought the belief that Hedda's unusual character was caused
by her being brought up without a mother by a military father who
raised her like a boy was quite bizarre. The only thing the play says about
her father is that she went riding with him. Which seems like a nice

thing for a father and daughter to do. And that she looked beautiful in her riding outfit. They say that the fact that he raised her as a boy was what made her turn out the way she did. I wrack my brain trying to figure out what in Hedda's character is masculine when she is the perfect picture of the glamorous, stylish, camp superbitch with a great sense of humor. What boy do you see pulling his friend's hair the way she is said to have pulled poor Thea's hair. That she has a picture of her father in the living room seems to me more to indicate that the house is her house and not Tesman's house rather than that she has some sort of fixation on her father. When I read the play I didn't believe for a moment that she is in love with Lovborg. Just look at the way she treats him and you'll see that she's not in love with him.

Being curious about the name Lovborg I looked up the word in a Norwegian dictionary and discovered that it means "dead leaf". Not very likely the name an author would choose for the romantic hero, (unless Norwegians find dead leaves romantic). I also suspect that Ibsen did not intend Hedda to be pregnant, that when he had her say…"In my condition…" rather than implying she is pregnant, he is showing her gall and cunning, pretending to be pregnant (as if pregnant women go around burning manuscripts) to justify the burning of Lovborg's book, which she burns, not as the romantics believe, because the book represents Lovborg's and Thea's child, but because the destruction of the book means that Lovborg will not get the job Tesman seeks. I think Ibsen was more interested in showing her cunning that in justifying her.

Each detail of what is the prevalent interpretation of the play seems to be as if concocted by a Hollywood team of script writers trying to turn a fine play into a laughable soap opera. Audiences at the turn of the century may have needed a justification to enjoy and love Hedda but today we can get a kick out of people like her as long as they are not part of our real life. In the play it is quite clear that Lovborg is not a dashing romantic hero, that Hedda had no interest in the house Tesman bought for her. She says, in their rides when he took her home, she talked about the house to make conversation and relieve him of his discomfort because the poor man had no conversation. However the public and critics insist that Tesman bought her the house of her dreams.

It was these recognitions that first got me thinking. There were also some details like Lily Langtry being cast to play Hedda Gabler in the first English production. She couldn't do it so they kept cutting bits from the play. Then Elizabeth Robins, an American actress who was living in London, got the rights to stage the play. I thought there were enough interesting things about getting the production together which would let me discuss the interpretation of the play. While they are rehearsing I can have them talking about the play.

DELGADO: So the first production of *Hedda Gabler* in London becomes a narrative framework for you to hinge a new reading of the play?

FORNES: Yes, but what then happened was that I found the person of Elizabeth Robins so interesting. She was a novelist, playwright, and actress who then went on to perform in other English premieres of Ibsen plays like *The Master Builder* where you also have a young woman who takes possession of a man. Ibsen was obsessed with the personality of a woman who was very attractive, enigmatic, and interesting. She's not just a little sexy, there's something a little odd about her. Before he wrote *Hedda Gabler*, when he was around sixty-three, Ibsen met Emilie Bardach, a young girl of around eighteen or nineteen, in the place where he spent his family summer vacations. He and his wife and son went there to Gossensass in the Tyrol when his son was little. One year, I think he went alone and he met this young girl who was also there with her mother for the summer. He had a platonic relationship with her that was in a sense similar to Hedda's relationship with older men. Either the girl was controlling or else he was so afraid of being enamored of her that he saw her as manipulative. When he went back to Oslo, he told his medical doctor, who was a good friend of his, that he had met this girl who was enigmatic and fascinating. He claimed she wanted to grab him, but instead it was he who grabbed her for his play. So it's quite clear that what he was writing was not a little social soap opera. You can see that when you read the play. Hedda has a power that is almost mystical. She subjugates all the men in the play. As badly as she treats people there is something so attractive about her.

I wrote a draft of the play but didn't get fully to the question of interpretation because I got so involved in the first production of the play and Elizabeth Robins. I found out how she produced the play with very little money but help from George Bernard Shaw and Arthur Archer, the translator of Ibsen who was a good friend and possibly her lover. Robins wrote novels and plays and became a suffragette. In the first production of *The Summer in Gossensass* in January 1997, Elizabeth Robins was taking over. I had to think that maybe if I wanted to write a play about Elizabeth Robins, it should be another play and I should just finish this play about *Hedda Gabler*. As a playwright I find the question of interpretation a nightmare. People don't understand something that to me seems very clear in the play. They don't understand it because their sensitivity doesn't go to that place. Even if someone were to try and explain it to them, they would say, "Yes, but that is not interesting."

DELGADO: You're continuing to work on the play. Did you know how you were going to rewrite it after the first workshop production?

FORNES: Sometimes I have ideas about what I want to do, but what happens is that I put away the play for a few months and sometimes I don't get a chance to come back to it. With *The Summer in Gossensass* the first workshop production in 1997 helped me to understand what things are there but without full force or full clarity. It is not as though I have made a list of the things. It's almost as if I know some things are not there yet and if you asked me to give you a list of what the things are, maybe I don't know yet. But when I have put away the play for some time and I next read it I immediately see it. I work on what I'm now looking at fresh. In the case of *Gossensass* it's a little more than that. I want to get to that point which inspired me to write the play, which had to do with the question of interpretation and misinterpretation. Usually when I write a play, I don't want to make a point, but in this case I do.

DELGADO: Do you find critics want to read your plays in certain ways?

FORNES: Oh, yes. I think there is a degree of prejudging, of assuming what a work is or should be according to who the writer is and what is happening at the moment regarding criticism. We probably all do that in one way or another but I think a critic has a professional responsibility the rest of us don't have. The critic has a responsibility not unlike a doctor when he diagnoses a patient. A friend can give you an aspirin and say you'll be fine when you have an aneurysm but a doctor ought not to do that.

I see that happening with my work. Young people in college read essays and literary criticism on my work that distorts their viewing of the work, and I doubt that they will ever see it any differently. I think it's probably because they are looking for something dramatic and meaningful.

People want things to add up. They need a number two for the addition to come out right, so they see a number two. It is not a two, they just bring it in as a two. It's about what they want to say. Academics listen to each other. If they don't understand something or even if they understand it, rather than read it again to see if that's indeed there, they have more trust in the explanation of another academic. It is as if you are a detective and you don't follow the real clues, but make them up. That's criminal.

I don't care so much if in an essay something is being misinterpreted, but then when I see production after production of the play where this happens, it makes me sad. It's like when you buy a dress and it says silk on the label but when you touch it you see it's not silk. You're not going to buy it because it says it's silk you're going buy it because you know what it is. People more and more believe the essays and not the work.

DELGADO: Do you think it has happened a lot with your work? That it has been misinterpreted by critics?

FORNES: I think it happens with everybody. The thing is that *I* mind it.

DELGADO: Do you read what the critics write about your work or do you tend to avoid it?

FORNES: I tend to avoid it, because I just get upset. But then I love learning more about my work, and sometimes I learn by reading about it. This has happened a couple of times. For example, Susan Sontag said that my work was about heartbreak.[1] Or somebody saying my work was about immigrants as the plays all deal with a person going to another world. It's not necessarily a physical world of another city or another country but it has to do with being a stranger or something. But if I see critics having an idea and then looking for proof and but not even proving it, it's just a twisted thing. To me that's a mistake. In my work — and in any work that is worthwhile — what's important is the spirit of the thing not the interpretation. The spirit of the thing is where something hits you and you don't know what it is. This is much more powerful than when it speaks to your rational mind and something that you agree with, so you like it, and you praise it. To me that's not as profound as when what you have experienced is something that you don't even understand.

DELGADO: How do you respond to negative reviews of your work?

FORNES: They annoy me of course. Who likes a negative review? If the critic is wrong I feel murderous naturally. How can you take it lightly when someone is prejudicing the world against you? But if the critic is right I am the first to agree. Writers rewrite their work time and time again because they know something or other is wrong or is not quite right yet. If a writer doesn't have the ability to look at his work objectively I don't see how they could ever create anything of interest.

DELGADO: You are often referred to as an avant-garde writer. Do you perceive your work as "avant-garde"?

FORNES: No, I think that if the work is based on character and story it is not avant-garde. My work is based on character and story and I think that those elements place the work in the realm of the traditional. Avant-garde characters seem to be subject to the imagery and the tones of the piece while traditional characters are mainly subject to their relationship with other characters. In the vanguard we frequently see a detached character, a stranger in an eerie world. One who sees the eerie world as normal. Or we see extroverts, characters who speak and act without inhibition and without understanding of traditional norms. My work, in its structure, is not traditional, but in its content it deals with the real world and it is basically humanitarian. In the early sixties my work may have been considered avant-garde when a great many people believed that the Aristotelian "well-made" play was the proper form for a play. But I believe by now people prefer a theatre that is exciting because of the singular way in which it is written and performed, as well as because of its content. I feel that today we want the play to follow its own impulses and to let those impulses determine the play's form. The playwright must form the play but the form must respond to its content, not the content to the form.

There is also a question of time. The creative avant-garde in theatre has been marching on since before the beginning of the century. Something that has been with us that long cannot be called avant-garde. By now it has become part of the main body. When the existing forms become tired artists and audiences alike wish for new forms and as with any other art theatre must renew itself again and again. Old forms are dear and beautiful but there is always an excitement, a freshness to doing things and seeing things in a new way.

DELGADO: Do you think of yourself as a writer, a director, an artist? Do these roles merge and converge?

FORNES: Yes, I started drawing and painting before I did any writing or even imagined I would be working in theatre.

I believe the work of the writer, the director, the artist, the actor, the composer, the dancer is all one at the onset. I think the creative impulse, the energy that makes us interested in studying something, analyzing something or creating something is all the same. The form that it takes when the creative process starts will differ, but at the root they all spring from the same place. In theatre especially, each person's work depends on the others in such a way that one cannot think of one as independent of the other. Practicing music, for example, will develop our sensitivity to tempo and tone of voice, to the importance of silence, of violent, abrupt and stormy tones. Music will make a director more aware of sounds, the sound of steps, the sound of voices in other rooms.

Painting, of course will make us aware of the importance of tones of light, of mood created by tones of light, but also of the dimensions in space, the mystery of the space of a hallway, a person stopping at the landing on a stairs, a person leaning out a window. A director who looks at paintings will be a better director, one who has acted will be a better director and so will an actor who writes or directs be a better actor.

DELGADO: You started writing in the hope of inspiring Susan Sontag to write.

FORNES: Oh, yes. It was a sort of game. We were in a cafe in Greenwich Village, hoping we would see a friend or someone who would know of a party and invite us. It was not very likely. I had been in Europe for three years and I didn't know many people in the Village any more and Susan had only lived in New York as a child. In the meantime Susan starts talking about how she is not too happy because she wants to start writing and doesn't seem to find the time or the way to start. I was in a positive and optimistic mood and said, "Start right now?" And she said, "I know, I keep postponing it." And I said, "Do. Start right now. I'll write too." She said, "Now?" and I said, "Sure, let's go and start now. I'll write too." She was quite surprised at the idea and so was I. We start to look for the waiter when, suddenly the devil puts his hand in. Someone I had met in Paris two years before walks in. Friendly greetings, the unimaginable, he is going to a party and invites us. Temptation. We look at each other. Susan is thrilled at the idea of a party and so am I. But I become virtuous. I say, "Oh, what a pity, we can't go. We have work to do." Susan says, "You mean it?" I say, "Sure, aren't we going to go write?" "You're going to write too?" I say, "Sure." I am trying to act as if writing is the easiest thing in the world. Like even a painter can do it. We go to her place and sit at the table. She at the typewriter. I have paper and pencil. She starts typing and my mind is blank. I reach for a book on the bookcase hoping I'll find the way. I start writing a sentence using the first word on the top left corner of the page. That sentence leads to another and another. I continue writing until the flow stops. Then, I look at the word on the top right corner of the same page and again I start writing using that word. I continue writing using my system. I have now two pages. My writing was not extraordinary but was not lacking in charm. More importantly, it taught me how to put aside a writer's block. And Susan started an essay that was published shortly after.

DELGADO: How did you write your first play? Was it soon after that night?

FORNES: I don't believe it was soon. After that I started translating letters that were written to my great grandfather in Cuba by his cousin Angela who had lived in Cuba in her youth but was at the time living in Seville with her mother and aunts. The letters were written in 1906–07. But concerned events that took place from 1860 on. I translated the letters to become more intimate with them and to offer them to my friends to read.

Then, soon after — I don't remember how soon — one day I woke up with an idea for a play. This idea was obsessive. For a few days I thought about nothing else. I started writing and wrote day and night obsessively. Nineteen days later I had written a rough first draft.

DELGADO: And this became *Tango Palace*.

FORNES: Yes. I didn't know anything about theatre. I had never been involved in rehearsals, never known an actor, never known a director, never known a playwright. But I had, five years earlier, a very profound experience seeing the first production of *Waiting for Godot* in Paris. I didn't know French so I didn't understand a word and yet this was theatre like I had never seen before. It never occurred to me then that seeing this play would later inspire me to become a playwright. But I have no doubt that it did. Soon after I finished the play, Herbert Blau, a very distinguished director of a theatre in San Francisco, by chance read my play and decided to stage it. I was amazed. I was invited to attend rehearsals (the first rehearsals I had ever seen). The production was extraordinary and I became a produced playwright.

DELGADO: Of course this was the time when Off-Off-Broadway started developing and you were very involved in forging that alternative theatre culture with figures like Sam Shepard, Ellen Stewart, Lanford Wilson, and Tom O'Horgan.

FORNES: I think about writing a play around some of those writers just because it's interesting how each one of us was so different from the others. We were working in the same theatres, we were extremely interested in each other's work. It was also the start of the *Village Voice*, whose brilliant critic, Michael Smith, contributed greatly to the Off-Off-Broadway scene's becoming a movement rather than just an accident. We were not consciously breaking ground or doing anything extraordinary. We were writing plays that were very natural to us. We just thought we were doing things that were interesting and that delighted us.

But it wasn't just the theatre that was stimulating us. The whole world of art was doing somersaults, the painters were doing happenings. These were more like theatre than living paintings. In them people spoke words. Not words that resemble everyday conversation, but short sentences, as personal outbursts, or statements that reflected a thought process. The dancers were doing work that reflected more states of being than aspects of human grace.

The Off-Off-Broadway movement was very small when it started, four spaces of which two were churches and two coffee houses. The churches were Judson Church, the person in charge was the junior minister, a composer and wonderful singer Al Carmines; Theatre Genesis at Saint Mark's Church, with Ralph Cook as artistic director, Cafe La MaMa run by the extraordinary Ellen Stewart and Caffe Cino run by the very charming Joe Cino where theatrical "camp" had its birth. Each was running a theatre filled with talent, charm, and imagination, playwrights with genius and personal styles, actors with individuality and charm, choreographers and dancers who were breaking ground in the most simple, natural, and magical form possible. Each brought a new vocabulary to the twentieth-century art. Theatre, dance, and musical pieces were done in all spaces. Directors started forming companies of actors who through improvisations developed important pieces namely Joe Chaikin with the Open Theatre, Tom O'Horgan with Theatre Genesis, Andrei Serban at La MaMa, Richard Schechner with the Performance

Group. These companies were not exclusively dependent on language. Physical dexterity was important to them and nonverbal sounds were sometimes their way of communicating. This freedom from language enabled them to perform in foreign countries. The playwrights' works could be done in non-English speaking countries only if translated.

Feeling that at that time playwrights work was beginning to take a second place to the company work, the playwright-actress Julie Bovasso and I decided to apply for a "non for profit" status which would make us eligible for Government and Foundation grants and produce our own work. We received some grants, named the organization "The New York Theatre Strategy" and started production. I was appointed President which meant doing everything in the world toward production. This included bookkeeping, hammering sets, making costumes, and applying for more grants. This meant that for three years I worked around the clock helping put on other people's plays. At the start of the fourth year I began to write a play. I asked a director and friend, Barbara Rosoff to be the managing director for the season and she agreed. I started work on my new play, *Fefu and Her Friends*. It was the start of the feminist movement. I had attended several consciousness-raising meetings where I had discovered how many of the things I had experienced as a woman were things that many other women shared.

I started writing scenes, speeches, some things I was saying to myself in my head. I had a file of material that I started to assemble and work into a play. I enjoyed very much the manner or technique that I used to construct the play. It resembled the making of a collage. When I was about to finish the first part, Barbara suggested we see a loft that was advertised as a performance place. We went to see it and I liked it. The person running it was used to renting it for parties or concerts. He took us to his office which was simply a small partition in the loft. There he had a beautiful Persian carpet, a lovely antique desk, bookshelves on the walls filled with books, and several lovely Victorian chairs. I said to Barbara, "This could be Fefu's study." I asked the man if we could use the whole space and he said "Yes. Would you like to use the kitchen too?" How thrilling. I said to Barbara, "I think I'm going to do the play here."

I did and it was thrilling. Besides the living room, the study, and the kitchen, there was a room in the back that became the bedroom, and the lawn was part of the set to the side of the living room.

DELGADO: *Fefu and Her Friends* also has characteristics that have been features of your plays since then. I'm thinking particularly of setting your plays in specific times and places in the past. We see this in *Sarita*, *Abingdon Square*, *What of the Night?*, and *The Summer in Gossensass*. Do you find it helpful to go back to a specific period in the past?

FORNES: Thinking of the present creatively is like thinking of Grand Central station as a place to write. Things are on top of you all around you. It is difficult to have any perspective. When you think of the past you not only have a better perspective. But your mind can also pick up nuances of behavior and feelings that are very subtle. It may be that we romanticize other times. People sometimes ask me why do you do this or that in your plays. For example, I have been asked, "Why do you have people read out loud in your plays?" I never realized I did that, or rather I had not realized that other writers don't do it. I do it because it is a lovely and harmonious thing for people to do. As simple as that. And because my father spent a few hours each day with a book in his hands. And sometimes he would read a passage to us and often would talk to us about what he was reading. It was peaceful and charming and exciting. If it happens in a play of mine, it's because it is natural to me. It doesn't seem like something extraordinary. It reflects a moment of harmony. Sometimes it happens because there is a text, something written by someone else, that I want to have as part of the play. And of course it has to be clear that it is not something I wrote. For example, in *Mud* I looked for a grammar school text to bring to a rehearsal of a new scene where Mae was learning how to read. I picked up a book on mollusks in a thrift store. At rehearsal I looked through the book and chose the starfish. I handed it to the actress playing Mae and asked her to read it as someone who is just learning how to read. She did and I was amazed that the description of the starfish's primitive eye is an accurate and poetic description of Mae's mind.

A certain speech in my play *Fefu and Her Friends* actually comes from a little book I found called *Educational Dramatics* written by Emma

Sheridan Fry. The book was published in 1917. Emma had been teaching children at the Educational Alliance, in New York's Lower East Side from 1903 to 1909. Her method of teaching children acting involved a few children performing a play. Then on Sundays the kids would come to the Educational Alliance, which still exists on the Lower East Side, and watch the play. When the play was over, she would say to the kids: "Now, which one of you would like to come on stage and do the play?" And some of them would come up and maybe they would put on a little bit of costume, whatever. They would then do the play. They improvised and recreated the play. I thought this was so incredibly creative, and ahead of its time.

I found her book in a little secondhand store full of dust and I thought: "One day, I'm going to write a play about this woman." Of course I have plans to write many plays which don't get written. In fact I did not write a play about her, but I thought she'd be a character in *Fefu*. Then it turned out that I couldn't, but the character of Emma in *Fefu* recites from the prologue to *Educational Dramatics*. If people don't notice the note in the program, they think that I wrote this and that Emma Sheridan Fry is my invention. But this was inserted specifically to honor that person.

DELGADO: I remember when Rod Wooden interviewed you for the Manchester City of Drama conversation series he made the point that in all your work since *Fefu,* especially the more realistic plays like *Mud, Sarita,* and *Abingdon Square,* you do great honor to the characters. These individuals may be extremely disadvantaged or they may be obliged to perform very menial domestic tasks, like Olimpia in *The Conduct of Life* or Mae in *Mud.* Are you conscious of wishing to honor them?

FORNES: Indeed. I think Rod is a true gentleman to have noticed that. I don't think I would enjoy writing if I had to demean a character. I will deal with a character's darkest side, but I think I will always feel interest or a degree of tenderness or compassion, except for the character of Orlando (the military torturer in *The Conduct of Life*) for whom I feel no compassion. The best feelings I've had for him were when I felt he was too stupid to know better.

DELGADO: Your plays are very pictorial. There's always very detailed specific stage directions at the opening which allow us to imagine and create an environment for the action. Do you think that your painting background has influenced your writing and directing?

FORNES: When I write a play, I visualize a place or places, the characters, the action in detail but I never place them on a stage. The scenes I visualize are in real and varied places. Or perhaps in imaginary places. But never on a stage. This is just because like with real people, the characters' behavior will be much more genuine if they are in a real place rather than on a stage. I truly believe that to imagine the stage as you write will limit the characters' responses and thoughts. Of course after the scenes are written, the locations must be adapted to the possibilities of the stage. In this part of my creative process my training was the years I spent drawing and painting. The other part was the time I spent at the Actor's Studio observing the actors and directors sessions with Lee Strasberg. And some very basic Method acting classes I took at the Gene Frankel Theatre Workshop in New York.

In general all these points of view are necessary in theatre work. When I direct a play I prefer to think of the set after I have seen the theatre space. The space itself can sometimes suggest interesting things. Of course this is not always possible. But when it is possible I find that the theatre space has a spirit and that that spirit begins to suggest the way the play should be done in that space. I don't mean to be done on a bare stage but what structure should the set have in that space. I like space to be solid.

DELGADO: Is directing part of the writing process?

FORNES: It is with a new play. A play is not really finished until it is on a stage. No matter how much experience you have. You have to see it on a stage before you know the work is done.

DELGADO: How and when you did you start directing your own plays?

FORNES: The very first thing that I directed was not my own play. After I wrote *Tango Palace* in 1963, I started going to the Actor's Studio.

I became very interested in the acting techniques there. The techniques aimed at getting the actors to get in contact with their instincts and with personal memories which, if used in connection with the role, begin to form part of the unconscious of the character. I was fascinated and I started taking acting classes at the Gene Frankel Theatre Workshop where "Method" techniques were taught. I also took a directing class there where I directed a scene a friend wrote. I was terrified to tell the actors what to do and I was surprised that when I did tell them, they did do it without blinking an eye. Although terrifying, the whole thing was fascinating to me. I realized that the actual stage practice would contribute greatly to my ability as a playwright.

I was present at rehearsals when *The Successful Life of 3* was done at the Open Theatre. There were a number of things that I thought should be done differently, however every time I tried to explain to the director how I thought it should be done she would say that she didn't agree. I thought what a peculiar thing that she would not listen to me when it was I who wrote the play (little did I know). I told Joe Chaikin what was happening, and he looked at me kindly and shrugged his shoulders with a philosophical and sympathetic expression on his face. I didn't know if I would know how to accomplish what I wanted even if I had the opportunity to direct it, but it surprised me that no one thought I should have been allowed to work on it.

A little later, *Tango Palace* and *The Successful Life of 3* were being done at the Firehouse Theatre in Minneapolis. I asked the director if I could direct the second play. He said yes. Here too I felt tentative when I gave direction to the actors. I also had the problem that the people who were acting were not experienced actors, especially the young girl. She objected every time I changed the blocking — she would say "Why do you keep changing your mind. First you tell me to go here and now you tell me to go there." And I told her that that's how you direct a play. First you do it one way and then you change it. I knew that directors don't just stage the thing and keep repeating it until the actor memorizes it. That is really what I remember: how difficult it was dealing with the other people. If I had been using paper dolls and doing the scene, I would not have gotten nervous whether it was working or not working. My nervousness had to do with so intimately telling people what to do. It's not that I didn't accomplish anything or learn anything. It's just that I did not do a particularly good job.

Then, Judson Church in New York did my play *Promenade*. It was a musical. The piece I wrote was tiny, only a few pages. Al Carmines wrote music for it and Larry [Lawrence] Kornfeld directed it. Watching them work was a delight. Each improvised the most magical and beautiful things at the spur of the moment. I wrote more and more lyrics, Al wrote more and more delightful music and Larry created more magical moments on the stage.

Larry is a director who doesn't spend much time with how the characters should be interpreted. He is interested in what happens on the stage and what a character does and how he does it. This is the way I feel one should create. Larry has genius and a real talent for creating a wonderful dynamic on stage. He has people behave in a manner that is charming, natural, and spontaneous. When he is directing an avant-garde play, his work is so attentive and full of charm.

Watching people direct, I didn't know that I was learning how to direct. I was just admiring how someone does something. The first time I directed after that, I paid attention to the things that really make life on the stage interesting. I realized the importance of physical movement, changes in rhythm, tempo and time and allowing for things to happen even accidentally.

Watching people like the choreographer Remy Charlip, observing the way Al Carmines would write music — improvised in the moment of rehearsal — I saw people who were connected to their own creativity and to the space they worked in.

I became a Judson addict. I helped in whatever way I could. I made costumes or props for other works of Al Carmines', Larry Kornfeld's, Remy Charlip's, Harry Koutoukas' and others' productions. I was still a frequent visitor at the Open Theatre sessions and saw wonderful people who were working with techniques that involved them physically and mentally as well as emotionally. They were fruitful and joyful days. The move to directing happened naturally.

DELGADO: As well as directing your own work, you direct the work of other writers. We've talked about your production of *Hedda Gabler* and how that fed into your own writing. You've directed *Uncle Vanya* and the work of your students at INTAR. I'm thinking particularly here of Caridad Svich's *Any Place But Here* in 1995 and Ana María Simo's *Going to New England* in 1990. How did you begin directing other people's work and what attracts you to the works you chose to stage?

FORNES: Both Ana María and Caridad were in my playwriting workshop at INTAR, a theatre in New York City that presents works written in Spanish and translated into English and new plays written in English by Hispanics living in the United States. Ana María and Caridad wrote these plays in that workshop. I had a deep feeling for the work the writers were doing there, especially for these two plays. There was something I saw in the work that made me want to spend time with it. Sometimes there is a mystery about a work that is compelling, sometimes it is the passion in the work, sometimes it is a sadness and sometimes a joy, or a sense of life that the characters have. Sometimes it is something you learn from spending time with these people. It could be many things that make me want to spend time with these characters; a sense of life that is tragic or philosophical, sometimes it is the joy of the piece, and so on. What I notice may be different from what other people notice, but it's something that is there. I never think I have to bring something to the piece. If the piece is there it's there. All you have to do is be sensitive to it and put it on. Directors are told you have to have a concept. I wonder if that is what you need.

DELGADO: Is it very different for you to work on other people's writing?

FORNES: With other people's work, when I start I'm aware that I don't know it well. I feel as if I found the work and have adopted it and it begins to feel no different than when I wrote it myself.

DELGADO: What if when you are rehearsing, there is a line that you feel doesn't work, you might change it with your own writing, do you change it with other people's?

FORNES: Yes if the playwright is not around I'm convinced that they will be delighted that I changed it. If the playwright is around, I ask them if I can do it. Sometimes they explain why the line is there. In that case I will put the line back and suggest something to avoid the confusion that I myself felt.

One time, I made so many changes in a scene of Ana María Simo's work that I called her and said, "Ana María, I have to meet with you because I made some changes." I met with her in a restaurant with my copy of the script. I was apprehensive because there were so many changes. The page was full of things crossed out and arrows changing the position of sentences. It looked messy. I showed it to her and she read it with great concentration. She held the script against her chest and closed her eyes. I thought, "Oh no, she hates it." I waited and she still held the script against her chest. I said, "You don't like it." She said, "You have no idea how much I have thought about this scene, how much trouble I have had and you took care of it." I was ecstatic because I didn't know what I would do if she refused to make the changes. I felt that these were important changes to make.

The same thing happened with Caridad Svich's *Any Place But Here*, except that Caridad was not present during rehearsals. She came from Los Angeles to the last performance at Theater for the New City. I was scared because if she didn't like the changes there was nothing to be done about it. Luckily, she liked them. I do take possession of a play when I direct it. I find it difficult not to feel as if I wrote the play.

DELGADO: There are a lot of directors who might do a play once and never return to it. But you return to your own works and stage them again and again.

FORNES: When you love someone, don't you want to see them again? When you hear music that you love, don't you want to hear it again? When you work with a play you love, you want to work with it again. Then, if I have a new cast it's always different. With a new cast, you have to find ways of working that are different because *they* are different. Then, of course, what I love is when there are moments in a play where I can do a little rewrite and improve something. When a scene is well written, it will always work. But there are times when a scene is passable, but not really right — there may be a moment that one hopes would go-fast-so-that-no-one-would-notice-that-it-wasn't-very-good. When I do the play again and I find out what is needed in terms of writing to make it right, it's wonderful.

DELGADO: You've recently been reworking *Fefu and Her Friends* for a single space.

FORNES: Yes, I have converted the four middle scenes into one scene that takes place in the living room, rather than in other rooms of the house. Theatres which have no adjacent spaces can do this version of the play on the main stage. I feel this version is not just a second best alternative. It turned out to be as interesting as the original draft. In some ways I think that this version may even have more resonance than the original.

I first made these changes because I was asked to translate the play into Spanish for a Latin American publication. It occurred to me that this would be the time when I could do a rewrite of the middle part, which I had for some time intended to do. In the process of translating, contrary to the idea that translation is simply a question of knowing both languages well, I needed to re-enter my original creative state of mind.

DELGADO: As well as translating your own work you've worked on translations of other plays, like Virgilio Piñera's *Cold Air*.

FORNES. I translated it because I wanted to stage it. When you translate you cannot just translate literally; a word may be the same in both English and Spanish but in each language it could have a different nuance. In my own plays I think I know what the mood should be, what the rhythms of the scene should be, the temperament of the characters, the character of the scene. The character may have a quiet temperament, but if I need a scene that has more dynamic, then the characters will have to become a little more dynamic than usual. When translating a play, you have to be careful not just to be accurate in the meaning of the words, but also to be sensitive to the connotation and the mood of the language. If you substitute one word for another, a sense of mood can be sharper. It could even be a question of rhythm or sound. I think if an actor translates maybe he will be more aware of what I am talking about because the actor needs to speak the words and the sound of the word is part of the meaning of the word.

DELGADO: How does this work in team translation when there's a group working on an English version?

FORNES: The first time I was involved in a project like this was at INTAR. We had to work very quickly on a play by the Peruvian novelist Mario Vargas Llosa. A team of three was set up to speed up the process. Someone suggested we each translate a third of the play. I was against that. I thought we would end up with three different styles. I suggested the three of us work together. We did. It happened purely by chance that each one of us had different origins and skills. This variety provided for a perfect team for the job. One was a perfectly bilingual Peruvian. The other was an American writer with some knowledge of Spanish. The third was me, a playwright whose native language was Spanish, but who had no sense of Peruvian connotations.

It was decided that since I was a playwright I would start so that the translation would have a conversational rather than literal tone. The Peruvian would make sure that my translation didn't miss Peruvian nuances. The American writer had his ear on the naturalness of the English translation. One can say he did a second draft. We did it so fast. In three or four hours the final draft was finished. This is what people should do when translating. A team like this would get translations done in no time at all.

DELGADO: Bearing in mind that English is your second language, did you ever think of writing in Spanish?

FORNES: If somebody asked me to write a play in Spanish I might find that if I do it, it's easy and natural, but I might find that it isn't because I don't speak Spanish that frequently. I have now been speaking English for over fifty years. I think in English.

DELGADO: How important is your Cuban heritage?

FORNES: Very important. I think your life is divided in three parts. The first is between birth and the age of sixteen, the second between sixteen and forty, and the third is from forty on. I was fourteen-and-a-half years old when I came to New York. In New York I turned from childhood to adulthood, so this is my home. Cuba was the place of my birth and the start of my life. I will always be a Cuban even if I adore my new country, New York. New York is my country. Cuba is my country of birth. New York is my country of growth. The first part of your life is very important unless you want to forget it and I never did. But even if you have forgotten it, it has left traces in you. My writing has an off-center quality that is not exactly deliberate, but that I have not tried to change because I know its origin lies in the temperament and language of my birth. Besides, my primary interest has never been to reproduce a realistic, everyday world. Outside of the language itself, I know there are character values and priorities that suggest a foreign source. I know that sometimes I am moved by something because of my Cuban upbringing and I know that sometimes I notice something because of my Cuban upbringing. At the same time, in many ways, I think the way Americans think, and I feel very much at home in the United States.

DELGADO: You've often spoken of as a kind of mentor for a generation of Latino dramatists in the US...

FORNES: Most of them came out of my workshop at INTAR. Rather than teaching them how a play should be written in the sense of a formula, I tried not teaching them how to write but to present to them ways where they could find their creativity, how to become in touch with their own imagery and their own aesthetic.

DELGADO: Could you talk a bit about your workshops at INTAR. How did they come about?

FORNES: Well, they came about because at some point I was talking to Max Ferrá, the artistic director at INTAR, telling him that we must do a playwriting workshop for Hispanics. A workshop that doesn't just give them a formula to write a play, but a place where, through some form of meditation, visualizations, and writing exercises, I could lead them to exercising their imagination and creativity. I also thought that they should receive some sort of payment, at least the equivalent of what they would receive in a job for the same amount of hours they spent in the workshop. This would be three hours, three times a week, so they would not be too overwhelmingly burdened by financial need. The playwrights should be paid because if the playwrights were not paid it would never take off. Americans can dangle a carrot for young Americans who want to be playwrights. There are role models. Young people can say, "I want to write like O'Neill." They may not be very interested in writing but they think it will be attractive and romantic to be that kind of person. The immigrant Hispanic doesn't have any kind of person like that so there has to be another kind of stimulus for them to make the overwhelming effort. They have to be paid.

A grant was allowed and the workshop worked beautifully for three years. Most of the Hispanic writers active in theatre today came out of that workshop. To receive the grant, I needed to write a description of it. At first I thought that would be difficult. But then, it occurred to me that I should just try to imagine an ideal workshop which, if I heard of it, I myself would wish to attend. I proceeded to imagine a system which consisted of stretching exercises, meditation, visualization of character, drawing of spaces and characters, and other creative exercises common to actors' training, but not at all to playwrights' training. I decided we should start work at nine o'clock in the morning when everyone starts work so they would apply themselves with the same sense of duty as anyone going to work in the morning. From the beginning, I said, "At nine o'clock sharp the door is locked. And if you are not here, don't knock at the door, because the door will not be opened. And if you don't come you won't get paid." This I never did. I never didn't pay them. But they got the idea and they were as punctual as soldiers.

DELGADO: How long would a writer be in the workshop?

FORNES: As long as I felt that they were profiting by the workshop. The workshop went on for seven years and some of them were there for as long as six years.

DELGADO: Did any become writers in different mediums?

FORNES: Some did some work in other mediums, but it was mostly in theatre.

DELGADO: Of course these workshops were not just confined to INTAR. You've been running writing workshops across America and beyond for many years now. Do you think playwriting can be taught?

FORNES: Of course. You can teach playwriting the way you can teach any other art. You don't teach an art by giving the person a bunch of rules. You teach it by encouraging the person to pay attention to their own imagination. To trust and respect their own imagination. To allow the work to be a meditation. To open their imagination and their sensitivity to the themes and aspects of human character that interest them. To trust their imagination in the most intimate and delicate way. To commit themselves to the integrity of the work. Not to drive the very work out of their hands by burdening it with external concerns. Those are the main things that people have to learn. You can teach a person how to breathe, how to meditate, how to listen to their own consciousness, even how to listen to their own desires. Why wouldn't you be able to teach a person how to find their own creativity?

Maybe the word is not teach but train. Some people have talent but they don't know how to use it. There are techniques to train people how to act. They don't know what the practice of what they are attempting to do consists of. Every art has methods of learning. A good method would usually consist of an application to a process rather than to seeking a result. A good teacher can make the student aware of errors in his approach to the work. A lot of my ideas about teaching playwriting have to do with my understanding of acting techniques. The Method exercises are creative techniques. They are not techniques dealing with style and certainly not theme. People believe that Method is a style.

Lee Strasberg may have limited his interest to psychological social drama but his intelligence, sensitivity, and sophistication in regard to the quality of acting was superb. He was a genius at inventing and developing exercises to keep the student focus on a genuine creative goal. That is, I suppose, the opposite of imitation and fakery.

DELGADO: Do the exercises have different aims and objectives?

FORNES: No, they are different approaches to arrive at the same thing, namely a fresh perspective toward the work. That is, a constant viewing of the work from a different point of view and with a fresh mind which really means a new viewing of the character from a different point of view. When you let your mind relax, you stop worrying about the scene you have to write, or about whether you are a good writer or not. The main point of my exercises is the same as acting, to try to stop people from concentrating on the result.

I have people do a visualization exercise. For example, I would have people remember a moment in their lives before the age of nine where there was something that had to do with water. I am not asking for something dramatic or significant. It can be the simplest thing. My aim is to make them understand that they can and should concentrate on simple things, as well as important, dramatic, and extraordinary things. It is indeed the opposite of what people teach a beginner student in a dramatic writing class. They would say, "Think of a moment that has great consequences." I would say, "Think of a moment that has no consequences." For me, to think of something that has great consequences is anti-productive. When you write a play, you have to start by putting seeds in the ground. Don't think of the great tree that will come out of it. I say to them, "Don't try to think of a memory that would be important. Just let your mind try to visualize a moment that has to do with water." The reason I say with water is because it is simple and has a variety of forms and uses. It could be a day on the beach, or it could be someone drinking a glass of water, or taking a shower, or looking at the ocean. I ask questions: Is the image outdoors or is it indoors?, What kind of day is it? I ask them about the tone of the light, the temperature, the sounds, the colour of clothing of each person, the hands, the arms — are they hairy or smooth? I force them to stay within themselves, moving into it. When you keep trying to move into it, then you really do transport yourself.

I ask them to make a drawing of it. After making the drawing, I give them about three lines of dialogue that I pick out from a book or something. They write the lines.

DELGADO: Do they have to use those three lines?

FORNES: I tell them that they don't have to use them in the writing. The lines are there just to trigger speaking, to trigger sound. Then the process of creative writing is a process of listening to the characters and being curious about what you hear and what you see them do rather than a planning and deciding what they will do. It is almost as if you are watching the characters through a window. If you start deciding what they will do, the characters will go flat and start speaking like puppets, only not as cute. They will be dull. You have to allow for the character to surprise the writer.

Characters must have as much autonomy in their world as the characters in our subconscious have in our dreams. If we provide a trustworthy environment for them (that means an environment that is real and secure, not because it is safe but more because it is real), they will not let you down. When you daydream, things are happening in your mind; you're not controlling them. There is perhaps, a deeper wish that is controlling it, but it is not our rational will. The rational mind has pulled back and has stopped controlling things. When that happens you will have a knowledge of the characters. The exercises are not as complicated as they may seem. The imagination has a component of reality and it also has a side that is fake. The writer has to keep his eye on this question and not let the fake side take over.

In the workshop I don't give the writer's dramatic criticism. I concentrate on developing their ability to connect with the characters' truest and central state of mind. At the end of each session, two or three of them will read what they have just written in the session. Their reading is beneficial for those listening as well as for the one who is reading. When the writing is genuine, the characters immediately come alive.

DELGADO: But isn't it also about observation?

FORNES: Yes, it is about observation. Observation as a means of moving closer to the subject. Understanding the subject's physical and mental state. Becoming one with the subject and noticing what he or she says. And how they say it. Sometimes a person says something you may notice that they may say something other than what they mean. When you write dialogue, it could ring false if you don't pay attention to what they say or how they say it. If you don't have an ear for what rings true or false, you're not going to be able to write a good play unless the play is called "Bad Ear." Having a great idea doesn't mean you'll write a good play. When actors get hold of a play that rings true, they are in heaven and they perform well. I've seen satisfaction in actors' faces when they say true lines. The lines are activating them, rather than they having to activate the lines through labor and craft.

During rehearsals for a workshop production of *Abingdon Square* in 1984, John Aylward — the actor who played the role of Juster, the betrayed husband — and I were working on a scene where his emotions were painful and his response toward his wife was brutal. We kept doing it again and again. At some point, I began to feel guilty about putting him through this nastiness over and over and I said to him, "Are you tired? Would you like to break?" And he said, "No! This is good stuff!" The actor smiled and I was thinking, "What does he mean?" The situation and the lines were motivating him and he was flying with the scene. I was amazed that in spite of it being a moment where his character was in pain, humiliated, betrayed, he was enjoying it. I realized that an actor's most thrilling moment of his craft is when the material gives him enough fuel to take off without having to laboriously construct a state of mind.

In their training, writers are instructed to create a text where the subtext is evident, where there is a hidden emotional subtext. It is then evident that their duty is to reveal the subconscious motivation of the character. In some ways doing this is asking the playwright to betray the character. The existence of the subconscious in the human mind is a powerful and real emotion that the person so abhors that it becomes a neccessity to conceal and deny it. A psychoanalyst has to work very hard to make the patient aware of these emotions that have been so successfully hidden. The person has been operating in all sincerity with the belief that what they are expressing or going through is the reality of their emotion. If the writer and the actor are directed to reveal that subconscious, they are betraying the behavior and reality of the character. There is a difference between having repressed emotions and lying.

DELGADO: You recently worked with the Florida Grand Opera Company on the libretto for a new opera with music by Robert Ashley which you called *Manual for a desperate crossing* but was later titled *Balseros/Rafters*. Was this very different from writing a play?

FORNES: Yes. The text for an opera should be closer to a poem than to natural speech. Another thing that is very different is that, as the music is written, the importance of the words begins to subside to the power of the music. The music can change the nature and meaning of a text. It can therefore begin to act as co-writer. The music can also begin to act as director. It can turn a lyrical solo into a lively quintet. The composer can turn a serious piece into comedy, or the other way around. What was wrong with *Manual for a desperate crossing* is that Ashley had no respect for my work as is evident in his changing the title of the piece without even consulting me.

DELGADO: Was it very different working on an opera like *Lovers and Keepers*?

FORNES: *Lovers and Keepers* was not an opera. For one, there was much more spoken language than is customary in opera. Then, the music had a very definite popular flavor; Tito Puente and Fernando Rivas wrote it. I would call it a play with songs.

DELGADO: Like a musical?

FORNES: In a way it was like a musical but the dialogue in a musical seems to be lighthearted and inconsequential. Some of the dialogue in *Lovers and Keepers* was humorous, but a great deal of it was naturalistic and in some cases crude and blunt like a play rather than a musical. It is three stories about three couples. In the middle story, for example, Elena and her husband are going through a stormy and desperate period. She becomes pregnant by another man. She delivers a desperate song sitting on her bed. There is a blackout. When the lights come up the sheets are full of blood. She delivers a song that is profoundly painful and tragic.

I did another piece called *Cap-a-pie* in 1975 with the composer Jose Raul Bernardo which was based on events, stories, experiences in the performers lives. These were collected during a period of workshops where the actors reminisced on childhood memories, first impressions of New York and other memories. Each told a story which I selected from what they had recounted in the workshop. I chose, from their narrative, two tales from each. Trimmed down the story, selected a moment where I turned the narrative into lyrics for a song. Jose Raul Bernardo wrote the music and each actor told his or her story and sang their song. Here are two extremes: one imperfect and two perfect collaborations.

DELGADO: And after directing the next production of *The Summer in Gossensass*, what next?

FORNES: To work on *What of the Night?*, to look over the text. I made some minor changes on *Springtime* when I worked on it last time. Then I'll put it aside for a while. *Springtime* was wonderful. Molly Powell played Greta. She has an interesting quality, an internal stillness. At the end of the play, she finds Rainbow's letter where Rainbow explains why she has left her. After she reads the letter, she stands center stage looking toward the window, her back is to the audience. The lights start to fade, leaving her in a pool of light. There is a visible tremor in her body. The lights fade to black. I gave Molly a note asking her to make the tremor smaller. The next day, the tremor was still too strong. I asked her to make it smaller and she said, "I am not making it happen this way. I can't help it. This is how it happens after I read the letter." I then said, "This is much much later, Rainbow is still gone, and you are still waiting for her." And she said, "I see what you mean. The reason I could not control it is because I thought the moment of the letter is immediately after Rainbow has left." And then, in the last performance, the stage lights began to come down as her pool of light started to come up, and the tremor was much more gentle. And the end of the play was beautiful. And it seemed that Greta would spend the rest of her life in great sorrow, waiting for Rainbow.

## POSTSCRIPT

DELGADO: It's now August 1999, we've just looked over the interview we did in 1997 and revised it for publication. You redirected *The Summer in Gossensass* at the Judith Anderson Theatre in 1998, wrote a new short play called *The Audition* staged at Theater for the New City later that year, and have recently directed *Fefu and Her Friends* at Santa Fe Stages. What comes next?

FORNES: The Signature Theatre, which is dedicating this season to my work, has commissioned me to write a new play. The play is about three friends, a playwright, a dancer, and a designer who have had a long and profound friendship. It starts with a conversation between the designer and the dancer about a creative crisis the playwright is going through. He cannot get a grip on his play and is restless, unpleasant and accusatory. The other two are concerned and try to find the way to help. Gradually the playwright's condition has created such tension that it starts to poison each of their relationships. An atmosphere of artistic jealousy, treachery, and despair has set in. The play is a study of the delicacy and susceptibility of the creative mind. A peaceful state of mind can allow it to flow steadily and be fruitful or it can make it go dormant. Tension and despair can block it or it can inspire it and cause it to burst open like a volcano.

* From an interview conducted in Brighton and London on October 26, 1997. Additional unpublished material from Rod Wooden's interview with Maria Irene Fornes for Manchester's City of Drama conversation series, November 20, 1994. The interview was revised for publication in July and August 1999.

1 See p. 19.

Maria Irene Fornes and Jerome Robbins during rehearsal of
*THE OFFICE*
Henry Miller Theatre, New York City, 1966

# ❀ DEIRDRE O'CONNELL
*actress*

## A FINAL THOUGHT

IRENE HAS THE MOST FUN OF ANYONE I know. People that don't know her and see her plays might think she is sad or dark, but I have never seen her sad.

Ever since I saw *Mud* a million years ago, I have sat at her feet and if she had been a sad person it wouldn't have been nearly as much sheer pleasure to do so.

She is always funny.

She is always inspiring.

She always speaks in direct language about how art is actually made, and the art she makes is the great art. She can drive you insane in the quest for the great art.

She does not suffer fools at all or weakness at all.

She does not allow you to be less brave than she is. She pretends the terror doesn't exist, and she banishes it.

When you fall in love with her she is like a riddle — why is this woman so joyful?

So quick to laugh and so utterly engaged?

I think maybe the answer is that she only and absolutely does what she wants to do and only and absolutely makes the art she wants to see.

She is completely true.

# ✸ A CHRONOLOGY OF WORK
# BY MARIA IRENE FORNES

## PRODUCTIONS OF PLAYS BY MARIA IRENE FORNES
## (* DIRECTED BY THE AUTHOR)

**Tango Palace** (first titled **There! You Died!**)

| | |
|---|---|
| 1963 | Actors Workshop, San Francisco, CA |
| 1964 | Festival of Two Worlds, Spoleto, Italy |
| 1964 | Actor's Studio, New York City, NY |
| 1965 | Firehouse Theatre, Minneapolis, MN |
| 1968 | Tempo Theatre, Boston, MA |
| 1968 | Trinity College, Hartford, CT |
| 1973 | Theatre Genesis, New York City, NY * |
| 1973 | US Information Service, Calcutta, India |
| 1974 | Academy Theatre, Atlanta, GA |
| 1976 | Ohio University, Athens, OH |
| 1978 | Rio de Janeiro, Brazil |
| 1986 | Found Space Theatre Group, Vancouver, BC, Canada |
| 1991 | California State University, Pomona, CA |
| 1992 | Amherst College, Amherst, MA |

**The Widow**

| | |
|---|---|
| 1978 | Universidad de Mexico, Mexico, D.F. (Radio) |

**The Successful Life of 3** (OBIE Award)

| | |
|---|---|
| 1965 | Firehouse Theatre, Minneapolis, MN* |
| 1965 | The Open Theatre, New York City, NY |
| 1967 | Judson Church, New York City, NY |
| 1968 | Baird Hall, Chicago, IL |
| 1968 | Little Theatre, London, England |

| 1968 | Teatro Studio, Caracas, Venezuela |
| 1968 | Kansas State College, Fort Hays, KS |
| 1968 | Trinity College, Hartford, CT |
| 1968 | Studio Theatre, Amsterdam, Holland |
| 1969 | Stockholm, Sweden (Radio Broadcast) |
| 1969 | California State College, Fullerton, CA |
| 1969 | Traverse Theatre Club, Edinburgh, Scotland |
| 1969 | Northeast Missouri State College, Kirkville, MO |
| 1969 | Ohio University, Athens, OH |
| 1969 | Dade Junior College, Miami, FL |
| 1970 | The Little Arhus Theatre, Svalegange, Denmark |
| 1971 | University of Delaware, Wilmington, DE |
| 1971 | Queens College, New York City, NY |
| 1971 | The Odyssey Theatre, Los Angeles, CA |
| 1972 | The Proposition, Cambridge, MA |
| 1973 | US Information Agency, Calcutta, India |
| 1973 | Theatre Intime, Princeton University, NJ |
| 1973 | University of California, Irvine, CA |
| 1974 | Muhlenberg College, Allentown, PA |
| 1974 | Eastern Iowa Community College, IA |
| 1975 | The Orphans, Chicago, IL |
| 1975 | The Oxford Players, Oxford, England |
| 1977 | Direct Theatre, New York, NY |
| 1987 | Lakeside Players, Evanston, IL |
| 1988 | Kentucky Contemporary Theatre, Louisville, KY |
| 1989 | Stanford University, Stanford, CA |
| 1989 | University of Alaska, Anchorage, AK |
| 1992 | Lewis & Clark College, Portland, OR |

**Promenade** (music by Al Carmines)

| 1965 | Judson Church, New York City, NY (OBIE Award) |
| 1968 | California State College, Fullerton, CA |
| 1968 | Arlechino Theatre, Sweden |
| 1969 | Promenade Theatre, New York City, NY |
| 1970 | Manhattan College, New York City, NY |

| 1971 | Pace College, New York, NY |
| 1971 | Center Players |
| 1971 | Diablo Light Opera Company |
| 1971 | Kalamazoo College, Kalamazoo, MI |
| 1972 | Kingston Mines, Chicago, IL |
| 1975 | Cricket Theatre, Minneapolis, MN |
| 1977 | Camera Three, CBS, Songs from *Promenade* |
| 1977 | Seattle, WA |
| 1979 | Ohio University, Athens, OH |
| 1981 | Santa Barbara, CA |
| 1982 | Manhattan Clearing House, Dallas, TX |
| 1982 | De Pere, WI |
| 1984 | Theatre Off Park, New York University, NY |
| 1985 | Playmakers, Tampa, FL |
| 1986 | Alberta, Canada |

## The Office
| 1966 | Henry Miller Theatre, New York City, NY |

## A Vietnamese Wedding
| 1967 | Washington Square Methodist Church, NY* |
| 1967 | Moore College, Philadelphia, PA |
| 1968 | The Changing Scene, Denver, CO |
| 1969 | Yale Cabaret Theatre, New Haven, CT |
| 1969 | La MaMa, New York City, NY |

## The Annunciation
| 1967 | Judson Church, New York City, NY* |

## Dr. Kheal
| 1968 | New Dramatists Committee, New York City, NY |
| 1968 | Village Gate, New York City, NY |

| 1968 | Judson Church, New York City, NY |
| 1968 | Berkshire Theatre Festival, Stockbridge, MA |
| 1968 | Act IV, Provincetown, MA |
| 1968 | The Changing Scene, Denver, CO |
| 1968 | University of Colorado, Boulder, CO |
| 1968 | Adelphi College, Garden City, NY |
| 1968 | Rutgers College, Camden, NJ |
| 1969 | Yale Cabaret Theatre, New Haven, CT |
| 1969 | Smith College, Northampton, MA |
| 1969 | Bucks County Theatre, PA |
| 1969 | University of Michigan, Ann Arbor, MI |
| 1969 | New Arts Laboratory, London, England |
| 1970 | Community Center, Los Angeles, CA |
| 1971 | Dawson Creek, BC, Canada |
| 1971 | The People Playhouse, New Orleans, LA |
| 1971 | Monash Teachers College, Melbourne, Australia |
| 1972 | US Department of Information Agency, Austria-Germany |
| 1972 | University of North Carolina, Chapel Hill, NC |
| 1972 | Concord Academy Center, Concord, MA |
| 1972 | Princeton University, Wilford College |
| 1973 | Theatre Genesis, New York City, NY* |
| | (co-directed with Michael Smith) |
| 1973 | Arkansas College, Little Rock, AR |
| 1973 | Wesleyan University, Middletown, CT |
| 1973 | Grace Episcopal Church, Washington, DC |
| 1973 | Dickinson College, Carlisle, PA |
| 1973 | University of Colorado, Boulder, CO |
| 1974 | American Place Theatre, New York City, NY* |
| 1974 | Academy Theatre, Atlanta, GA |
| 1974 | George Street Playhouse, New Brunswick, NJ |
| 1978 | Concord Academy, Concord, MA |
| 1978 | New York Stageworks, New York City, NY |
| 1986 | New City Theatre, Seattle, WA |
| 1987 | Young Vic, London, England |
| 1988 | Santa Fe Actors Theatre, Santa Fe, NM |
| 1989 | University of Houston, Houston, TX |

| 1997 | Goodman Theater, Chicago, IL |
| 1999 | La Companie du Horla at Théâtre des 3 Bornes, Paris, France |

### *The Red Burning Light*
| 1968 | Open Theatre, Zurich, Milan, Copenhagen |
| 1969 | La MaMa, New York City, NY |
| 1974 | University Theatre, Urbana, IL |

### *Molly's Dream* (music by Cosmos Savage)
| 1968 | Boston University-Tanglewood Workshop, Lenox, MA |
| 1968 | New Dramatists Committee, New York City, NY* |
| 1973 | New York Theatre Strategy, New York City, NY* |
| 1974 | Hartford University, Hartford, CT |
| 1975 | Northern Illinois University, Dekalb, IL |
| 1988 | Novus Theatre, Vancouver, BC, Canada |

### *The Curse of the Langston House*
| 1972 | Cincinnati Playhouse in the Park, Cincinnati, OH* |

### *Aurora* (music by John Fitzgibbon)
| 1974 | New York Theatre Strategy, New York City, NY* |

### *Cap-a-pie* (music by Jose Raul Bernardo)
| 1975 | INTAR, New York City, NY* |
| 1975 | INTAR, Lincoln Center Plaza, New York City, NY* |
| 1976 | INTAR, The Cloisters, New York City, NY* |

### *Washing*
| 1976 | Theater for the New City, New York City, NY* |

**Fefu and Her Friends**

| 1977 | New York Theatre Strategy, New York City, NY* |
|------|-----|
| | (OBIE Award) |
| 1978 | American Place Theatre, New York City, NY* |
| 1978 | Wesleyan University, Middletown, CT |
| 1978 | University of Melbourne, Parkville, Victoria, Australia |
| 1979 | Victoria College of the Arts, Melbourne, Australia |
| 1979 | Padua Hills Festival, Los Angeles, CA* |
| 1979 | University of Kinosha, Kinosha, WI* |
| 1979 | Bard College, New York City, NY |
| 1979 | Pasadena Playhouse, Pasadena, CA* |
| 1980 | Los Angeles Community College, Los Angeles, CA |
| 1980 | American Musical & Dramatic Academy, New York City, NY |
| 1981 | Eureka Theatre Company, San Francisco, CA |
| 1981 | The Empty Space, Seattle, WA |
| 1981 | University of Ottawa, Ottawa City, Canada |
| 1982 | Victoria College for the Arts, Melbourne, Australia |
| 1982 | University of Calgary, Alberta, Canada |
| 1983 | Paradise Island Express, Washington, DC |
| 1983 | Theatre Off Park, New York University, NY |
| 1984 | The Blind Parrot Company, Chicago, IL |
| 1984 | Theatre Aside, Toronto, Canada |
| 1985 | St. Frazier University, Burnaby, BC, Canada |
| 1985 | State University College, New Paltz, NY |
| 1985 | Ohio Theatre, New York City, NY |
| 1986 | At the Foot of the Mountain, Minneapolis, MN* |
| 1986 | Davidson College, Davidson, NC |
| 1986 | Center Stage, Montpelier, VT |
| 1986 | Trinity College, Hartford, CT |
| 1987 | At the Foot of the Mountain, Minneapolis, MN* |
| 1987 | New York University, New York City, NY |
| 1987 | University of Regina, Saskatchewan, Canada |
| 1987 | Wellesley College, Wellesley, MA |
| 1989 | De Paul University, Greencastle, IN |
| 1989 | University of Texas, Austin, TX |
| 1989 | Contemporary Arts Center, New Orleans, LA |

| 1989 | Iowa State University, Ames, IA |
|------|--------------------------------|
| 1989 | Princeton University, Princeton, NJ |
| 1990 | Kent State University, Kent, OH |
| 1990 | New City Theatre, Seattle, WA* |
| 1990 | LA Theatre Collective, Los Angeles, CA |
| 1990 | Arts Alliance, Evanston, IL |
| 1990 | Algonquin Cafe Theatre, Amarillo, TX |
| 1990 | University of California, La Jolla, CA |
| 1992 | University of California, Los Angeles, CA |
| 1992 | Yale Repertory Theater, New Haven, CO |
| 1999 | Santa Fe Stages, Santa Fe, NM* |

**Lolita in the Garden** (music by Richard Weinstock)
| 1977 | INTAR, New York City, NY* |
|------|---------------------------|

**In Service**
| 1978 | Padua Hills Festival, Los Angeles, CA* |
|------|----------------------------------------|

**Eyes on the Harem** (OBIE Award for Directing)
| 1979 | INTAR, New York City, NY* |
|------|---------------------------|

**Evelyn Brown (A Diary)**
| 1980 | Theater for the New City, New York City, NY* |
|------|----------------------------------------------|

**A Visit** (music by George Quincy)
| 1981 | Padua Hills Festival, Los Angeles, CA* |
|------|----------------------------------------|
| 1981 | Theater for the New City, New York City, NY* |

**The Danube**
| 1981 | Theater for the New City, New York City, NY* |
|------|----------------------------------------------|
| 1982 | Padua Hills Festival, Los Angeles, CA* |

| 1983 | Theater for the New City, New York City, NY* |
| 1984 | American Place Theatre, New York City, NY* (OBIE Award) |
| 1984 | New City Theatre, Pittsburgh, PA* |
| 1985 | Eureka Theatre, San Francisco, CA |
| 1988 | Organic Theatre, Chicago, IL |
| 1988 | New City Theatre, Seattle, WA |
| 1989 | University of California, Berkeley, CA |
| 1990 | Alumnae Theatre, Toronto, Canada |
| 1991 | Schauspielhaus, Vienna, Austria |
| 1994 | Shared Experience at the Gate Theatre, London, England |

## *Mud*

| 1983 | Padua Hills Festival, Los Angeles, CA* |
| 1983 | Theater for the New City, New York City, NY* (OBIE Award) |
| 1983 | Magic Theatre, Omaha, NE* |
| 1985 | University of California, San Diego, CA |
| 1985 | New York Theatre Workshop, New York City, NY |
| 1985 | Empty Space, Seattle, WA |
| 1986 | Court Theatre, Chicago, IL |
| 1986 | Invisible Performance, New York City, NY |
| 1987 | York University, North York, Canada |
| 1987 | Wesleyan University, Middletown, CT |
| 1987 | J. Weiser, New York City, NY |
| 1987 | University of El Paso, El Paso, TX |
| 1987 | A Stage Above, Irvington, NY |
| 1987 | Columbia University, New York City, NY |
| 1987 | SUNY, New Paltz, NY |
| 1988 | Espacio Cero, Madrid, Spain |
| 1988 | Lucre, London, England |
| 1989 | Moscow Actors Theatre, Moscow, ID |
| 1989 | University of California, Los Angeles, CA |
| 1990 | Citrus College, Glendora, CA |
| 1990 | Lewis and Clark College, Portland, OR |
| 1990 | Theatre Outlet, Allentown, PA |
| 1990 | Seven Stages, Atlanta, GA |

| 1990 | Miami University, Oxford, OH |
| 1991 | New City Theater, Seattle, WA* |
| 1998 | Minc Theater, Dublin, Ireland |
| 1999 | Signature Theatre, New York City, NY |

## Sarita (music by Leon Odenz)

| 1984 | INTAR, New York City, NY* (OBIE Award) |
| 1987 | Lorraine Hansberry Theatre, San Francisco, CA |
| 1987 | Tulane University, New Orleans, LA |
| 1988 | Soho Poly, London, England |

## No Time

| 1984 | Padua Hills Festival, Los Angeles, CA* |

## Drowning

| 1985 | Acting Company National Tour |
| 1988 | Padua Hills Festival, Los Angeles, CA |
| 1992 | Magic Theatre, San Francisco, CA* |
| 1999 | Signature Theatre, New York City, NY |

## The Conduct of Life

| 1985 | Theater for the New City, New York City, NY* (OBIE Award) |
| 1986 | UCLA, Los Angeles, CA |
| 1986 | Amherst College, Amherst, MA |
| 1986 | Williams College, Williamstown, MA |
| 1986 | URSA, Vermont |
| 1988 | Organic Theatre, Chicago, IL |
| 1988 | Union 212, Gate Theatre, London, England |
| 1988 | Pacific Theatre, Los Angeles, CA |
| 1989 | Amherst College, Amherst, MA |
| 1989 | Brown University, Providence, RI |
| 1989 | University of Iowa, Iowa City, IA |

1990     University of Miami, Ann Arbor, MI
1990     Open City Theatre, San Francisco, CA
1990     University of North Carolina, Greensboro, NC
1990     Rights of Reason, Providence, RI
1990     Drama League, New York City, NY


**Lovers and Keepers** (music by Tito Puente and Fernando Rivas)
1986     INTAR, New York City, NY*
1986     New City Theatre, Pittsburgh, PA*
1988     Blind Parrot, Chicago, IL
1989     Amherst College, Amherst, MA
1989     Brown University, Providence, RI


**A Matter of Faith**
1986     Theater for the New City, New York City, NY*


**The Mothers** (a study for *Nadine* for *What of the Night?*)
1986     Padua Hills Festival, Los Angeles, CA*


**Art (Box Plays)**
1986     Theater for the New City, New York City, NY
1986     INTAR, New York City, NY


**Abingdon Square**
1987     The Women's Project, New York City, NY* (OBIE Award)
1988     Studio Arena, Buffalo, NY*
1989     Shared Experience, Soho Poly, London, England
1989     Amherst College, Amherst, MA
1989     Passe Muraille, Toronto, Canada
1990     National Theatre, London, England
1990     Next Theatre, Chicago, IL

| 1990 | New City Theatre, Seattle, WA |
| 1990 | Belvoir Theatre, Sidney, Australia |
| 1990 | Malthouse, Melbourne, Australia |
| 1990 | Boston College, Boston, MA |
| 1990 | Source Theatre, Washington, DC |
| 1991 | Agnes Scott College, Atlanta, GA |
| 1992 | San Diego Repertory Theater, San Diego, CA |

*La plaza chica* (Spanish Translation of *Abingdon Square)*
| 1992 | San Diego Repertory Theater, San Diego, CA* |

*Hunger* (A study for *What of the Night?)*
| 1988 | En Garde Arts Productions, New York City, NY* |
| 1988 | New Radio, Radio Broadcasters |

*And What of the Night?* (Pulitzer Prize Finalist)
Later *What of the Night?*
| 1988 | Milwaukee Repertory Theatre, Milwaukee, WI* |
| 1989 | Trinity Square Co, Providence, RI* |

*Oscar and Bertha*
| 1991 | Padua Hills Playwrights Festival, Northridge, CA* |
| 1992 | Magic Theater, San Francisco, CA* |

*Springtime* (From *What of the Night?*)
| 1992 | For Your Life Productions, New York City, NY |
| 1992 | LA Comunity College, Los Angeles, CA |
| 1993 | Vineyard Playhouse |
| 1997 | Theater for the New City, New York City, NY* |

## Terra Incognita

1991      INTAR, New York City, NY (with music by Roberto Sierra)*

1992      Dionysia Playwrights Festival, Siena, Italy *

1993      Yale University, New Heaven, CO

1997      INTAR/Women's Project Productions, New York City, NY *


## Enter the Night

1993      New City Theater, Seattle, WA*

1994      Dallas Theater Center, Dallas, TX*

1999      Signature Theatre, New York City, NY


## Ibsen and the Actress (A study for *The Summer in Gossensass*)

1995      The University of Iowa, Iowa City, IA*


## Manual for a desperate crossing

later ***Balseros/Rafters*** (libretto for an opera by Robert Ashley)

1996      Florida Grand Opera, Miami, FL


## The Summer in Gossensass

1997      The Women's Project at The Harold Clurman Theatre,
           New York City, NY *

1998      The Women's Project at The Judith Anderson Theatre,
           New York City, NY *


## The Audition

1998      Theater for the New City, New York City, NY *

# TRANSLATIONS AND ADAPTATIONS

1980   *Blood Wedding* by Federico García Lorca
        Translation and adaptation
        INTAR, New York City, NY
        Directed by Max Ferrá

1981   *Life is a Dream* by Pedro Calderón de la Barca
        Translation and Adaptation
        INTAR, New York City, NY
        Music by George Quincy
        Directed by Maria Irene Fornes

1985   *Cold Air* by Virgilio Piñera
        Translation and Adaptation
        INTAR, New York City, NY
        Directed by Maria Irene Fornes

1987   *Hedda Gabler* by Henrik Ibsen
        Revision of Translation
        Milwaukee Repertory Theatre, Milwaukee, WI
        Directed by Maria Irene Fornes

1987   *Uncle Vanya* by Anton Chekhov
        Revision of Translation
        The Classic Stage Company at the CSC Repertory Theatre,
        New York City, NY
        Directed by Maria Irene Fornes

# DIRECTION OF PLAYS BY OTHER AUTHORS

1981    *Life is a Dream* by Pedro Calderón de la Barca,
        INTAR, New York City, NY

1982    *Exile* by Ana María Simo,
        INTAR, New York City, NY

1985    *Cold Air* by Virgilio Piñera,
        INTAR, New York City, NY

1987    *Hedda Gabler* by Henrik Ibsen,
        Milwaukee Repertory Theatre, Milwaukee, WI

1987    *Uncle Vanya* by Anton Chekhov,
        The Classic Stage Company at the CSC
        Repertory Theatre, New York City, NY

1990    *Going to New England*, by Ana María Simo,
        INTAR, New York City, NY

1990    *Dogs* by Leo Garcia,
        Ensemble Theater, Los Angeles, CA

1990    *Shadow of a Man* by Cherríe Moraga,
        Eureka Theater, San Francisco, CA

1993    *It Is It Is Not* by Manuel Garcia Pereiras,
        Theater for the New City, New York City, NY

1995    *Any Place But Here* by Caridad Svich,
        Theater for the New City, New York City, NY

# PUBLISHED PLAYS
## (LISTED CHRONOLOGICALLY)

*The Widow,* in *Cuatro obras de teatro cubano* (Havana: Casa de las Americas, 1961).

*Tango Palace* and *The Successful Life of 3,* in *Playwrights for Tomorrow* (Minneapolis: The University of Minneapolis Press, 1966).

*Promenade,* in *The Bold New Women,* ed. Barbara Alson (Greenwich, CT: Fawcett Publications, 1966).

*The Successful Life of 3,* in *Eight Plays from Off-Off-Broadway,* eds. Nick Orzel and Michael Smith (New York: Bobbs Merrill, 1966).

*Promenade,* in *The New Underground Theatre,* ed. Robert J. Schroeder (New York: Bantam Books, 1968).

*Dr. Kheal,* in *Yale Theatre Review,* 1968.

*Dr. Kheal,* in *The Best of Off-Off-Broadway,* ed. Michael Smith (New York: E.P. Dutton, 1969).

*Tango Palace,* in *Concepts of Literature,* ed. James William Johnson (Englewood Cliffs, NJ: Prentice Hall, 1971).

*Tango Palace, The Successful Life of 3, Promenade, A Vietnamese Wedding, Molly's Dream, The Red Burning Light,* and *Dr. Kheal,* in *Promenade and Other Plays,* introduced by Richard Gilman (New York: Winter House, Ltd, 1971).

*Molly's Dream,* in *The Off-Off Broadway Book,* eds. Albert Poland and Bruce Mailman (New York: Bobbs Merrill, New York, 1972).

*Fefu and Her Friends,* in *Performing Arts Journal,* Vol. II, No. 3, 1978, pp. 112–40.

*Dr. Kheal,* in *A Century of Plays by American Women,* ed. Rachel France (New York: Richard Rosen Press: 1979).

*Promenade,* in *Great Rock Musicals,* ed. Stanley Richards (New York: Stein and Day, 1979).

*Fefu and Her Friends,* in *Word Plays* (New York: Performing Arts Journal Publications, 1980).

*The Conduct of Life,* in *Plays from Padua Hills,* ed. Murray Mednick (Pomona, CA: The Pomona College Theatre Department, 1982).

*The Danube,* in *Plays from Padua Hills,* ed. Murray Mednick (Pomona, CA: The Pomona College Theatre Department/New York: Performing Arts Journal Publications, 1984).

*Fefu and Her Friends* (excerpts), in *Buying Time* (St. Paul, MN: Greywolf Press, 1985).

Trans. of *Cold Air* by Virgilio Piñera, in *Plays in Process,* Vol. 6, No. 10 (New York: Theatre Communications Group Publications, 1985).

*The Danube, Mud, Sarita,* and *The Conduct of Life* in *Plays* (New York: Performing Arts Journal Publications, 1986).

Trans. of *Cold Air* by Virgilio Piñera, in *New Plays USA 3* (New York: Theatre Communications Group Publications, 1986).

*Drowning,* in *Orchards: Seven Stories by Anton Chekhov and Seven Plays They Have Inspired* (New York: Alfred A. Knopf, 1986).

*Promenade, Tango Palace, The Successful Life of 3, A Vietnamese Wedding, Molly's Dream, Dr. Kheal,* in *Promenade and Other Plays* (New York: Perfoming Arts Journal Publications, 1987).

*The Conduct of Life*, in *On New Ground: Contemporary Hispanic-American Plays*, ed. M. Elizabeth Osborn (New York: Theatre Communications Group Publications, 1987).

*Lovers and Keepers*, in *Plays in Process*, Vol. 7, No. 10 (New York: Theatre Communications Group Publications, 1987).

*Abingdon Square*, in *American Theatre*, Vol. 4, No. 10, February 1988, pp. 1–10.

*Fefu and Her Friends* (New York: Performing Arts Journal Publications, 1989).

*Abingdon Square*, in *Womens Work: Five New Plays from the Women's Project*, ed. Julia Miles (New York and Tonbridge: Applause, 1989)

*Abingdon Square*, in *Plays International*, April 1990, pp. 42–9.

*Springtime*, in *Antaeus*, ed. Daniel Halpern, No. 67, Spring 1991.

*Oscar and Bertha,* in *Best of the West,* eds. Murray Mednick, Bill Raden and Cheryl Slean (Los Angeles: Padua Hills Press, 1991).

*A Vietnamese Wedding,* in *Literature-An Introduction to Fiction, Poetry and Drama* (New York: Harper Collins, 1991).

*What of the Night?*, in *Women on the Verge: Seven Avant Garde Plays,* ed. Rosette C. Lamont (New York and Tonbridge: Applause, 1993).

*Terra Incognita*, in *Theater,* Vol. 24, No. 2, 1993, pp. 99–121.

*The Conduct of Life*, in *Telling Tales: New One-Act Plays*, ed. Eric Lane (New York: Penguin, 1993).

*Springtime*, in *Facing Forward: One Act Plays and Monologues by Contemporary American Women at the Crest of the 21st Century,* ed. Leah D. Frank (New York: Broadway Play Publishing, 1995).

*Fefu y sus amigas,* in *Teatro: 5 autores cubanos,* ed. Rine Leal (New York: Ollantay Press, 1995).

*Enter the Night,* in *Plays For the End of the Century,* ed. Bonnie Marranca (Baltimore and London: John Hopkins University Press, 1996).

# TEACHING AND LECTURING (SELECTED)

| | |
|---|---|
| 1966 | Judson Workshop, New York City, NY |
| 1967 | New School for Social Research, New York City, NY |
| 1968 | Sarah Lawrence College, Bronxville, NY |
| 1971 | National Theatre Institute, Waterford, CT |
| 1971 | Teachers Writers Collaborative, New York City, NY |
| 1978–91 | Padua Hills Playwright Festival, Los Angeles, CA |
| 1978–91 | INTAR Playwrights Workshop, New York City, NY |
| 1982 | Bay Area Playwrights Festival, Marin County, CA |
| 1984 | Bay Area Playwrights Festival, Marin County, CA |
| 1985 | Theater for the New City, New York City, NY |
| 1985 | Princeton University, Princeton, NJ |
| 1986 | Florida University, Tallahassee, FL |
| 1986 | Carnegie-Melon University, Pittsburgh, PA |
| 1986 | At the Foot of the Mountain, Minneapolis, MN |
| 1987 | Nevada University, Las Vegas, NV |
| 1987 | Northwest Playwrights Guild, Seattle, WA |
| 1987 | New York University, New York City, NY |
| 1988 | Miami Dade University, Miami, FL |
| 1988 | Manhattanville College, Rye, NY |
| 1988 | The Blind Parrot, Chicago, IL |
| 1988 | Southwest Playwrights, Atlanta, GA |
| 1988 | Northwest Playwrights Guild, Seattle, WA |
| 1988 | West Coast Playwrights, San Francisco, CA |
| 1988 | Tapestry Players, Albuquerque, NM |
| 1988 | Puget Sound University, Tacoma, WA |
| 1988 | Playwrights Center, Minneapolis, MN |
| 1989 | Iowa University, Iowa City, IA |
| 1989 | Boise University, Boise, ID |
| 1989 | USIS Lecture Tour, Mexico, Caracas, Santiago, Montevideo |
| 1989 | New York University, New York City, NY |
| 1990 | New City Theatre, Seattle, WA |
| 1990 | West Coast Playwrights, San Francisco, CA |
| 1990 | Mark Taper Forum, Los Angeles, CA |
| 1991 | Hamilton College, New York City, NY |

| 1991 | University of Washington, Seattle, WA |
| 1991 | West Coast Playwrights, San Francisco, CA |
| 1992 | USIS Lecture Tour, Madras, Calcutta, New Delhi, Bombay. |
| 1992 | Brown University, Providence, RI |
| 1992 | University of Texas, Austin, TX |
| 1992 | Mark Taper Forum, Los Angeles, CA |
| 1992 | California Institute of the Arts, Northridge, CA |
| 1992 | San Diego State University Foundation, San Diego, CA |
| 1992 | Yale University, New Haven, CO |
| 1993 | Wesleyan University, Middletown, CO |
| 1993 | The University of Iowa, Iowa City, IA |
| 1993 | University of Washington, Seattle, WA |
| 1994 | Traverse Theatre, Edinburgh, Scotland |
| 1994 | Contact Theatre, Manchester, England |
| 1995 | New York University, New York City, NY |
| 1996 | The University of Iowa, Iowa City, IA |
| 1996 | UCLA, Los Angeles, CA |
| 1997 | The University of Iowa, Iowa City, IA |
| 1998 | ASK Theater Projects Common Ground Festival, Los Angeles, CA. |
| 1999 | Cal Arts, Valencia, CA |

# ❈ SELECT BIBLIOGRAPHY

Austin, Gayle, "The Madwoman in the Spotlight: Plays of Maria Irene Fornes," in *Making a Spectacle: Feminist Essays on Contemporary Women's Theatre,* ed. Lynda Hart (Ann Arbor: The University of Michigan Press, 1989), pp. 76–85.

Betsko, Kathleen and Rachel Koenig, *Interviews with Contemporary Women Playwrights* (New York: Beech Tree Books/Quill, 1987).

Cohn, Ruby, *Anglo-American Interplay in Recent Drama* (Cambridge: Cambridge University Press, 1995).

Cole, Susan Letzler, *Directors in Rehearsal: A Hidden World* (London and New York: Routledge, 1992).

Cummings, Scott T., "Seeing with Clarity; The Visions of Maria Irene Fornes," *Theater*, Vol. 7, 1985, pp. 51–6

Cummings, Scott T., "Maria Irene Fornes," in *American Playwrights Since 1945,* ed. Philip Kolin (Westport: Greenwood, 1989), pp. 111–23.

Cummings, Scott T., "Fornes's Odd Couple: *Oscar and Bertha* at the Magic Theatre," *Journal of Dramatic Theory and Criticism*, Vol. 8, 1994, pp. 147–56.

Cummings, Scott T., "Psychic Space: The Interiors of Maria Irene Fornes," *The Journal of American Drama and Theatre*, Vol. 10, No. 2, Spring 1998, pp. 59–73.

Delgado, Maria M. and Paul Heritage, eds, *In Contact with the Gods?: Directors Talk Theatre* (Manchester: Manchester University Press, 1996).

Dolan, Jill, *The Feminist Spectator as Critic* (Ann Arbor: The University of Michigan Press, 1988).

Fornes, Maria Irene, "I write these messages that come," *Drama Review*, Vol. 21, No. 4, 1977, pp. 25–40.

Fornes, Maria Irene, "The Playwright as Director," in *Conversations on Art and Performance,* eds. Bonnie Marranca and Gautam Dasgupta (Baltimore and London: John Hopkins University Press, 1999), pp. 288–95.

Geis, Deborah R., "Wordscapes of the Body: Performative Language as *Gestus* in Maria Irene Fornes's Plays," *Theatre Journal*, Vol. 42, No. 3, October 1990, pp. 291–307.

Gruber, William E., "Individuality and Communality in Maria Irene Fornes's *The Danube*," in *Public Issues, Private Tensions: Contemporary American Drama*, ed. Matthew C. Roudané (New York: AMS Press, 1993).

Gruber, William E., *Missing Persons: Character and Characterization in Modern Drama* (Athens: University of Georgia Press, 1994).

Kent, Assunta Bartolomucci, *Maria Irene Fornes and her Critics* (Westport: Greenwood Press, 1996).

Keyssar, Helene, "Drama and the Dialogic Imagination: *The Heidi Chronicles* and *Fefu and Her Friends*," in *Feminist Theatre and Theory*, ed. Helene Keyssar (New York: St. Martin's Press, 1996), pp. 109–36.

Lee, Josephine, "Pity and Terror as Public Acts: Reading Feminist Politics in the Plays of Maria Irene Fornes," in *Staging Resistance: Essays on Theatre and Politics,* eds. Jeanne Colleran and Jenny Spencer (Ann Arbor: The University of Michigan Press, 1997), pp. 166–85.

Marranca, Bonnie, "Interview: Maria Irene Fornes," *Performing Arts Journal*, Vol. 2, No. 3, 1978, pp. 106–11.

Marranca, Bonnie, *Theatrewritings* (New York: Performing Arts Journal Publications, 1984).

Marranca, Bonnie, *Ecologies of Theater: Essays at the Century Turning* (Baltimore and London: John Hopkins University Press, 1996.

Moroff, Diane Lynn, *Fornes: Theater in the Present Tense* (Ann Arbor: University of Michigan Press, 1996).

Murphy, Brenda, ed., *The Cambridge Companion to American Women Playwrights* (Cambridge: Cambridge University Press, 1999).

O'Malley, Lurana Donnels, "Pressing Clothes/Snapping Beans/Reading Books: Maria Irene Fornes's Women's Work," *Studies in American Drama*, 1945–*Present*, Vol. 4, 1989, pp. 103–11.

Pevitts, Beverly Byers, "Review of *Fefu and Her Friends*," in *Women in American Theatre*, eds. Helen Krich Chinoy and Linda Walsh Jenkins (New York: Theatre Communications Group, 1987), pp. 314–17.

Robinson, Marc, ed., *The Theater of Maria Irene Fornes* (Baltimore and London: Johns Hopkins University Press, 1999).

Savran, David, *In Their Own Words: Contemporary American Playwrights* (New York: Theatre Communications Group, 1988).

Schuler, Catherine, "Gender Perspective and Violence in the Plays of Maria Irene Fornes and Sam Shepard," in *Modern American Drama: The Female Canon*, ed. June Schlueter (Rutherford, NJ: Fairleigh Dickinson University Press, 1990).

Wetzsteon, Ross, "Irene Fornes: The Elements of Style," *Village Voice*, April 29, 1986, pp. 42–45.

Wolf, Stacy, "Re/presenting Gender, Re/presenting Violence: Feminism, Form and the Plays of Maria Irene Fornes," *Theatre Studies*, Vol. 37, 1992, pp. 17–31.

Worthen, William B., "Still Playing Games: Ideology and Performance in the Theater of Maria Irene Fornes," in *Feminine Focus: The New Women Playwrights,* ed. Enoch Brater (Oxford: Oxford University Press, 1989), pp. 167–85.

Zinman, Toby Silverman, "Hen in a Foxhouse: The Absurdist Plays of Maria Irene Fornes," in *Around the Absurd: Essays on Modern and Postmodern Drama* eds. Enoch Brater and Ruby Cohn (Ann Arbor: University of Michigan Press, 1991), pp. 203–20.

# ❀ INDEX